E. Irene Arth

DATE DUE

DEMCO 38-297

LABOR AND
SOCIAL ORGANIZATION

ECONOMICS AND SOCIAL INSTITUTIONS

VOLUME I
Development of Economic Society
by MODLIN and DEVYVER

VOLUME II
Introduction to Economic Analysis
by MCISAAC and SMITH

VOLUME III
Social Control of Industry
by MODLIN and MCISAAC

VOLUME IV
Money, Credit, and Finance
by LUTHRINGER, CHANDLER, and CLINE

VOLUME V
Population, Resources, and Trade
by DELL and LUTHRINGER

VOLUME VI
Labor and Social Organization
by MCCABE and LESTER

ECONOMICS AND SOCIAL INSTITUTIONS

Volume VI

LABOR

AND

SOCIAL

ORGANIZATION

—— *by* ——

DAVID ALOYSIUS McCABE

AND

RICHARD ALLEN LESTER

Department of Economics and Social Institutions,
Princeton University

BOSTON

LITTLE, BROWN AND COMPANY

1938

PREFACE

THIS book deals with labor organization, labor legislation, social security, and social reorganization. It describes and analyzes those problems of modern economic society that are directly related to and arise from the wage system. Constituting the final volume of a six-book series designed to serve as an up-to-date and flexible text for an introductory course in economics, *Labor and Social Organization* may also be used as a textbook for courses in labor problems. As a text for labor courses, it is sufficiently compact and inexpensive to permit wide use of supplementary readings such as periodical articles, government reports, special studies, and "case" material.

The need for a concise, up-to-date textbook, applying modern methods of economic analysis to the field of labor, becomes more and more apparent with the growing interest in labor relations and worker security. With labor issues on the front pages of the newspapers, there is no lack of "news" and "facts", which may soon be forgotten. What is lacking is an analysis and understanding of the economic factors and forces that underlie the current disputes and issues. For this purpose a textbook that is less encyclopedic and more analytical has definite advantages.

This book, as one volume in a series, integrates the treatment of problems in the field of labor to other aspects of the economic system. It enables the student to appreciate, for example, how the principles of economic theory and of public finance apply in such matters as labor legislation, unemployment relief, social security, and social reform. Moreover, the analysis in this volume is in accord with the economic theory presented in the other volumes.

The first volume of the six-book series describes the development of economic organization and institutions since the Middle Ages, thus serving as background material for the succeeding volumes. The second volume presents methods of economic analysis, based on the recent realistic approach of imperfect markets and monopolistic competition. The remaining four volumes in the series present a survey of the major problems of the modern economic system. In each of these books the emphasis is placed not merely on the description of economic problems, but also on the study of underlying economic and social processes.

This series of small textbooks has been prepared by a group of men who have been teaching in the respective subjects for many years, and it was used at Princeton in preliminary book form during 1936–1937. Constructive criticisms by students and instructors were thus available to the authors when preparing the books for publication. The size of the volumes not only facilitated revision by the authors but was readily appreciated by both students and instructors.

JAMES G. SMITH
Editor

Princeton, N.J.
December 1937

CONTENTS

PART FOUR · SOCIAL REORGANIZATION

LABOR AND
SOCIAL ORGANIZATION

Introduction

A LARGE part of this volume is devoted to what are ordinarily called "labor problems." These are problems arising out of the wage system. In this country, at the present time, a large proportion of the population is dependent for livelihood on securing wage employment. What the wage earners receive for their work, the amount of work they get, and the conditions under which they do their work, are all matters of social importance.

One of the major inadequacies of our economic system is low wages. Many wage earners cannot earn enough, even if fully employed, to support themselves and their families in health and decency, according to standards generally accepted as reasonable. The continuance of low wages for a large section of the working population stands out in clear contrast with the advances that have been made in the production of the goods on which the wage earners are employed.

Moreover, wage earners' incomes are notoriously uncertain. The risk of unemployment is one of the major hazards of the wage earners' life. The liability to unemployment, coupled with the fact that the wage earner has, ordinarily, little or no source of income other than wage employment, makes the worker's economic position peculiarly insecure.

Other hazards confront the wage earner in his place of employment. The mechanization of industry has greatly increased the danger of accident to the worker while at work. The wage earner cannot control the hours of his work, or the pace of his work, to the same extent as can the farmer, the self-employed worker, or the professional man. There is no doubt that both hours and pace affect the risk of accident and of injury to health that the individual wage earner faces while at work.

Wage earners have frequently attempted to cope with some of these problems by organized action among themselves. The wage system has produced the labor organization. Because it originated before protective labor legislation became important and because it is still a form of voluntary action by the employees themselves, labor organization will be considered first in this book.

The growth of labor organization has itself created a set of social problems concerned with the relations between such organizations and employers. Failure on the part of organized labor to arrive at an agreement with the employer results, ordinarily, in a strike. In addition to the loss of immediate income by the strikers and the loss occasioned to the employer, a strike may have important social consequences. It may interrupt the supply of essential goods or services. It may lead to violence and disorder. Whatever the particular causes of the development of labor strife, such economic warfare is a matter of grave public concern.

To solve this problem by legislation alone is obviously impossible. Good relations between employers and labor organizations cannot be established by government fiat. The law can reach only overt acts. Yet the law can do much to prevent certain types of conduct that tend to lead to strikes. Recently, in this country, the employer not only has been forbidden to interfere with organizing activities among workers but also has been required to allow the workers, if they wish, to bargain collectively with him through a labor organization. The coercive measures used by organized workers also come within the province of the law. In addition, the government intervenes at times in labor disputes with the purpose of averting strikes or bringing them to a settlement after they have begun. The legal aspects of collective action by labor and the intervention of the government in labor disputes will be discussed in Part Two.

Voluntary action by wage earners to improve their terms of employment has been supplemented by legislation on such matters as hours and physical conditions in the place of employment and even by the fixing of minimum wages by law. This type of labor legislation will likewise be treated in Part Two.

Efforts have also been made to meet the problem of the other hazards confronting the wage earner —

industrial accident, unemployment, and old-age dependency. The conviction has grown that some form of social insurance must be developed to cover these risks and thereby cushion the effect of their impact on the wage earner. For the unemployed, there has also been a resort to employment by the government itself of those who cannot find employment with private employers. These measures to assure a greater degree of economic security to the workers are treated in Part Three.

The development of the capitalistic wage system has been followed by a series of movements for the replacement of Capitalism by one or another different type of economic system. These movements have not aimed merely at securing particular reforms, through voluntary action or through legislation, but at a fundamental overhauling of the economic system. Because it has been assumed that the proposed recasting of the economic system would effect a fundamental change in the whole social order, these programs have been regarded as programs of "social reorganization."

For many years the dominant note in the demand for the supersession of Capitalism was for ending the exploitation of the workers. The only solution of labor's problems, it was contended, was the overthrow of Capitalism or at least a gradual but none the less thorough remaking of the economic system. Whether the method advocated was a sudden scrapping of Capitalism or a gradual, conscious transformation of it into a new economic order, the primary plank in the platform was the rescue of the workers from exploitation. There was thus a close association between social reorganization and the elevation of labor. Social reorganization was regarded by many as an alternative to voluntary action and reform through legislation under the capitalistic wage system.

In the programs of social reorganization that are receiving most attention today, a less prominent place is accorded to labor as such. In Russia, under a dictatorship established in the name of the proletariat, the mass of workers is controlled, not controlling, and the immediate material welfare of the workers is apparently still subordinated to other aims. In Italy, under a dictatorship committed to a totalitarian nationalism, strict control of labor is an important feature of the new political and economic order. In such countries, the problem of the mass of the workers has become more acute, in important respects, than it is under the capitalistic wage system in democratic countries.

There has been another important change in the background for the discussion of social reorganization. Until recently, programs for social reorganization were merely programs offered by groups that lacked the political power to put their plans into effect. That was true as late as twenty years ago. But for two decades there has been a communist dictatorship in Russia and, for nearly the same length of time, a fascist dictatorship in Italy. Under each of these dictatorships the economic system is markedly different, on the surface at least, from Capitalism as it exists in the United States. Social reorganization is no longer merely a matter of theories and of paper programs offered as alternatives to Capitalism. A study of social reorganization, therefore, includes not only the consideration of proposed plans and programs, but also the consideration of the existing economic systems of such countries as Russia and Italy. Social reorganization, proposed and actual, is the subject matter of Part Four of this volume.

PART ONE

LABOR ORGANIZATION

CHAPTER I

Rise and Growth of Labor Organization

THE term "labor organization" covers any continuing association of workers that has for its primary purpose the promotion of the economic interests of its members as wage earners. Broad as this definition is, it is not intended to cover every association made up predominantly, or even exclusively, of wage earners. It limits the term to organizations primarily concerned with the economic interests of their members and especially with their economic interests as employees. A labor organization may have fraternal, cultural, or spiritual aims, and it may concern itself with the interests of its members as consumers or as taxpayers, but the activities that make it a "labor organization" are those that have to do directly with the economics of the employment relation. If the latter is outside the scope of its action, it is not a labor organization even though all of its members are wage earners. On the other hand, if it serves as the instrument of combined action of its members with respect to the terms of their employment, it must be considered a labor organization, even though its declared ultimate purpose be the elimination of the capitalistic wage system. The practical test is whether it here and now busies itself with the terms of employment of its members.

For over a century the method followed by labor organizations to advance or defend the terms of employment has been predominantly that of collective bargaining.[1] Indeed, it is commonly assumed that labor organization and collective bargaining are related terms, related to the extent that the latter is the reason for the former. In very large measure that has been true, and is still true. We must recognize, however, that labor organization and collective bargaining are not coterminous. A labor organization may fail to attain, or to hold, collective bargaining for its members. More than that, a labor organization may resort to political action to secure through legal enactment hours of labor, working conditions, or even wages, that it cannot secure at the time by direct bargaining with employers. The line between what is won by collective bargaining and what is won by political action has become hazier in recent years. And there are indications that political action may play a still more important part in the future activity and effectiveness of labor organizations.

Labor organization is no new phenomenon. Nor does it owe its initial appearance to the factory system.

[1] Collective bargaining is discussed below, in Chapter IV.

Rather is it an offspring of the wage system, and the wage system long antedates the Industrial Revolution.[2] During the late Middle Ages there were, in some trades in some towns, associations of *journeymen* (skilled craftsmen who had emerged from the status of *apprentices* but continued to work for master craftsmen). These associations busied themselves to some extent with the terms of employment as well as with the fraternal and religious functions which characterized the vocational associations of that period. There are evidences, too, of strikes by the journeymen. But both the moral code and the law were opposed to the use of economic coercion by workers to change the terms of employment. The most they could do, legally, was to appeal to the employers to grant them their due according to the customary standards, and, failing to secure proper treatment by this means, to appeal to the government. The consequence was that such journeymen's associations as were allowed to continue took on the appearance, if not the reality, of organizations subordinate to the respective masters' gilds. In England none of these associations, so far as we know, lasted beyond the sixteenth century. On the Continent, they lingered longer but there, too, they were gone before the modern type of labor organization came on the scene.

The beginnings of modern labor organization are found in England in the seventeenth century. Not only had the number of skilled workmen who had no ex-

[2] See Modlin, G. M., and de Vyver, F. T., *Development of Economic Society* (1937), pp. 95 and 410–411.

pectation of rising from the wage-earning status increased, but the need for defensive organization to preserve the customary standards was becoming increasingly evident. The old statutory apprenticeship requirements were being more and more ignored, and the provisions on the statute books for the fixing of wages were fading into general nonobservance. Moreover, this increasing obsolescence of legal regulation was accompanied by a widening toleration by employers of organization among the wage-earning craftsmen. Through the eighteenth century an increasing number of associations of craftsmen dealt with their employers on the terms of employment and attempted to enforce the customary apprenticeship as a prerequisite to employment as a journeyman. When the legal prohibition of combinations among workmen was extended and tightened at the close of the eighteenth century, the movement for organization had developed sufficient strength to endure in spite of legal proscription and even instances of severe punishment. And after legal freedom to organize was granted in 1824 the labor movement in England grew rapidly.

The early English trade unions were organizations of skilled craftsmen, confined to their several trades and localities. In these respects they followed the medieval tradition. They differed from the craft gilds, of course, in the important economic particular that they were organizations of employees, not of masters; of wage earners, not of enterprisers. But it is equally important to remember that, like the earlier craft gilds, they were made up of skilled craftsmen. Skill in a

craft no longer served as a passport to self-employ-
ment; for the majority it had to be marketed through
an employment contract. Nevertheless, the journeymen
still believed that they had a vested interest in the
protection of the market for their skill, an interest
superior to freedom of contract or a free labor market.
Thus, their organizations concerned themselves with
the conditions of entrance to the trade as well as with
wages. They were, first of all, organizations of members of a craft, with a common interest separating
them from all outside the craft. Their policies and
their methods were those of craftsmen; they were not
organs of mass action by labor in general.

EARLY AMERICAN ORGANIZATIONS

The first labor organizations in the United States
belonged to the same category as the early English
trade unions. They were local craft organizations. Like
their English prototypes they preceded the factory system. They were born of town conditions in the old
skilled trades, such as printing, shoemaking, and tailor-
ing, at the end of the eighteenth century and the beginning of the nineteenth. They were interested in
regulating apprenticeship as well as in raising wages.

These early workers' organizations were ephemeral.
Formed because of some problem confronting the
trade at the time, the organization seemed unable
long to survive either success or failure in meeting the
emergency; a few years later it would be succeeded by
another association with the same intention of perma-
nence and the same shortness of life. It was not until

after 1840 that the persisting recourse to organization resulted in the formation, in an appreciable number, of local associations that have lasted through to our own time.

That skilled workmen should have organized in the cities of the northern seaboard before the development of mills, factories, mines, and railroads is not remarkable in view of the English tradition of craft organization. Nor is it strange that, when new occupations requiring special training arose, the men engaged in those occupations should have followed the example of the older trades and organized not only for the direct protection of their wages, hours, and working conditions but also for the regulation of entrance to the trade. Thus, by the Civil War period there were organizations among such newcomers as iron puddlers, iron molders, locomotive engineers, and coal miners.

FACTORS AFFECTING GROWTH OF LABOR ORGANIZATION

EXTERNAL FACTORS

Technological Methods. The existence of a permanent wage-earning class does not necessarily produce labor organization, nor does an increase in the number of wage earners necessarily mean a corresponding increase in the number of organized workers. The backbone of labor organization in the United States has, until recently at least, been composed of skilled workers in recognized crafts. Exceptional conditions have

led to the inclusion of semi-skilled, and even some unskilled, workers along with the skilled in strong
unions in some industries, but enduring separate unions
of workers with little or no skill have been uncom-
mon. At times there has been a rising tide of organization that has swept in large numbers of the less skilled
and unskilled, but the tide has later receded, leaving
the unskilled and less skilled but little more organized
than before. It is possible that a more vigorous and
sustained attempt by the already well-established unions
of skilled men to organize the semi-skilled and unskilled workers, female as well as male, might have
resulted in considerably larger degree of permanent
organization among them. But the historical fact is
that the mass of semi-skilled and unskilled wage earners, and especially female workers, has not yet been
organized to any considerable extent, even though
their terms of employment have been far from satisfactory according to American standards.

  The methods of production in vogue have had an
important influence on the degree of organization.
Those methods that call for skill of a craft type have
been favorable to labor organization, and those that
require no skill, or skill of a highly specialized kind
which can be acquired in a short time, have been unfavorable. This does not mean that the skilled workers
are, or ever have been, fully organized. The point is
that the possession of a skilled trade has been the usual
prerequisite of lasting organization. It is in this sense
that the development of new skilled trades has been a
favorable factor for labor organization and that a trend

away from the need of skilled craftsmen has been an unfavorable factor.

It has been pointed out that the growth of new industries and the introduction of new methods and processes of production have, by enlarging the number of skilled occupations, led to a great increase in the number of organized workers. The iron industry, the construction industry, coal mining, and railroading furnish conspicuous examples. But the introduction of new methods that lessen the demand for skill in an existing industry, through subdivision of labor or the use of automatic or semi-automatic machinery, has tended to have the opposite effect. Technological changes in many of the older industries in the last quarter of a century have, on the whole, been unfavorable rather than favorable to the maintenance of labor-organization membership in those industries.

Nor have the methods of production in the important new industries that have developed in the last two or three decades been favorable to the extension of craft unionism to them. They have created many skilled jobs, to be sure, but these, for the most part, neither fall within old craft lines nor constitute new crafts; the skill is too specialized and too closely identified with the operations of a particular plant to make its possessors members of a separate craft, uniform throughout the industry and changing little from year to year. The rapidity of change in American industrial employment, and the trend of the changes in production methods, have been unfavorable to the extension of craft organization of the traditional protective type.

Whether the workers in the mass-production industries of the present can be permanently organized into a different type of labor organization remains to be seen.[3]

Prosperity and Depression. In addition to the underlying factor of technological methods, which has affected the growth of labor organization among particular groups through the years, the sharp upward and downward movements in business conditions have resulted in temporary expansions and recessions in the total labor organization membership. When business is booming and producers' prices are rising, there is greater opportunity to secure quick gains through organization, and this has led both to the swelling of the membership of existing unions and to the organization of new unions. If the cost of living is rising at the same time, the push of necessity is added to the pull of opportunity. These pulls and pushes have generally affected the less skilled and unskilled as well as the skilled, and organization has spread rapidly among them in such periods.

The business reaction following the period of boom has always wiped out a large part of the gain in total paid-up membership. With the demand for labor greatly reduced and the cost of living falling, unions are forced to take the defensive against wage reductions. In time of depression even strong unions may have to compromise on the wage-reduction issue. Some workers who join the union as a means of pushing up their wages on the upward swing are un-

[3] See below, Chapter II.

willing to stand by the union when it is unable to
ward off a wage cut. Some drop out because they are
unwilling to hold out for the union wage rate when
employment is scarce. Many, having lost the jobs they
had when they joined the union, seek work in unorganized plants or occupations and disappear from
the union rolls. The old unions of skilled workers
usually suffer less recession in membership than more
recently organized occupations or localities. But even
the old unions experience some decline in paid-up
membership in times of unemployment, and it is
paid-up membership that is usually taken as the basis
of comparison of membership totals through the years.

Attitude of the Government. The attitude of the
government toward labor organization has had an important influence upon the degree of organization.
The law and its operation will be discussed more
fully below.[4] At this point, it is merely necessary to
note that court decisions prior to the Civil War removed the uncertainty as to the legality of combinations of workmen to improve their terms of employment by concerted action, including striking. It was
not until the end of the nineteenth century that court
decisions and court orders curtailing the activities of
labor organizations became a source of loud complaint
from the organized workers. More recently the rights
of the workers in these matters have been extended by
statute. In addition, recent legislation has deprived
the employer of the legal right to interfere with the
organization of his workers, or to refuse to bargain

[4] Chapter V

with them through an organization of their own choosing.

Apart from the law itself the attitude of the government, in the sense of the Administration in office, may lend positive encouragement to labor organization. If the Administration recognizes the officers of national labor organizations as the spokesmen for the interest of the wage earners in their respective trades or industries, or of labor in general, the prestige of the organizations is heightened with the workers. This was especially marked during our participation in the World War. Officials of national labor organizations were appointed to high administrative or advisory posts, and the government, in its wide-flung activities as an employer, dealt with the national labor organizations on an unprecedented scale in the determination of wages and hours of work. The attitude of the Administration became much less encouraging in 1919. It was not until the advent of the National Industrial Recovery Act in 1933 that the leaders of national labor organizations were again recognized in the make-up of national advisory and administrative boards to a degree that recalled the days of 1917 and 1918.

Employer Attitudes and Policies. Among the factors affecting the growth of labor organization must be reckoned, of course, the attitude of employers and the policies followed by them within the limits allowed by law. Employers have seldom encouraged the organization of their workmen into unions. They have differed widely, however, in the policies they have pursued with respect to attempts at organization. Some have left the

matter to the workmen themselves and, if and when
the latter have effected a strong organization, have
dealt with them through their organizations. Others
have met attempts at organization with immediate discharge of any worker discovered to be a union member.
Still others have gone so far as to require all their employees to agree in advance, as a condition of accepting
and retaining employment, to refrain from membership
in a labor organization; this is the "yellow-dog contract." And some have even used labor spies.

The contention of the employers who took these active steps "to keep out the unions" was that unions dis-
turbed labor relations and interfered with production;
it was therefore merely good business for the employer
to use the economic weapons at his command to prevent any union from getting a foothold in his establishment. So far as collective bargaining was concerned,
these employers would have none of it; to them collective bargaining meant unionism, hostility, and the
holding back of the industrious and ambitious worker.
Down to the World War, at least, the employer who
refused to deal with a union usually declared that it
was his policy to treat with each workman individually
and reward him according to his merits.

The stand of employers for "individual bargaining",
even apart from discrimination against men for union
membership, obviously made organization of the workers more difficult than it would otherwise have been.
As a permanent labor policy, however, such a stand
had certain drawbacks, especially for corporations employing large numbers of workers. There was a growing public sentiment, even before the World War,

that it was unfair for a large employer to compel the individual worker to accept a "take it or leave it" basis of settlement for everything from an individual grievance to the fixing of the hours of labor. Moreover, many of the workers resented such a policy and, although their resentment might not carry them into labor organizations or into strikes, it militated against willing, co-operative service. Here and there, employers, especially those with a large labor force, began to experiment with plans for enlisting the co-operation of their workers by dealing with them as a group, but not through a labor organization.

Employer-Initiated Group-Relations Plans. Many of the plans inaugurated by the employers have been concerned with supplying services to workers or providing them with financial benefits in addition to the terms of the wages contract in the narrower sense. Such plans have covered matters as diverse as recreational facilities, education, free lunches, housing, sick benefits, pensions, and group life insurance, all paid for in whole or part by the employer. They have also embraced profit sharing in various forms, including purchase of the company's stock on terms more advantageous than those open to the general public. Their aim is to secure the loyal co-operation of the workers with the management and the continued service with the company of those workers whom the company wishes to retain. It cannot be said that generally these services or benefits have been given in exchange for working for less than the prevailing wages. Rather are they intended to be extras, beyond the prevailing or going rate of wages. Many of them, however, have been related to length of service and good behavior. That they have made it more difficult to organize the workers into trade unions is undoubted.

Until recently, one of the most conspicuous elements in group-relations plans initiated by employers was the substitution for purely individual dealings, on terms of employment and on particular grievances, of dealing on these matters with representatives elected by the company's own employees from their own number. Usually without any more formal machinery than was necessary for the conduct of elections and the holding of conferences, "employee representation" provided an opportunity for consultation between the management and the workers' representatives on "all matters of mutual interest." Sometimes there was a formal association of the employees which elected the representatives, but more often not. In neither case was there a labor organization in the generally accepted meaning of the term; there was only a method of dealing between the management and the employees of the particular company, or even the particular plant. In most cases, too, this company-initiated method was only a part of a larger plan of enlisting worker co-operation that included some of the services or benefits mentioned above. It did, however, set up a form of group dealing through representatives chosen by the workers which looked like an alternative to independent labor organization and was often intended to be just that. Indeed, these plans and associations were dubbed "company unions" by organized labor, a name that has gained wide usage.

Even before the United States entered the World War a few employers were experimenting with plans under which the employees in the plant chose representatives from their own number to consult with the management on matters of general interest to the workers and to handle individual complaints and grievances. The best known of these was that established by the Colorado Fuel and Iron Company in 1915, after a long struggle in which the company defeated the coal miners' union, the United Mine Workers of America. During the period of American participation in the World War there was a very large growth of employee representation, under various names. Not only was this a period of rapidly changing labor conditions, but one in which government influence upon forms of labor relations was unusually important. This was made evident in "essential" industries not under direct government operation, through the activity of the War Labor Board appointed by the President. The board had no statutory powers of enforcement of its decisions, but as a government board in time of war its actual power was great. The board generally insisted that the employer should deal with his workers as a group — through a union if they had one, or through representatives chosen by them in some other way if they had no outside union. This policy gave great stimulus to the formation of employer-initiated machinery for employee representation.

Many of the wartime plans subsequently disappeared, but new ones were established after the war in a number of plants. In 1932 there were some three hundred of these plans in existence, with a coverage of about a million and a quarter workers. Upon the passage of the National Industrial Recovery Act, in June 1933, there was another wave of installation of employee-representation plans, generally on employer initiative, which more than doubled the number of workers covered by such plans.

We are not concerned at this point with the advantages or disadvantages of employee-representation plans or kindred associations established on employer initiative, as compared with independent labor organizations. Whatever their merits, they did serve to check the growth of labor organizations. To be sure, these plans or associations were, for the most part, instituted for workers not at the time organized into unions. But had there been no such plans or associations in existence — if the only alternative to labor organization had been isolated individual bargaining — the growth of labor organization would doubtless have been greater, especially in periods when conditions were otherwise favorable to such growth.

The employee-representation, or company-union, obstacle to independent labor organization, however, has now been removed by legislation, wherever the National Labor Relations Act or similar state legislation applies.[5] Indeed, it may well be that the fact that workers had already been introduced to representative dealing, even under employer auspices, made it easier to enroll them into national industrial unions after the law was changed. Another possibility is that some

[5] See below, Chapter V.

of these plans or associations may be transformed by the workers into independent plant organizations. There are indications that something of the kind has been going on in some plants, especially since the Supreme Court upheld the constitutionality of the National Labor Relations Act in April 1937.

INTERNAL FACTORS

It is, of course, not external factors alone that affect the numerical strength of labor organizations. What may be called "internal factors" may also stimulate expansion. For example, the development of a new type of organization may cause a rapid expansion, even if but a temporary one, among hitherto unorganized workers. On the other hand, reaction against the methods pursued by union officials, or quarrels over methods or over affiliations with political or revolutionary groups, may check the growth of an organization or even reduce its membership. Such internal dissensions, however, are likely to affect but a relatively few unions at any one time; they are seldom general enough to account for an important recession in the aggregate membership of labor organizations in any particular period.

NUMERICAL GROWTH AND RECESSION BY PERIODS

The survey in the preceding section of the factors affecting the growth of labor organizations indicates that the movement of the aggregate membership has been neither at an even pace nor always forward. These factors, operating in varying strength and in varying combinations, have produced periods of rapid expansion and periods of rapid decline in the aggregate of union membership.

Until about 1880, the condition of business seems to have been the most important single influence. Even before the foundations of permanent local organization were laid, there were alternate periods of organizing activity and disappearance of the organizations, as in the inflationist boom of 1833–1836 and the depression following the panic of 1837. The more tenacious growth that followed was also accompanied by spectacular expansions and recessions in periods of boom and depression. It is estimated that the number of union members in New York City fell from 44,000 to 5,000 between 1873 and 1877. Nevertheless, the number of organizations that survived this historic depression, albeit with greatly reduced membership, was greater than that which lived through any preceding depression.

The years of industrial expansion immediately following the depression of 1873–1878 were marked not only by an increase in the membership of national unions organized along craft lines but also by the meteoric rise of a different type of organization known as the Knights of Labor. The structure and policies of this organization will be discussed in the next chapter. We must note here, however, that it set out to organize all classes of labor. In a period marked by rapidly changing economic conditions it had an appeal to labor outside the skilled groups, and to many skilled workers as well, an appeal which swept into its ranks close to three quarters of a million workers, most of them in the years 1885 and 1886.

But after 1886 the membership of the Knights of Labor fell almost as rapidly as it had risen. The organization proved itself unable to serve the interests of its various classes of members with sufficient promptness and effectiveness to hold their allegiance. The skilled workers either turned to organizations independent of the Knights or gave up organization altogether, while the less skilled and unskilled generally fell back into the mass of unorganized labor.

Meanwhile, the organizing activities of the Knights of Labor, and the policies that some of its local units pursued toward existing national unions organized on craft lines, had brought it into conflict with one national trade union after another. Whether or not the conflict might have been avoided, the fact is that the Knights of Labor and the national unions along craft lines were unable to work side by side in friendly rivalry. There were many instances of co-operation in a common cause, and frequently workers held membership both in the Knights of Labor and a national trade union. However, cases in which orders from the officials of the Knights of Labor conflicted with orders from a national union became more and more common. Members of one organization refused to co-operate in strikes called by the other or in settlements negotiated by the other. Charges of undercutting, "scabbing", and "knifing in the back" were hurled back and forth. This internal war within the ranks of organized labor undoubtedly contributed to the reduction in the total labor organization membership that took place between 1886 and the panic of 1893.

Organized labor emerged from the depression of 1893–1897 with slightly less than a half-million members. But with the issue of the form of organization apparently settled in favor of national trade unionism, organized labor took advantage of expanding industrial employment and generally good business to raise the membership to about two million by 1904. Its growth was then checked by vigorous anti-union campaigns by some employer groups, in which both economic pressure and appeals to the courts were utilized.

The membership figures resumed their upward swing in 1910, to reach two and three-quarter millions before the business recession of 1914–1915. But by 1916 another upward swing was in progress in the boom that preceded America's entry into the World War. The demands of warring nations had stimulated a very profitable expansion in industrial production at a time when the practical cessation of immigration and some re-migration had caused a relative shortage of labor. Moreover, the cost of living was rising rapidly.

The participation of America in the war greatly intensified the economic conditions favorable to organization. The demand for labor in war employments, the withdrawal of millions of men for military and naval service, the absence of the resistance offered in normal times to increasing labor costs, the soaring cost of living, all stimulated recourse to organization as a means of securing speedier and greater wage increases. In addition, the government was seeking the co-operation of labor leaders in a way that greatly enhanced the prestige of organization, while the government's policy as an employer — in transportation and shipbuilding especially — made organization in these employments not only easy but almost automatic. This was capped by the virtual suspension of the open use by employers of coercive methods against organization by the workers in the "essential" industries under private operation. This truce had been agreed to by well-known representatives of large employing interests who served, along with representatives of organized labor, as members of the War Labor Board, and it was enforced by that board with the active support of the Administration. To the momentum generated during the days of the war was added the push of the further rise in the cost of living and the opportunities offered by the feverish post-armistice activity to meet demands in this country held back during the war and to help meet the needs of European countries as yet unable to care for their own wants. By 1920 the paid-up membership in labor organizations in this country reached approximately five million.

That this figure could not be maintained was by no means due entirely to the sharp depression of 1921–1922. It was not only business conditions that changed. The retirement of the government as an employer brought the unions face to face with employers much less disposed to deal with labor organizations. With the disappearance of the War Labor Board, too, the principle that the employer should deal with whatever organization his workers wanted to represent them was also apparently demobilized. Nor could the Administration be counted on any longer to intervene on behalf of freedom for the workers to organize and be dealt with collectively. This had become evident in the unsuccessful strike in the steel industry in the autumn of 1919, in which the question of organization and collective bargaining was a prominent issue. When the depression came in 1921 the unions had to struggle against many employers who were determined to deflate not only wages but the unions as well, without government intervention in the unions' favor on either issue. That paid-up union membership shrank more than a million in two years is not surprising. What is perhaps more noteworthy is that union membership entered the new era of prosperity (1924–1929) over half a million above the pre-war level of three millions.

This time a period of general prosperity, accompanied by great industrial expansion along new lines, did not bring an increase in labor-organization membership. Indeed, losses in some industries, notably in coal mining, were hardly balanced by gains in other quarters. One factor that helps account for this result was that the fall in wages had been checked by 1923 at a point that left real wages, generally, well above the 1916 level; thereafter, the cost of living remained almost stationary. With employment good, save in a

few apparently declining industries, most of the wage
earners were receiving earnings that gave them a higher
standard of living than they had ever before enjoyed.
·Furthermore, the technological advances that brought
within the wage earners' reach "comforts beyond the
dreams of medieval kings" were unfavorable to the
extension of the craft type of unionism that still predominantly characterized American labor organization.
The maintenance of employee-representation plans by
many large companies was also a barrier to the spread
of outside labor organization among their employees.
The growth of the existing labor movement had apparently not only been checked but had entered upon
a slow decline in a period of unprecedented prosperity.

For more than a year after the bubble burst in 1929
the unions held their membership very well, at least
in the published figures. But unemployment and the
eventual insistence upon wage cuts by the employers
reduced the ranks, until, by the end of 1932, the membership was down to the pre-war level.

RAPID GROWTH SINCE 1933

The passage of the National Industrial Recovery Act,
in June 1933, brought a sudden and deep-reaching
change in the prospects for labor organization. It was
not merely that the law forbade employer interference
with organization for the purpose of collective bargaining.[6] The act also gave positive encouragement to col-

[6] See below, Chapter V.

lective bargaining as an implement of recovery; and, to the workers and the public at large, collective bargaining connoted labor organization. Once more, too, as in wartime, the leaders of organized labor were recognized by the Administration as the spokesmen of labor generally in matters relating to the recovery program.

The number of workers who affiliated themselves, nominally at least, with labor organizations in the months following the passage of the National Industrial Recovery Act will probably never be accurately known. Certainly it was far greater than the increase subsequently recorded in the sober figures of paid-up membership. In contrast with the period of wartime expansion in labor organization, the economic condition of the workers in 1933 and 1934 was unfavorable to the payment of initiation fees and dues. Wage rates were increased in the summer of 1933, but the number of hours per week was low, many were still unemployed, and the employment of many others was uncertain.

The operation of the clauses of the Recovery Act promising noninterference by the employer with organization for collective bargaining proved a bitter disappointment to the union organizers and to many workers who joined labor organizations on the strength of those promises. The prohibition of discharge for union membership was widely disregarded, and no effective measures of enforcement were applied by the government. Requests for collective bargaining through organizations of the workers' own choosing were frequently refused outright or evaded. That employee-representation plans were also used to check the growth of outside labor organizations was abundantly and indignantly testified by the leaders of those organizations. The Recovery-Act phase ended in May 1935. In July 1935 the National Labor Relations Act was passed to establish the workers' rights more clearly with respect to organization and collective bargaining and to provide a method of enforcement; but the constitutionality of that act was not established until April 1937, and in the meantime most employers had refused to be bound by it.

Although the net increase in labor-organization membership during the Recovery-Act period fell far short of what had been confidently predicted, the estimated total of approximately four millions in 1935 represents a gain of one third over the 1932 membership.

Then followed an unusually favorable combination of factors that carried union membership to a higher total than ever before reached. The important external factors accounting for this growth were the continued upswing in business, the results of the November 1936 elections, which were favorable to the unions, and the decisions of the Supreme Court on the National Labor Relations Act in April 1937. Accompanying these was a more aggressive drive for the organization of the unorganized workers, especially in the mass-production industries. The total membership claimed by labor officials in September 1937 was seven and a half millions. No doubt the figures included many whose membership was still merely nominal, but the previous high of five million paid-up members (in 1920) was unquestionably greatly exceeded.

The outstanding characteristic of this marked expansion was the spread of organization to hitherto unorganized mass-production industries. In 1935 over half of the total union membership was found in railroading, coal mining, the building trades, and printing and publishing. In manufacturing, the only large industries well organized were the clothing industry and the boot and shoe industry. But during 1937 the Committee for Industrial Organization, the so-called C.I.O., made great gains in the newer mass-production industries such as the automobile, rubber, electric equipment and appliances, and radio industries. The most spectacular gain was in the steel industry, long regarded as enemy country to the union. The C.I.O. enrolled the great majority of the workers in that industry. The unions affiliated with the American Federation of Labor also made considerable gains after the break between the Federation and the C.I.O. unions in 1936.

Structural Pattern of Organized Labor

TYPES OF ORGANIZATION

Primary Organizations. It has long been common to classify labor organizations according to the membership base chosen by the organization in question. The membership base of the earliest unions was the single craft; membership was confined to workers skilled in the same occupation, with a common apprenticeship and, in general, a common ability to do the same kind of work. Much later came the so-called *industrial union,* in which membership is based upon employment in a particular industry, regardless of craft or occupation. In between these two there are many unions whose membership coverage is not restricted to one craft but widened to include two or more closely associated crafts. Some of them also include helpers or specialists or other workers not "all-around journeymen." Most of the American unions are of this third type — neither single craft nor industrial unions. They, as well as the single craft organizations, are commonly called *craft unions* today.

The term *trade union,* which originally meant a union of men in the same craft or trade, is now generally applied to all three of these types. In contrast with the trade union, of whatever type, there is a fourth type of labor organization, usually called a *general labor organization.* In this type the coverage transcends all lines of craft, occupation, or industry. The most notable example of this type of organization in American labor history was the Knights of Labor. It is not now an important type of labor organization in this country.

Federation. All four of the types just described are *primary* labor organizations; the individual member belongs directly to the labor organization in question and owes his allegiance primarily to it. The primary organization is thus distinguished from a supplementary federation of labor organizations, formed for the promotion of common interests. The individual worker does not belong to the federation; he belongs to his primary organization; it is the primary organizations that are members or, more accurately, "affiliates", of the federation. For example, the "union" printer belongs to the Typographical Union, which is affiliated with the American Federation of Labor; the individual printer is not a member of the American Federation of Labor.

National and Local Unions. Whatever the membership base chosen by the particular primary organization, it is likely that the workers will attempt to make their organization nationwide, or at least wide enough geographically to cover all the workers included in that base throughout the entire country. Many unions have also included workers in their respective categories in Canada, hence the title "international" in the name of many American unions.

The movement toward national organization by the primary labor organizations in this country began relatively early. The mobility of labor or the widening of the area of competition between employers, or both, led the local unions in the particular craft, crafts, or industry to unite with their fellow workers in other localities. At first their aim was to provide an interchangeability of membership for workers migrating from one locality to another, and to secure closer cooperation in time of strike. Eventually they sought, through national organization, to assure a greater degree of uniformity in policy with respect to admission to the trade and the introduction of labor-saving devices and even a closer approach to uniformity in hours, wages, and other terms of employment. A few of the present national unions date back to the Civil War period, and the oldest of them, the International Typographical Union, was established in 1852.

The establishment of a superstructure of national organization has generally been followed by the absorption of functions and powers by the national union from the constituent local unions. The degree of control exercised by the national union, as distinct from the local union, varies greatly. It depends upon the importance of financial support from the national union in local strikes, upon the degree of uniformity required for the successful maintenance of regulatory policies, and upon whether a wider than local system of collective bargaining and agreements with employers is feasible. In some organizations the national union is practically supreme in determination of the policies, in bargaining, and in control of strikes; the "locals" are little more than administrative units. In others the local unions still retain a large degree of autonomy in deciding upon their demands on the employers and in the calling and conduct of strikes. In the building trades, for example, the local unions generally reserve the right to strike without referring the matter to the national union. The market is local; the local unions of the several different national unions frequently act in concert in the matter of striking; and rapidity in calling a strike against an offending employer is considered essential to success because of the brief duration of most of the jobs.

KNIGHTS OF LABOR

A General Labor Union. The earliest local labor organizations, as it has been pointed out, were craft organizations. The first permanent national organizations were also craft unions. When the Knights of Labor came into prominence, its structure and program and its underlying philosophy carried a challenge to the existing national trade unions. It aspired to be a national general labor organization, transcending all craft and industrial lines. It was not a federation of autonomous unions but was itself a primary organization, with final authority resting, nominally at least, in a national assembly and national executive officers. The membership base and the structure of the Knights of Labor reflect a belief that autonomous craft unionism offered little hope for the great majority of the workers. And although many of its local "assemblies" were constituted on craft lines and although some of its "district" assemblies were also "trade" assemblies, the leaders generally, although not consistently, opposed the formation of national trade organizations within the Knights of Labor. Moreover, its constitution denied autonomy to such trade organizations as were allowed.

The avowed program of the Knights of Labor was more ambitious and more general than that of the individual national craft union, although it contained little that was novel in the history of the American organized labor movement. Education of the workers and social reform through legislation were particularly emphasized. The use of the strike was, in principle, discouraged. However, in practice the membership of the Knights of Labor seemed just as prone to resort to the strike as any trade unionists, and in the middle 1880's the Knights were involved in a sensational series of strikes and boycotts. In spite of the idealism of its professions and the preaching of its leaders, the organization found itself put to the test as a fighting organization. And it failed to meet the test successfully.

Causes of Failure. The failure of the Knights of Labor has generally been attributed to the heterogeneity of its membership and to its structural organization. Had its expansion in membership been less rapid, and had its leadership been firmer and more energetic, it might have made a better showing for that type of organization. As it was, the leaders failed either to control the membership or to assist it vigorously after it had involved the organization in struggles with employers. It is doubtful if the Knights of Labor could have succeeded, in the economic and political conditions prevailing in the 1880's and 1890's, in welding American labor into an effective, all-inclusive, primary organization even if there had been no national trade unions in the field. But the presence of the autonomous national unions as a rival type of organization undoubtedly contributed greatly to the rapid disintegration of the Knights of Labor. And whether or not the experience under the Knights of Labor was a fair test of the value of a general primary labor organization, the fact is that the workers, especially the skilled workers, became convinced that more satisfactory results could be obtained through autonomous organizations on a narrower base.

INDUSTRIAL UNIONISM VERSUS CRAFT UNIONISM

In recent years the most important issue concerning the type of organization has been industrial unionism versus organization along craft lines. The contention that the industry rather than the craft should be generally accepted as the base of primary organization is by no means new, but in the past few years the advocacy of industrial unionism has become much more militant, especially with respect to the large industries that long withstood all attempts to organize them.

The Sphere of Conflict. The challenge of industrial unionism finds organization along craft lines much more firmly entrenched than did the challenge offered craft unionism by the Knights of Labor a half century ago. The industrial base cannot be adopted generally now without separating a much larger number of craftsmen from their fellow craftsmen in long-established unions organized on craft lines. Organizing machinists, blacksmiths, carpenters, painters, stationary engineers, truckmen, and so on, into different unions according to the particular industries in which they are employed — automobile, steel, radio, etc. — would mean cutting the organizational lines along which national unions for these respective occupations have long been operating, even if not wholly successfully. For those occupations that are peculiar to a particular industry, as is the case, for example, with many of the railroad crafts, industrial unionism would mean the merging of the separate craft organizations into a single union, but it would still leave these craftsmen in the same union with their fellow craftsmen. It is with respect to craftsmen whose work is found within the boundaries of different industries that the issue between industrial or "vertical" unionism and craft unionism is most acute.

The Economic Basis of Craft Organization. The unwillingness of unions organized on craft lines to surrender their organizational autonomy is not without an economic basis. Craft unionism is not merely a matter of collective action for bargaining on immediate terms of employment; it has had as one of its main purposes the protection of those already in the craft from the competition of too many newcomers and from the substitution of new methods that threaten to reduce the demand for their skill.[1] To do this most effectively, their collective action must embrace all those who use the craft process, regardless of the particular industry in which they are employed. To split the members of the craft among a number of organizations, in which their interests would be subordinated to those of a larger group in which they would be but a minority, would make more difficult, if not impossible, that united action among the members of the craft which is essential to the enforcement of craft protective regulations.

Even where the crafts are peculiar to the industry, there may be a reluctance to subject the craft's interests to those of a larger group that might not have the same respect for craft rights as the members of the craft. And when it comes to collective bargaining with the employer, many craftsmen still prefer to keep their freedom to use their skill as a bargaining lever for their own craft instead of throwing it into a common pool of strength with all the other employees of the same employer, including the less skilled and unskilled as well as the skilled.

The Economic Basis of Industrial Organization. The chief economic basis of industrial unionism, on

[1] See below, pp. 57–69.

the other hand, is unified action in collective bargaining by all the employees of the same employer or group of employers in the same industry. The maintenance of craft protective regulations is not excluded from the functions of industrial unionism. Indeed, for those crafts that are confined to one industry, an industrial union controlled by a group of crafts that respect each other's craft rights may be the most effective form of organization. But the kind of industrial union envisaged by most advocates of industrial unionism is one in which special craft interests are subordinated to the lifting of the standards for all, skilled and unskilled alike, through unified collective action by all. Such a program cannot be made effective if the skilled groups, whether their skill is peculiar to that industry or not, are to have separate autonomous organizations. Thus, while craft unionism is based on control of the craft wherever practiced, industrial unionism is based on control of all the workers in the industry, whatever the craft or whether craftsmen or not. With respect to many crafts these two bases are obviously in conflict.

There seems to be little doubt that recent economic trends have weakened rather than strengthened the economic bases of craft unionism as contrasted with industrial unionism. Technological changes have already reduced the relative importance of craft skill and have lessened thereby the workers' ability either to control the supply of workers in the craft or to resist further substitution through changes in methods.[2]

[2] See below, pp. 61–63, 68–69.

Moreover, integration in ownership has more and more substituted, as the employer, a large industrial unit for the old master craftsman or the relatively small "contracting shop." The employer has gone farther and farther beyond the boundaries of the craft or the associated crafts. This has seriously reduced the bargaining power of the craft as compared with that of the employer, and has made it seem more desirable for the craftsmen to make common cause with the other employees of the same employer. There are many exceptions, of course, but the general trend has been in this direction.

AMERICAN FEDERATION OF LABOR

Based on Autonomy for National Trade Unions. The rise of the American Federation of Labor to prominence in the world of organized labor was a reflection of the victory of the national trade unions over the general labor union. The Federation is not a primary labor organization; it is the creature of the national trade unions, established to secure that degree of community of action that can safely be combined with autonomy for each national union in trade policies, collective bargaining, and strikes. It represents the answer of the national trade unions to the attempt of the Knights of Labor to make a single general labor union the paramount organization of American labor. Although it now dates its birth at 1881, it was organized in its present form and under its present name in 1886, when the Knights of Labor was apparently at its crest. The Federation then had an affiliated membership of less than 150,000. In 1936, there were 111 national unions in the Federation with an aggregate membership of approximately 3,340,000.[3] The four big "Brotherhoods" in the railroad engine and train service were the only important group of national unions then outside the Federation; no one of them has ever been affiliated with it.

Local Unions Directly Affiliated with the Federation. There are some local unions directly affiliated with the Federation. However, this is intended to be but a transitional arrangement. In its capacity as the agent of the affiliated national unions for the promotion of organization among those yet unorganized, the Federation organizes workers, in occupations for which there is no national union, into local unions attached directly to the Federation. The constitution stipulates that they are to remain in this status only "until such time as there is a sufficient number to form a National or International Union, when it shall be the duty of the President of the Federation to see that such [national] organization is formed." No local union may continue in direct affiliation with the Federation when there is a national union for that trade affiliated with the Federation. If a directly affiliated union is made up of workers in one trade it is known as a "local" trade union; if its membership is mixed, from the standpoint of occupation, it is called a "federal labor union." In 1937 there were 1406 of these

---

[3] This includes the ten national unions suspended for supporting the activities of the Committee for Industrial Organization. The figures for 1937, which are exclusive of national unions suspended or withdrawn, show one hundred affiliated national unions with 3,039,026 members.

local trade and federal labor unions with an aggregate paid-up membership of 232,700.

As the Federation stands somewhat in the relation of a national union, for the time being, to the local trade and federal labor unions, it has some measure of control over them and requires an initiation fee from the members and a per capita tax of thirty-five cents per member per month, of which twelve and a half cents is set aside as a defense fund for them. In 1937 the balance in this defense fund was $533,139, out of the $586,567 total balance which the Federation then reported. These local trade and federal labor unions must be sharply distinguished from the local unions of the national unions affiliated with the Federation; the Federation has practically nothing to do, directly, with the latter local unions.

Powers and Functions Limited. The functions and powers of the Federation are limited by the controlling principle, laid down in its constitution, that it should further "the establishment of National and International Trade Unions, based upon a strict recognition of the autonomy of each trade." The spread of organization among the yet unorganized workers, the encouragement of the sale of union-made goods, the influencing of "public opinion, by peaceful and legal methods, in favor of organized labor", the encouragement of "the labor press of America", the securing of "legislation in the interest of the working people" — these are its chief functions. They indicate the limits of the community of interest recognized by the national trade unions. The constituent national unions have reserved to themselves the determination of their policies with respect to such matters as admission to membership, labor-saving devices, methods of payment, rates of wages, hours of labor, collective bargaining, and strikes. The officers of the Federation may exercise some moral influence upon them in these matters, but the Federation leaves the final decisions to the respective affiliated national unions; it does not lay down their policies for them, nor does it carry on collective bargaining for them, nor order them out on strike, nor order them back to work after they have struck.

The Federation may not tax or collect dues from the individual members of any affiliated national union. The constitution provides that each affiliated national union shall pay to the Federation a per capita tax of one cent per member per month, on its paid-up membership. On a membership of three million in the affiliated national unions this would amount to but $360,000 a year, an amount certainly insufficient to give the Federation financial control over the policies or strikes of the national unions. In addition, the constitution permits the Executive Council of the Federation to levy an assessment on all affiliated unions of one cent per member per week for a period of not more than ten weeks in any one year, "to assist in the support of an affiliated National or International Union engaged in a protracted strike or lockout", but this authority has rarely been used. In 1937 the constitution of the Federation was amended to permit the levying of an assessment by majority vote of the convention; no limit as to the amount is specified. The 1937 convention voted an assessment of one cent per member per month; this is in addition, of course, to the regular per capita tax of the same amount.

Nonpartisan Policy of Political Action. Although the promotion of legislative and administrative action favorable to labor, and especially to labor organization, is one of its most important functions, the American Federation of Labor is not, and never has been, a separate labor party. Its policy for the past thirty years has been that of "rewarding its friends and defeating its enemies" at the polls regardless of party. It makes known the labor record of the candidates of the leading parties and urges the organized workers to support their friends and defeat their enemies in whatever party they are found. It also analyzes and passes judgment on the national party platforms on points affecting labor directly, but it does not endorse a party as such. This program is known as "the nonpartisan policy." Even when the Federation's "Nonpartisan Campaign Committee" clearly indicates a preference, its action is only advisory to the members of the affiliated unions. It has never assumed to make the support of a favored candidate a condition of affiliation with the Federation.

Jurisdictional Disputes between Unions in the Federation. The chief internal problem of the Federation is that of conflicting jurisdictional claims on the part of affiliated national unions. When a national union is affiliated with the Federation, it makes a statement of the categories of workers that it will accept for membership and this is approved by the Federation as denoting its jurisdiction. The constitution forbids the granting of a charter of affiliation to any union, national or local, "if the jurisdiction claimed is a trespass on the jurisdiction of existing affiliated unions without the written consent of such unions." But methods of production change, and a change in materials or tools or in the place where the work is done — whether in a shop or at the place of installation — may cause a conflict over jurisdiction of the work between two unions, each contending that the work falls within its accepted sphere of jurisdiction. For example, the introduction of metal window frames, instead of wooden ones, gave rise to a long drawn-out dispute between the Sheet Metal Workers and the Carpenters over which craft should put them in; the former claimed the work because the frames were metal, while the latter insisted that the work belonged to them because putting in window frames had always been their work. The building trades have been especially prolific of jurisdictional disputes of this kind.

The Federation has been drawn into jurisdictional controversies because one, or both, of the disputing unions complains that the other is trespassing beyond the jurisdiction on which its affiliation with the Federation is conditioned, and calls upon the Federation to make it desist or expel it from the Federation. The Federation usually tries to get the dispute settled by agreement between the warring unions, but in this it has met with many discouragements. However, if it renders a clear-cut decision, it will not necessarily settle the issue. Its decision may be ignored by the union decided against. It may then expel the offending union from the Federation. But this does not mean necessarily that the expelled union will not continue to refuse to work on the same job or in the same plant with members of the other union, or that it will not be given support in this by some local unions of national unions affiliated with the Federation. Thus, some of these jurisdictional quarrels have dragged on for years, to the discredit of organized labor and almost to the despair of the officials of the Federation, to say nothing of the loss suffered by employers.

Jurisdictional disputes of the above class, however troublesome, do not directly involve the issue of the type of organization to be followed; it is a question of *which* craft union shall have jurisdiction over borderline work. But an attempt to widen the base of unionism by including workers in occupations for which there are already separate national unions affiliated with the Federation raises a very different issue. Whatever may be the advantages of a wider union base under changed conditions, the constitution of the Federation forbids it to countenance the clear invasion of a jurisdiction already granted by it. At times a claim by a larger so-called "craft" union to a large part or all of the work claimed by a smaller craft union has led to the merging of the smaller union into the larger, with every appearance of reluctance on the part of the latter, but it has not been admitted that this solution involved a revocation of jurisdiction by the Federation.

The Conflict over Industrial Unionism. The demand that the Federation accept the industry as the base of organization, even if it involved the withdrawal of jurisdiction from unions organized on craft lines over those workers in their respective crafts who are employed in large industries, raised a much more difficult issue. The Federation is not committed to the principle of separate craft organization. If several crafts in the same industry, or otherwise closely associated in their bargaining activities, wish to unite in a single national union, the Federation will not refuse it affiliation. Nor will it object to the crafts peculiar to an industry taking into their organization semi-skilled workers whose work is also peculiar to the industry, or even unskilled workers, over whom, obviously, no existing craft unions claim jurisdiction. The Federation has never objected to "industrial unions" of this character; there are several of them in the Federation.

It was the fact that the unions in the "inter-industry" crafts were unwilling to surrender any of their jurisdictions that made so difficult the formation of vertical or industrial unions in the newer industries with the blessing of the Federation. For the Federation it was not a question of whether the vertical type of organization would be more successful for the workers as a whole in the particular industry. It was not even a question of the comparative failure of the unions organized along craft lines to get and hold the allegiance of the particular workers in the mass-production industries, over whom they have what has been contemptuously termed "paper jurisdiction." It was a question of openly disregarding jurisdictions once granted to a large number of national unions, against the will of these unions.

With several large industrial unions demanding, on the one hand, that a vigorous effort be made to organize the workers in the mass-production industries into single vertical national unions for each industry and, on the other hand, with most of the national unions in the Federation opposing the abandonment of the traditional principle that jurisdictions already granted must be respected, the Federation was finally split asunder. The defeat in the 1935 convention, after a long debate, of the advocates of a free hand for organization on the industry base, was followed by the formation by the defeated group of a Committee for Industrial Organization. It was soon apparent that this group was going ahead with an independent campaign for organization on industrial lines in the mass-production industries in defiance of the orders of the officers of the Federation. In September 1936, ten national unions affiliated with the Committee for Industrial Organization were suspended from the American Federation of Labor by the Executive Council of the Federation. The suspension was approved by the annual convention of the Federation in November. An open break between the C.I.O. and the A.F. of L. soon followed.

THE C.I.O.

The ten national unions suspended by the A.F. of L. had almost a million members at the time of their suspension. The most important of these unions were the United Mine Workers, the Ladies' Garment Workers, and the Amalgamated Clothing Workers (in the men's clothing industry). All three are strong unions; together, the three accounted for a fifth of the A.F. of L. membership in 1936. The C.I.O. has since drawn other unions away from the Federation. In addition, it has taken in several new national industrial unions that are rivals of national unions affiliated with the Federation. It has also affiliated with itself a large number of local unions scattered among many industries and occupations hitherto little organized. Some of its affiliates seem to be craft or vocational, rather than industrial, unions. The C.I.O. claimed 3,700,000 members in September 1937 in thirty-two affiliated national unions and approximately six hundred directly affiliated local unions.

The structure of this new organization has not yet been worked out. So far, the officials of the mine workers' and clothing workers' unions seem to have exercised a large measure of control over the organizing activities of some of the other affiliated national unions and to have taken an important part in the negotiations with employees for their members. But the intention is, presumably, to form a permanent federation of more or less autonomous national unions. There are indications of a leaning toward more united action among the industrial unions in carrying on strikes than has characterized the A.F. of L. There appears to be a greater preference, too, for open support of a separate labor party in the political field. On the financial side, the funds have been largely supplied by the mine workers' and clothing workers' unions. Since June 1, 1937, however, all affiliated national unions have been called upon to pay five cents per member per month to the C.I.O., and the directly affiliated local unions fifty cents per member per month.

CHAPTER III

Trade-Union Policies

THE primary purpose of trade unionism is the substitution of combination for competition among the workers with respect to the terms of employment. The terms of employment that are made the subject of collective action include not only wages but also the normal hours of work and the "working conditions", that is, the physical and other conditions in the place of employment that affect the health, safety, or comfort of the employees. The terms of employment may also include such matters as the order of advancement, the order of layoff when business is poor, and the procedure to be followed in discharging men. Another economic basis of trade unionism is the maintenance of regulations intended to protect the "vested right" of those already in the trade to the work of the trade. Such protective regulations cover the conditions of entrance of new workers into the trade and also the control of changes in methods of production that affect the demand for the labor of those already in the occupation.

Inasmuch as regulations of this kind are maintained, as a rule, only by workers who have a common skill to protect, these regulations may be called "craft protective regulations."

Most trade-union policies originate in the attempt to use one or the other of these types of collective action — collective action on the immediate terms of employment and collective regulation of numbers or methods of production. It is not intended to imply that unions do not have higher and more general aims than the improvement or safeguarding of the terms of employment of their own members. However, this has been their primary economic function and the more specific policies that they have adopted to accomplish this purpose must be given the first and largest place in the necessarily brief discussion that follows.

ADMISSION TO MEMBERSHIP

To make the substitution of collective action on terms of employment for individual bargaining complete, the trade union must include in its membership all the workers in the occupation. This, in general, is what is aimed at. The union may attempt to keep down the number of workers entering the trade, but once they are in the trade the need of controlling their competition dictates that they be included in the combination. Unless exclusion of workers from union membership means that they will not be allowed to work at the trade, the control of admission to membership cannot be used to control entrance to the trade. Union membership as a prerequisite for being allowed to work at a trade is seldom realized in practice; it requires not only that nonmembers be excluded from working in union shops but also that all the shops in which the trade may be learned be union shops. To be sure, unions have sometimes pursued an exclusive policy with respect to membership even when they have not had control of all the shops. In such instances, the control of a smaller supply of union labor, instead of an all-inclusive combination, is preferred in the hope that nonunion competition will not become important enough to break down the success of the combination in the field that it controls. Such a policy, however, has been the exception rather than the rule. Some unions, too, have excluded female workers or negro workers in the hope of keeping them out of the trade, but this also has been an exceptional policy and one frowned on by the members of most unions.

REGULATION OF ENTRANCE TO TRADE

Even before the days of trade unionism, the protection of the "vested interest" of the members of the craft in the work of the craft was a function of organizations of craftsmen; and it has been an important economic basis of labor organization from the earliest days. Indeed, the enforcement of craft protective regulations, which had behind them not only the sanction of custom but also the tradition of legal sanction, was a reason for labor organization in England before what is now called "collective bargaining" was recognized as legal.

The regulation of entrance to a skilled trade is a logically distinct economic function from that of collective bargaining on the terms of employment. Wage earners can raise wages, reduce the length of the working week, improve working conditions, and establish rights of tenure in the job by the use of collective bargaining, without restricting the number entering the occupation.[1] On the other hand, restriction of numbers would result in a higher level of wages for those in the trade even if the terms of employment were left to individual bargaining. Organizations of workers that attempt to control the number entering the trade almost invariably resort also to collective bargaining on the terms of employment. Nevertheless, the control of numbers must be considered as a separate factor affecting the ability of the workers to get better terms. The restriction of the "quantity" of labor of that class offered for "sale" exerts the same kind of upward pressure upon the "price" of the labor as does the restriction of the production of a commodity upon the price of that commodity. The restriction of the number admitted to the trade creates a monopolistic condition on the supply side.[2]

The control of entrance to the trade is today much more difficult than in the days when apprenticeship was the only avenue of admission to a trade. In those days, regulation of the conditions of apprenticeship meant control of numbers. This was not the only purpose of union apprenticeship regulations; the proper training of the future journeymen was another ob-

---

[1] The economic possibilities of gain through the use of collective bargaining are discussed in the following chapter.

[2] *Cf.* McIsaac, A. M., and Smith, J. G., *Introduction to Economic Analysis* (1937), pp. 268–269.

jective. But craft interest was joined with pride of craft in support of the limitation of the number of apprentices and the requirement of a minimum period of training.

Changes in methods of production have greatly reduced the relative importance of apprenticeship as a means of entrance to manual occupations. In only a small number of trades is it the exclusive avenue of entrance. In many trades in which the unions still maintain rules governing the number of recognized apprentices and the period and character of apprenticeship training, men who have never served a formal apprenticeship are admitted to the union as a matter of course; the practical requirement is that the candidate shall be a competent journeyman, and the practical test of competency is ability to get a job at the union rate of wages. This reflects the existence of opportunities to learn the trade under other than union auspices as well as a technological trend away from the need of the old-time apprenticeship training. It is the latter cause, of course, that is fundamental. Even in union shops, in many trades, apprenticeship no longer has the position it once had. Many employers have been unwilling to put on the number of apprentices the union rules allow. This situation has led the unions and the "union-shop" employers, in a few trades, to set up a new program of apprentice training that combines instruction in the shop with instruction in schools, in order to insure a supply of well-trained workmen for the future.

The decline of old-time apprenticeship has not pre-

cluded union control, through other means, over the
number of men learning the trade in union shops. In
those occupations in which the journeymen are re-
cruited from helpers who work along with them, the
unions generally regulate the rate of advancement of
helpers to journeyman status, whether the helpers are
called apprentices or not. In some occupations the rule
is that no one is to be advanced to journeyman status
unless there is a vacancy. In railroad engine and train
service not only is the advance from fireman to engineer
and from trainman to conductor governed by this rule,
but qualified men are advanced in the order of seniority.
Moreover, the last advanced must return to the lower
status when, because of a decline in traffic or a technological change, there is a surplus of men in the
higher status. They are not allowed to remain as competitors for jobs on the higher level.

When due allowance is made for the many surviving
examples of control of the numbers of eligible journeymen, the fact remains that the requisite conditions for
the successful use of the policy of restriction of numbers are not common in present-day industry. A restriction of numbers is enforced by the refusal of those
in the trade to teach newcomers, except under the
rules laid down, and by the refusal of those already in
the trade to work in establishments where men are
employed who have not learned the trade in conformity with the rules. The efficacy of these measures
of enforcement varies with the relative importance to
the employer of avoiding a break with the members
of the union and of the advantage to him of having

a freer hand in putting on new workers. If the employer is dependent upon the workers already in the trade for the performance of the bulk of the work, as well as for the training of the newcomers, a union that includes all the skilled workers will be able to maintain a limitation upon the creation of new journeymen. But, with changes in the methods of production, these conditions have become less and less prevalent.

CHANGES IN METHODS OF PRODUCTION

In the early days of trade unionism, craft protective regulations were primarily directed against competition from "unauthorized persons." But, as new technological methods were introduced in one industry after another, protection of the journeymen's market from invasion by substitute methods of production became an added feature of trade-union policy. An influx of new workers under the customary methods of production adds to supply; a change in the methods of production that reduces the need for skilled journeymen lessens demand. Skilled workmen have always shown a tendency to oppose the second quite as much as the first. If the workers are organized, this opposition is very likely to be reflected in a union policy either of exclusion of the proposed change from union shops or, in the case of an important technological advance, of imposing conditions upon its use.

The transfer of part of the "journeyman's work" to less skilled labor is a type of change that unions have opposed again and again. Insistence is general that only men who have qualified as journeymen shall

do journeyman's work and that no one shall do journeyman's work who does not receive the journeyman's
rate of pay — unless he is a recognized apprentice. The
union objection to "dilution" through subdivision of
work is based, of course, upon the assumption that it
will reduce the demand for skilled journeymen. The
argument that by lowering unit costs it will increase
rather than diminish the demand for journeymen
usually fails to convince the union members.

The same objection accounts for the opposition
unions have offered to minor labor-saving devices of
one kind or another. For example, painters have prohibited the use of brushes, for oil paint, that are
more than four and a half inches in width; marble
workers have opposed the use of pneumatic hammers.
Other building-trades unions have required that certain work be done "on the job" rather than prepared
in advance in the shop. The printers long prohibited
the use of "borrowed matter", that is, the transfer of
type set up for one newspaper to another newspaper to
be used without being reset — as in the case of advertising matter to be run in both papers.

The possibility of preventing a change in the methods
of production by collective resistance depends upon
the degree of reduction in labor costs involved in the
change as compared with the degree to which the employer would still require, after the change, the labor
of workers possessed of the old skill. A proposed subdivision of labor that would give only a small part
of the work, then done by journeymen, to relatively
unskilled men, would not bring a saving in cost suf-

ficient to offset the loss involved in a concerted with-drawal of the skilled men.

The exclusion by a union of the use of a single minor labor-saving device may be more irritating than important. The reduction in labor cost that would re-sult from its adoption may be small. Similarly, it may affect but little the demand for journeyman labor. Yet, if restrictions of this kind become numerous in a particular trade, their cumulative effect may be great enough to induce the employers to give battle for the general repeal, or at least the modification, of restrictive rules on methods. The question for the employers is one of whether a victory would be worth the cost.

The introduction of a machine or a new process is more spectacular than the substitution of less skilled workers or the introduction of a minor labor-saving device. However, the economic issue presented is the same in kind. There is the same question of how far the new machine or new process leaves the employer dependent upon the possessors of the old skill. Because it has so often happened that the employers have been able finally to secure satisfactory operators for new machines or new processes in spite of the opposition of the men who have been doing the work by the old method, it has come to be generally accepted that a union cannot successfully pursue a policy of exclusion in the case of an important labor-saving machine or process. It is impossible to keep it out of the industry by refusing to allow it in union shops. If and when there are nonunion shops using the new method with considerable competitive advantage over the union shops, the union must come to terms on its use in union shops or see the industry go more and more nonunion through the loss of business to the nonunion shops and, eventually, the breaking away of shops from the union. Therefore, the union policy toward machinery and new processes has come to be, generally, one of regulation rather than of exclusion.

The objectives of a policy of regulation of a machine or a new process are to slow down the displacement of workers from the old method, to transfer as many as possible of the members displaced from the old method to the new, and to get as good wages as possible for the new method. The last-mentioned objective is related, of course, to the first two. The higher the wages on the new method, the less rapid, other things being equal, will be the encroachment of the new method on the old and the greater will be the likelihood that the old-method men will take the jobs on the new method. If the policy of control places a handicap upon the new method in competition with the old, so much the better, from the union standpoint. The union members believe themselves justified in slowing down the rate of displacement and in gaining for the workers on the new method as large a share as possible of the gains from technological advance.

The effectiveness of a policy of regulation is dependent, as was pointed out above, upon the technical character of the new method. If it requires skill of the same kind as the old method, and to the same degree, the chances are excellent that the union may secure as good wages on the new job as on the old and also preference on the new jobs for the members displaced from the old. This was the case when the linotype machine was introduced to replace typesetting by hand. However, such favorable conditions are not common.

Another important factor is the proportion of the work on which the new method can be used. If it covers but part of the necessary operations, leaving the need for men of the old skill on operations preceding or following the operations taken over by the machine or new process, the union is in a good position to insist on higher wages than the kind and degree of skill required for the new operations would command in an unrestricted market. The same is true if the new method can be applied only on certain types of product. In more than a few cases a union has, by its control of the labor necessary for the other operations or the other types of product, secured as good terms as those on the old job, or almost as good, for new jobs that did not require as much skill as the old.

On the other hand, if the new operation requires little or no skill, or if the old skill is useless for the new method, and if the new method takes care of the bulk of the work, there is little that the union can do. The new method can be made an effective competitor without the use of any of the labor controlled by the union.

A good illustration of the difference between technological conditions that permit a large measure of control and those that make control impossible is found in the history of the glass bottle industry. The first machine introduced, the "semi-automatic", was one on which the skill of "hand blowers" gave them a considerable advantage over green men in operating the machine. Moreover, the machine was successful at first only on wide-mouthed bottles. The value of the old skill in the new operation, and the need of the employers for hand blowers for the general run of ware, enabled the union to gain control of the semi-automatic machine and to establish a level of earnings for it almost as high as that of the hand blowers. But several years later came the "Owens automatic", a machine in which the glass was fed and blown automatically. This machine was almost a complete glass factory in itself. The employer who installed one could operate without any of the labor controlled by the union. The union, therefore, had no lever by which it could gain control of the work done on this machine.

By way of summary it may be said that unions of skilled men may, for a time, prevent the introduction of a minor change in methods that reduces the need for journeyman labor for a given quantity of output. When the technical conditions are favorable, unions may also regulate the introduction of important machines or processes so as to keep up the demand, at relatively good wages, for the men already in the trade. There seems little doubt that unions in the building trades and in the publishing industry, for example, owe their strength in no small part to the successful use of such controls. However, there is a decided limit to regulation of methods as an economic basis of trade unionism. If the union restrictions get too far out of line with technological possibilities, they furnish an incentive to employers to attempt to produce without restrictions, and an incentive to other workers to accept the new jobs that promise to develop into better jobs than those they then have. This new competition will reduce the demand for the labor of the union workers and defeat the purpose of the union restrictions. The decisive factor is the character of the technological change. And the tendency has been toward technological changes that reduce rather than enlarge the economic possibilities of control through collective action by those already in the occupation.

WAGES AND HOURS

Trade-union policies as to the level of wages and the length of the working day or working week may be briefly summarized as raising wages and lowering hours as much as possible. There is no generally accepted trade-union principle that sets a limit to the increase of the one or to the decrease of the other. The arguments advanced in negotiations with employers, in arbitrations, or in appeals for public support, have varied from time to time and from union to union, according to the instant conditions, but the policy generally followed is that of raising the standard of hourly wages and shortening the working day whenever possible and by as much as possible.

Wage Principles. The arguments invoked to support requests for wage increases, or to ward off reductions in wages, include the principle of the family living wage, the right of labor to share in the increase of real income made possible by industrial progress, and the necessity of increasing the purchasing power of the workers to prevent depression — or to secure recovery from a depression. The first of these arguments is used chiefly by unions of less skilled workers, or for their less skilled groups by unions of the more vertical type. It is offered as a norm for the lowest permissible wage for adult males, and not as a standard in any way limiting wages above the lowest "living wage." Unions of workers in the more skilled brackets, and even the more skilled groups within unions of the vertical type, tend to insist upon the necessity of maintaining their "differentials" above the wages of the lower wage groups in the same industry. The argument for a share in the benefits of progress and the purchasing-power argument are used for all classes. The two arguments are closely related in periods of increasing per capita production. The cost-of-living argument is used by practically all unions also, but only when the cost of living is advancing. When living costs are dropping, the unions fall back on the necessity of raising workers' living standards and on the purchasing-power argument.

Reasons for Reducing the Number of Hours. The arguments for reducing the length of the working day include: the argument on grounds of health, safety, and prevention of premature superannuation; the claim to a fair amount of leisure; the claim to a share, in this form also, of the benefits of technological advance; and, most important of all in recent years, the argument that it is necessary to reduce the working week to provide for the employment of a larger number of workers. At times the reduction in the work week has been advocated as a means of securing greater regularity of employment through the year in seasonal industries, but the argument that reduction in the number of hours is necessary to prevent total unemployment of some has been used generally by trade unions for many years. It has been especially stressed, of course, in times of depression. More recently a drastic, permanent reduction in the length of the working week has been advocated as absolutely essential to the reabsorption of workers displaced by technological changes. The work week generally advocated now as necessary to this end is the "thirty-hour week", but it must not be assumed that the figure "30" has a fixed place in trade-union policy, either as the immediate practical demand of all unions or as a reduction to end reductions in the length of the working week.

The union policy of reduction in hours of work has not been one of accepting a reduction in the daily wage as the price of a reduction in the number of hours in the "normal" day. The policy generally followed has been that of demanding the same daily wage — and often an increased daily wage — for a smaller number of hours. The demand for a reduction in hours has meant in practice a demand for a corresponding increase, at least, in the hourly wage. And the one has seldom been accepted without the other; if both could not be obtained together, the reduction in hours has usually been postponed until it could be obtained without a reduction in the weekly wage. So far from believing that reductions in hours can be got only at the expense of wages, trade unionists generally hold that "reducing the hours increases the pay." This means the pay per day. And it is possible that a reduction in the normal number of hours may enable a union to hold a higher hourly wage by reducing the number of members seeking work.[3]

The union method of "enforcing" observance of the normal day upon employers is to set a higher hourly rate for hours beyond the normal than for the hours up to the normal number. The overtime rate is usually "time and one half" (150 per cent of the normal rate), with "double time" (double the normal rate) for the days or half days not included in the normal working week. These are known as "punitive overtime rates." They allow the employer to work the men overtime in emergencies but impose a tax to insure that it is an emergency. This practice has led to the charge that in demanding a shorter workday the men are aiming not so much at a reduction in actual hours as at an increase in the daily wages. However, most unions frown upon men working overtime regularly while other members of the union are unemployed.

Collective Action on Wages and Individual Outputs. Collective action on wages, if it is to supersede competition among the workers completely, must cover not only the amount of wages to be insisted upon

[3] See below, p. 94.

but also the amount of work to be done for the wages. If one man offers to do twenty-five per cent more work than another for the same wages, he is offering his labor, in terms of output, at a lower price. Where the wage rate is expressed in terms of output — so much per dozen, per hundred, per ton, etc. — as it is under the piecework system, the acceptance of a lower wage per piece is clearly recognized as a form of wage competition and is practically universally forbidden by unions as a negation of collective action on wages. But where the wage rate is stated as so much per hour, the wage rate does not expressly cover the quantity of work to be done for the wage, and collective action on the wage rate alone apparently leaves to individual action the matter of the output to be given for the wages. However, trade unions have tended to supplement collective action on wages with some degree of collective action, direct or indirect, on the quantity of output even under the "timework" system, wherever quantitative comparisons of daily output are feasible.

The union position on the connection between output and wages is, generally, that there should be no increase in output without a corresponding increase in pay. A bargain for a given rate of wages, they hold, assumes a given level of output; if output is to be increased it should be only with a proportionate increase in wages for all whose output is increased. Any "speeding up" by individuals that leads to an increase in the output exacted from all for the old level of earnings is frowned upon.

This view of the proper relation between output and

wages is reinforced by the well-known union opposition to speeding up on its own demerits. Speeding up is charged with injuring health, reducing the length of the working life, and reducing the number of employed. In these respects it is in the same category with the long working day. The reduction of the hours of work and the prevention of speeding up are part of the same general policy with respect to the "day's work", a policy that has been intensified in recent years by the pressure of widespread unemployment. The opposition to increasing daily outputs is logically independent of the policy toward changes in methods of production — it is followed even while the methods remain unchanged — but it proceeds from the same deeply rooted fear of unemployment. With this dread of the consequences of increasing daily outputs in mind, it is easy to understand the union opposition to such an increase when not accompanied by a proportionate increase in pay.

DISCHARGE AND DISTRIBUTION OF WORK

In general, trade unionists would agree that workers should be hired and retained on the basis of competency. They do not agree, however, that the employer should be given a free hand in discharging or in the selection of the workers to be laid off when work is scarce, without any so-called interference from the union.

Whether or not the union agrees to a general statement that freedom in hiring and discharge remains with the employer, most unions reserve the right to object to "arbitrary" discharge. To some degree this reservation is part of a policy of protecting its members from discrimination on account of union membership or union activity. But it proceeds also from a conviction that a man ought not to be discharged except for good cause. This means that, where the man complains, the organization should satisfy itself that the cause is really a good one. Unrestricted freedom to discharge does not exist, therefore, where the union is strong enough to resist what it considers discriminatory discharges or arbitrary discharges.

Unions also take a hand in the determination of the policy to be followed with respect to layoffs when work is scarce. The unions do not agree, however, in their policies on this issue. Most of them favor a policy of equal distribution of such work as there is among all the men, but some follow a policy of preferential rights to full-time employment, or to a minimum number of hours, with layoff for the remainder. The most frequent basis for such preference is that of length of service. In occupations in which the jobs are graded, the unions that have succeeded in establishing the rule of seniority in advancement or choice of jobs usually apply seniority — length of service — to the distribution of work as well. Layoffs are made in reverse order of seniority to the point necessary to leave a minimum number of hours or days for those retained. A notable example of this is found in the railroad engine and train service. In most organized trades, however, there are no seniority rights with respect to particular jobs and the unions in these trades generally favor the principle of "equal distribution of work."

Where the men are paid under the time system, the insistence on equal distribution of the work, as contrasted with freedom of the employer to select workers for complete layoff, prevents the employer from reducing his force by laying off the least competent workers and so rewarding the more competent with more regular employment. However, the principle of equal distribution of work in dull times appeals strongly to the men as the only just way of meeting the depressed condition of trade. If any have to be laid off, the unions generally favor the rule of seniority, modified perhaps by preference to married men. These are objective rules of preference that are independent of the employer's findings as to relative competency. It must be recognized that freedom on the employer's part to lay off would be almost tantamount in practice to unrestricted freedom to discharge.

OTHER POLICIES

The above discussion of union policies is not intended to be exhaustive. There are other policies followed by a few or many unions that cannot be discussed here for lack of space. Mention may be made, however, of insistence upon improvement of the physical conditions in the place of employment that affect the health, safety, or comfort of employees. It is true that these have usually been given a subordinate place to such matters as wages and hours in the schedule of union "demands" upon employers, and that in this sphere reliance upon legislation has been especially marked. But direct collective action for improvement of the physical conditions of employment has by no means played a negligible part in trade-union policy.

Co-operation with management in reducing costs of production, or improving the quality of the product, without either reducing earnings or speeding up the workers unduly, is another policy of which mention should be made. "Union-management co-operation" in railroad shops has been much advertised since 1924, but the policy that it reflects was not altogether new nor is it confined to the railroads. It cannot take root, however, until it is clear that the employer fully accepts trade unionism, not only as a bargaining agency but, in the case of the skilled workers, as a craft-protecting agency as well. This helps to explain why union-management co-operation was regarded in the middle 1920's as a "revolutionary" innovation and why formal co-operation is still the exception rather than the rule. Militant unionism and co-operation do not easily mix. Where the employer has accepted the union as a constructive agency, however, it has often been found that collective bargaining on the terms of an agreement every two or three years is consistent with peaceful and co-operative relations in the common business of production from day to day. This is even more likely to be true when the union and the employers are fighting nonunion competition — or foreign competition. "Co-operation" in the production process, always with due regard for the protection of the workers' jobs or their compensation in case of displacement, is of a piece with union promotion of the sales of union-made goods, a union policy of long standing.

It is not possible to discuss in detail the large volume of trade-union benefits of a more or less insurance character, ranging from sick benefits to death benefits, or of the maintenance by national unions of homes for superannuated members, or of the provision of hospitalization for members suffering from specified diseases.[4] These activities have not only provided assistance that could not, in many cases, have been secured in any other way; they have also, and designedly, made union membership more attractive and the loss of good standing more to be avoided. But they have, save in a few exceptional cases, been carried on apart from union dealings with employers. And, however important they have been in the past in providing a modicum of worker security against the contingencies of ill health, old age without income, last-illness and funeral expense, and unemployment, they are a bit aside from the function of collective action on terms of employment or craft protective measures affecting the supply of workers or the use of substitute methods.

[4] See below, Chapter VIII.

CHAPTER IV

Trade-Union Methods

COLLECTIVE BARGAINING

THE NATURE OF COLLECTIVE BARGAINING

Collective Action and Collective Bargaining. The method usually employed by trade unions to put into effect their policies as to the terms of employment is negotiation with the employer, or a group of employers, for an agreement. The term "collective bargaining" is applied to the method because it involves collective negotiation on the *workers'* side; collective bargaining is contrasted with individual bargaining. Collective bargaining presupposes some previous collective action among the workers with respect to proposals to be presented for inclusion in an agreement. Collective bargaining also assumes the probability of collective refusal to work if an agreement is not reached. Thus, collective bargaining is but one step in collective action, although, if successfully carried through to an agreement with the employer, it is the culmination of collective action. There may be successful collective action by workers on some matters, such as limits on individual outputs, without collective bargaining with an employer, but collective bargaining without collective action is a contradiction in terms.

Representative Bargaining and Union Recognition. Collective bargaining is, in practice, also representative bargaining. The workers might go to the employer *en masse* to present proposals and discuss them with him, but it is much more practicable to send representatives to deal with the employer as spokesmen for the group. The representatives, in the case of organized workers, are either full-time union officers or workers chosen for the purpose under union procedure. The union representatives may all be workers employed by the company, especially if they come to deal on issues arising out of conditions peculiar to the plant or on piece rates for products made in that plant alone. Dealing through "insiders" is not peculiar to company unions; it not only has an important place in trade-union practice but it is urged by many unions as the proper practice for handling certain types of questions and for the initiation of negotiations on other questions. The "insiders" come, however, as accredited representatives of the union that regards itself as the accredited agent of the workers in the plant.

If the employer receives and deals with the union representatives in their capacity as representatives of the organization, he is said to "recognize the union" as the agent of his employees or at least of those of his employees who are members of the union. At times, members of a union have carried on collective bargaining without formal recognition of the union. But, as collective bargaining through the union is one of the primary purposes of organization, union members generally consider union recognition essential to collective bargaining.

Collective Negotiation for Terms in Advance of Any Sale. Collective bargaining involves more than an agreement among the members of the group not to accept lower terms than those agreed upon among themselves. It goes beyond the analogy of a simple price agreement among sellers of a commodity that fixes the terms to which each seller will adhere in his individual dealings with prospective buyers.[1] Under collective bargaining the negotiation for terms is unified. The bargaining is carried on for all in advance of any "sale" by any member of the combination. In other words, it is understood that none will work until terms have been agreed upon by the combination with the employer (or employers) for all who are to be employed. Collective bargaining has this practical advantage, among others, over a simple agreement among the workers themselves on terms; namely, that it is more likely to result in terms that each worker knows will be adhered to.

Collective Agreements. Collective bargaining, when carried to successful completion, results in an agreement between the workers' combination and an employer or group of employers. This is often called a

---

[1] *Cf.* McIsaac, A. M., and Modlin, G. M., *Social Control of Industry* (1938).

"collective agreement." The expressions "joint agreement" and "trade agreement" are also used. The workers' side may include more than one union; on the railroads, collective agreements have often included several different national unions, as well as a number of roads. The term collective agreement is used here for all agreements between unions and employers, whether there be one union or several on the workers' side and a single employer or a group of employers on the other. The adjective "collective" signifies merely that the agreement is the result of collective bargaining.

It is important to note the essential character of a collective agreement. It is not a contract of sale. The union does not sell the labor of its members in block, nor does the employer agree to hire a given number of workers at the specified terms. The employer binds himself to grant the terms of the collective contract to such workers as he employs, in the designated classes. If the agreement permits the employment of workers who are not members of the union, it is usually understood, if not expressly stated, that the terms apply to all of the workers in the classes in question. In other words, it is the terms that are covered, not the amount of labor to be employed. What the union agrees to, for its part, is that it will not call strikes, or countenance strikes by its members, during the period for which that particular agreement is to run. Agreements are ordinarily made for a specified period of time — for one, two, or more years. In some cases, however, the agreement is to run for a minimum period and to continue in effect beyond that date until terminated or modified after a specified period of notice. This is, for example, the practice on the railroads.

ECONOMIC POSSIBILITIES IN COLLECTIVE BARGAINING

Collective bargaining plays such an important part in trade-union activity that it is well to consider at this point the sources of, and the limits to, the economic advantages that can be gained by the workers through the substitution of collective for individual bargaining. The analysis will be confined to the use of the method of collective bargaining in the determination of the general terms of employment — wages, hours, working conditions, and rights with respect to discharge, distribution of work, vacations with pay, and so on. It will not include the possibilities of gain through regulation of the supply of labor and of the methods of production; the economic possibilities with respect to such regulatory policies have already been discussed.[2] It is true that the method of collective bargaining is used to secure the observance of these regulatory rules by the employer. But the ensuing discussion deals only with the possibilities of securing better terms of employment for the existing supply of labor, under the existing methods of production, through substituting collective for individual bargaining.

The Limitations of Individual Bargaining. To appraise the economic possibilities of securing better terms of employment through the use of collective

[2] See above, pp. 57–69.

bargaining, it is necessary to bear in mind the conditions under which individual bargaining is carried on. What is called individual bargaining is ordinarily not "bargaining" at all, in the sense of higgling over terms. Except, perhaps, in small establishments, the terms offered by the employer are not subject to change through negotiation with the individual seeking employment. For the applicant it is usually a case of "take it or leave it" as first offered. Whatever advance the employer makes in his offer from time to time, because of the necessity of bettering his terms in order to get the number and quality of workers he needs, he makes on his own initiative; he does not depart from his first offer in dealing with the individual applicant. A worker who has been employed for some time by the same employer may, by individual negotiation, secure an advance over the "hiring rate" or "starting rate" for that class of labor in that plant, but the starting rate is ordinarily applied automatically until the worker has shown superior capacity. And the starting rate is not itself fixed by higgling with individual workers. Thus, the expression "individual bargaining" does not imply a bargaining process so much as it implies that the choice on the part of the worker between "taking it or leaving it" is made individually, that is, without any concerted action with other workers in the matter.

It must be remembered, too, that the terms of employment include much more than wages. The normal hours of labor and the working conditions are also of vital importance to the workers. The workers are not selling commodities with which they will have no further personal connection, but services, which cannot be rendered apart from their own personal presence. These services must usually be performed on the premises of the employer and under his direction. The workers are selling the disposal of their time under a physical environment provided by another. And there is even less chance for real bargaining by the individual worker over the normal hours of labor or the working conditions than there is over wage rates. To be sure, an employer may make the hours and working conditions in his plant more attractive in order to get and keep the workers he wants. But the individual worker has, in practice, slight chance of getting the hours or working conditions changed by isolated dickering. If the workers are to bargain directly on these matters they can do so only through collective action.

The same is true of rights concerning discharge, order of layoff, distribution of work, vacations with pay and similar matters. If such rights are to be established in advance through bargaining, it must be by collective bargaining. The employer may announce a policy with respect to these matters, and adhere to it, without collective bargaining, but the announcement of such individual "rights" by the employer does not mean that they are the result of bargaining, nor does it prevent their termination by action of the employer alone.

Individual Bargaining and Competition. Another important point to bear in mind in comparing the economic possibilities of collective and individual bargaining is that individual bargaining does not imply a condition of informed, two-sided competition. The introduction of collective bargaining on the workers' side does not mean that combination on one side is being substituted for pure competition on both sides. In general, the conditions under which labor is "bought" and "sold" fall farther short of that informed, two-sided competition suggested by the term "pure competition" than is the case with most commodities.

The terms offered by the employers are not generally the result of full and free competition on the employing side in the purchase of labor, whatever may be the degree of competition among the employers in the sale of their products. There may be a monopsony — a condition in which there is but one buyer of labor of the class in question in that locality. The town in which there is but a single employer in a particular industry comes readily to mind. Even where there are several employers in the locality using the same class of labor, there may be an oligopsony — a condition of imperfect competition on the buyers' side.[3] The restriction of competition in the purchase of labor may be due to an understanding between the employers or it may exist just as a matter of fact without any concerted agreement.

The "competition" on the workers' side under individual bargaining also falls short of the conditions

[3] For a fuller discussion of pure competition, monopsony and oligopsony, see McIsaac and Smith, *Introduction to Economic Analysis* (1937), pp. 248–254.

of pure competition. But here the difference is not that there is too little competition but that the competition is not informed. This applies with less force to skilled craftsmen than to unskilled workers. But for most groups it is safe to say that the competition among the workers for jobs is not carried on with full knowledge of what is being offered by employers and what is being accepted by other workers, or with full knowledge of what the employers would pay, if they had to, for the quantity of labor employed.

There is a more important, because fundamental, characteristic of the competition on the workers' side, under individual bargaining. The individual worker is relatively weak in resources that would enable him to refrain from a present sale of his labor in the hope of securing a better price by holding out for more. Most of the workers, and especially the less skilled workers, are dependent upon selling their labor at *some* price within a very short time if they are to provide for themselves and their families without charitable assistance or public relief. With them it is not a question of more or less profit, but of self-support or dependence. It is obviously more difficult for the individual worker to adhere to a minimum set of terms for his labor, below which he will not "sell", than for a seller to adhere to a minimum price for this or that quantity of his goods.

Thus, it seems that there is often a considerable margin between the terms of employment obtained under individual bargaining and what could be obtained without an appreciable reduction in the volume of employment. The lack of full competition in the purchase of labor and the character of the competition among the workers in the sale of their labor may well keep the wages below what could be paid for the same quantity of labor — which means, to the workers, the same volume of employment. To be sure, the actual wage rate paid under individual bargaining may, in some cases, be higher than it would be under pure competition. Not all employers are immune to personal, humane, or ethical considerations in deciding upon what wages to offer. But it is a reasonable assumption that, when employers are paying no more than they must pay to get the quantity and quality of labor they need, there is frequently a gap, under individual bargaining, between what is paid and what could be paid for the quantity of labor purchased.

The Margin of Possible Advantage in Collective Bargaining. The margin between the terms of employment under individual bargaining and the terms that could be given for the same quantity of labor furnishes the fundamental economic basis for collective bargaining. We must hasten to add, however, that the substitution of collective for individual bargaining does not necessarily secure the highest terms that could be given for that quantity of labor. Collective bargaining does not necessarily unearth all the facts as to what the buyer, or buyers, would pay for a given quantity of labor if they could not get it for less. Nor does it necessarily generate the resources to enable all the workers to hold out for those terms. Indeed, those classes of workers whose wages are lowest under individual bargaining are the least likely to be able to secure by collective bargaining the best terms that could be given for that quantity of labor, if they have to depend on their own economic resources. A combination of workers who are on or below the poverty line cannot hold out long unaided.

It is to be noted that this analysis is confined to the substitution of collective bargaining for competition *among those in the combination*. The analysis does not extend to what may be secured by persuading nonunion workers not to work, or by using other means of preventing them from working when peaceful persuasion proves ineffective. Unquestionably, the terms secured by a combination may be enhanced by the use of such other methods. Indeed, these other and more violent methods have so often been the accompaniments of collective bargaining that many would assume them to be included in it. It will contribute to clearness of analysis, however, to distinguish between unified bargaining among the members of the combination and persuasion or prevention of others not in the union from accepting lower terms. Therefore, the analysis of the economic possibilities of collective bargaining as such will assume only the first method; the other methods will be discussed later in this chapter.

That there is some advantage in substituting collective for individual bargaining seems clear. Certainly, collective bargaining should secure an improvement in terms more quickly than it could be secured under individual bargaining. In collective bargaining, the employer is confronted with the threat, express or implied, of a simultaneous collective withholding of labor, and not merely with an increased difficulty in getting a larger number of workers at his present terms or in holding some of those he has. Even when business is in a relatively poor condition, the threat of the immediate withdrawal of the whole group is frequently effective in postponing a reduction in wages or in narrowing its limits.

The full possibilities of gain through collective bargaining cannot be realized unless the combination on the workers' side is fully inclusive, that is, inclusive of all those workers who would otherwise compete in the sale of their labor. The most direct form of competition between workers for employment is that among workers seeking the same kind of work in the same locality. The competition may be intensified by the influx of workers from a locality in which the terms are less favorable, but the area within which the direct competition exists is the area in which the workers themselves are located. So long as all the workers of the same class in that area are in the combination, there is a suppression of direct competition on labor terms in that market for labor.

There is, however, a form of indirect competition for employment among workers employed in different localities that affects the terms that can be obtained in each. In a broad sense, the competition between workers for employment extends to all those doing the same class of work on products destined for the same market, wherever the producing units are located. The market for the product may be regional rather than local; it may even be nation-wide. And, what is more to the present point, the producing units may be widely separated geographically. The workers throughout the area that includes the firms producing for the same market are, unless they are included in the same bargaining combination, competing for jobs in that industry even though they remain in their respective localities. For example, coal miners in West Virginia were for many years competing with coal miners in Ohio; cotton mill workers in North Carolina are competing with cotton mill workers in Rhode Island; and printers and pressmen in smaller cities are competing with printers and pressmen in publishing houses in New York.

Interlocality competition among workers doing the same class of work for different terms is less direct and less apparent than that between workers seeking jobs in the same locality. Nevertheless, such interlocality competition is, in effect, competition for work through the medium of the terms that will be accepted for it. If other factors affecting costs are equal in the several localities, more of the work will go to the workers in the localities where the terms are lower, even though the workers in all the localities are carrying on collective bargaining locally. The workers in the localities with the better terms must eventually accept lower terms or suffer a reduction in employment. Other things being equal, the terms accepted in one locality affect the terms that can be got by the workers in another locality for a given volume of employment.

There is, then, room for raising the terms, in some localities at least, by making the combination on the workers' side inclusive of all the workers doing the same class of work on products destined for the same market. We are speaking now of better terms for the same aggregate volume of employment. To be sure, it might involve a different distribution of employment among localities from that existing under separate local collective bargaining. This is one of the greatest barriers to achieving unified collective bargaining covering all localities. Nevertheless, the economic possibility is present.

Improving the Terms and Reducing Employment. The discussion thus far has been concerned with the economic possibility of improving terms of employment by collective bargaining without reducing the volume of employment. It must now be recognized that the terms of employment may be advanced to, or held at, a level that is incompatible with the volume of employment that would result under individual bargaining. Even where there is a monopsony or an oligopsony on the employing side, there is obviously a limit to the terms that can be obtained without reducing the quantity of labor sold by the workers. And this limit is more likely to be exceeded under collective bargaining than under individual bargaining.

The raising of the level of wages through collective bargaining, at the cost of a reduction in the volume of employment, is analogous to the raising of the price of a commodity by a combination of sellers with an accompanying reduction in the quantity sold. In neither case can the combination among the sellers control *both* the price and the quantity purchased. Under some circumstances, of course, a considerable improvement in terms of employment can be secured with a relatively small reduction in the quantity of labor sold. In other cases, the demand for labor may be relatively elastic — that is, the amount of labor demanded may fall sharply with a relatively small increase in the price of the labor. Much depends on such factors as the degree of elasticity of the demand for the product itself, the degree of competition among the employers in the sale of the product, and the margin between existing labor costs and the cost of substituting mechanical methods for labor.

It is not intended to imply that an improvement in terms of employment at the expense of the volume of employment is not justifiable. Under individual bargaining the terms may have been kept below the minimum essential to general social welfare. In such a case it is better to raise the terms to the fullest extent possible by collective bargaining, and take care of the reduction in employment in some other way. This holds with especial force for "sweated" industries — industries in which low wages, excessive hours, and poor working conditions are the rule rather than the exception. The fact must not be overlooked, however, that, if competition among the employers for sales has resulted in selling prices dependent on low terms of employment for the workers, it may not be possible economically to raise the terms appreciably without a considerable reduction in employment.[4]

Finally, in considering the practicability of raising wages by collective bargaining, when the increase in wages involves a reduction in the quantity of labor that can be sold, it is necessary to take into account the effect of reducing the number of hours in the full-time working week. The number of hours established as the normal working week is an element in the quantity of labor offered at a given rate per hour. If the full-time working week is fifty hours and there are eight hundred workers offering their labor at a collectively fixed wage rate, the supply at that price is forty thousand man-hours; whereas, if the full-time working week were forty hours, the same supply would require a thousand men. Without assuming that the same number of man-hours could be sold at a given rate of wages under a forty-hour week as under a fifty-hour week, it seems likely that the forty-hour week would, under ordinary circumstances, give full-time employment to more men at the same hourly rate than would the fifty-hour week. Thus, a reduction in the number of man-hours of employment resulting from a higher wage scale could be absorbed in part by a reduction in the length of the full-time week instead of being left to fall entirely on one section of the workers through total unemployment.

---

[4] This analysis is confined to the effect upon the volume of employment in a particular trade or industry of raising the terms of employment in that trade or industry alone. The analysis does not extend to the effect on the demand for labor, through an increase in purchasing power, of a general increase in wages.

THE AREA IN COLLECTIVE BARGAINING

Relation to Area of Production for Same Market. The locality is the predominant area in collective bargaining in this country. In some industries, notably the building industry and newspaper publishing, the market for the product is also localized. But in some other industries, in which local bargaining still prevails, production is carried on in widely separated localities for a common market. This is the case, for example, in book and periodical publishing, in boot and shoe manufacture, and in most branches of the textile industry. In fact, a correspondence between the area of production for the same market and the area covered by a single collective agreement has not yet been generally attained.

Collective bargaining on a regional or national basis was at a low point in manufacturing and mining in 1932. The leading example of national collective bargaining was found on the railroads. There, national collective bargaining for all the crafts on the question of a uniform percentage change in wages had been superimposed upon bargaining with each road or system on particular wage rates and other terms of employment. In the anthracite coal industry the practice of negotiating an agreement for the whole industry had been continued. But in the bituminous coal industry, a highly competitive industry widely distributed geographically, the bargaining had been reduced to relatively small areas and covered in the aggregate less than a third of the output. In manufacturing there was regional or national bargaining in but a few industries, all relatively small.

The National Industrial Recovery Act, with its encouragement of collective bargaining on a market-wide basis, stimulated the extension of the area of collective negotiation. The Appalachian agreement in the bituminous coal industry now covers three fourths of the tonnage, and the terms that it sets are followed as a guide in fixing the terms in the unionized fields not included in the Appalachian negotiations. In the men's clothing industry an agreement was concluded early in 1937, the first of its kind, covering eighty-five per cent of the industry. There has also been an extension of the area covered in single agreements in some other manufacturing industries in which, since June 1933, unionism has been greatly strengthened.

The Problem of Geographical Differentials in Wages. The failure to bring about a greater correspondence between the area of production for the same market and the area of negotiation for an agreement with the union employees is not, generally, the result of union refusal to accept unitary bargaining on both sides for the whole market. Rather must it be ascribed to the reluctance of the employers in some of the localities to bind themselves to an agreement that, they fear, will not give sufficient recognition to varying local conditions. Wage rates, which constitute the principal item in terms of employment and, in consequence, the predominant element in collective bargaining, tend to vary from locality to locality on account of differences in the cost of living and in other factors affecting the supply of labor. It is difficult to overcome this tendency by organization of the workers alone; it is especially difficult to raise the wages in the lower wage localities when the union is new in such a locality or is kept on the defensive by a surrounding nonunion atmosphere.

Of course, lower wage rates do not necessarily mean lower labor costs. But it is difficult to measure the labor costs from wage rates alone, unless the operations are practically uniform and the work is paid for on a piece-rate basis, a situation that does not usually obtain. Where payment is on a time basis the employers in the lower wage-rate localities tend to minimize the competitive advantage from those rates and to resist attempts to fix the wage rates in an industry-wide agreement.

The making of an industry-wide agreement does not necessarily require that the rates of wages for each occupation shall be uniform throughout the industry. It does lead, however, to attempts to whittle down differences to a point that leaves no competitive advantage. Indeed, this is its logical purpose, from the union side. The union policy is the elimination of competition based on differences in wage rates for the same work, through geographical standardization — and this means making the rate in the highest wage locality the standard for all competing localities.

It must not be assumed that the policy of geographical standardization over the field of production for the same market is not pursued by national unions even when local collective bargaining prevails, or that the local variations have not been narrowed considerably as a result of this policy. The national unions generally encourage the local unions with the lower wage rates to attempt to bring up the local wages, and lend to the local efforts the financial and other support of the national union. But the local unions in the higher wage cities are inclined to attempt, meanwhile, to push forward their own rates. Experience shows that geographical standardization makes less progress under local collective bargaining than under industry-wide collective bargaining. Variations between localities in union rates of wages, in the face of a competition for business that is wider than local, remain a serious problem for some national unions.

National Union Rules and Local Collective Bargaining. Another result of the predominance of local collective bargaining is that craft protective regulations and other working rules are frequently enforced by the unions without having been made the subject of collective bargaining in the full sense. Many such regulations have been adopted by national collective action on the workers' side alone; they are "national union rules."

Where there is national collective bargaining, such rules can be made the subject matter of bargaining between the two sides, just as wage rates are. But, where the collective bargaining is local, the local unions usually take the position that they are powerless to bargain away a national rule or to submit it to arbitration; the local employers must take it or leave it. The rules are thus maintained, not by joint agreement after full negotiation, but by *ex parte* national collective action. The removal of this discrepancy between collective action and collective bargaining would, in the cases of many craft unions, require more than the bringing together of all employers (or those employing union members) who are producing for the same market; it would require bargaining between the national union and all the employers of members of that union whether or not these employers are in the same market as sellers. And if the former is difficult to attain, the latter seems almost impossible.

The widening of the area of collective bargaining to include all employers whose interests are affected by the union policies seems desirable for another reason. It offers greater opportunity for the extension of the sphere of employer-union agreement beyond the traditional scope of collective bargaining. A notable example of this is the agreement reached in May 1936 between twenty national unions of railroad employees and the railroads of the country, covering the matter of compensation for employees displaced by consolidations. Another possible, and very desirable, field for advance is that of union-management co-operation for the reduction of costs without sacrifice of the worker's interest in employment. These two fields are, of course, closely related; it seems evident that cost-reducing changes in methods can be introduced with union co-operation only if the workers are given assurance that there will be no consequent reduction in employment without compensation. Although there has been some joint action in cost reduction or improvement in quality of the product by co-operation between unions and individual employers, a greater promise of advance would be offered if the co-operation were based on a wider unit of collective bargaining.

THE CLOSED SHOP

The term "closed shop" is applied to any shop, plant, mine, or other unit of employment in which union membership is a requirement for employment at work over which the particular union claims jurisdiction. Sometimes the members of one union will refuse to work if the employer hires nonunionists on work claimed by any other union, but if the work of a particular craft is closed to nonunionists that craft has a closed shop, whether or not the employer has nonunionists in other occupations. Strictly speaking, a shop is not closed unless nonunionists are excluded as the result of an agreement by the employer to employ only union members, or as a result of the refusal of the union members to work with nonunionists. If there is no such agreement or no such refusal, the fact that all the workers in the shop do belong to the union does not make it a closed shop in the strict meaning of the term.

Not all unions insist on the closed shop. No doubt the unions that do not insist upon it would like to have all the shops "one hundred per cent union" and would be glad to have the employers agree to employ only persons in good standing in the union, but they do not carry this preference to the point of refusing to make an agreement without a closed-shop contract or refusing to work with nonunionists in the absence of such a contract. This is true of a number of unions that have been recognized and dealt with by the employers for years, including the four big Brotherhoods in the railroad engine and train service.

Arguments for the Closed Shop. Arguments are offered for both the necessity and justice of the closed shop. The argument from necessity is based on the assumption that one hundred per cent organization is essential to effective collective action in the fixing of the terms of employment, and on the further assumption that without it the terms once agreed upon will be whittled away by the competition of nonunionists and the union strength dissipated by employer discrimination in favor of nonunion men in hiring and in discharging. The argument for the justice of the closed shop is the simple one that as all the workers benefit by the activities of the union in raising and defending the terms of employment, all should help to defray the expenses of the organization. One very practical consideration is that the closed-shop rule compels those who have already joined the union to keep up their payments; the presence of some who shared in the benefits without paying might tempt others already in good standing to become delinquent.

Relationship to the Bargaining Position of the Union. Experience has shown that a union may, under favorable circumstances, protect the union members from the competition of nonunionists in the same shop on terms of employment, and from adverse discrimination as well, without a closed-shop rule. Where the terms of employment are agreed upon by the union and the employer, it is usually with the understanding, if not the explicit contract, that these terms are binding upon the employer with respect to all employed on the class or classes of work covered, whether or not the worker is a member of the union. The employer is not free to employ nonunionists at less than the rates agreed upon. Similarly, apprenticeship rules and working rules with respect to methods of production or other matters apply to the shop as a whole. As for discrimination against union members in favor of nonunionists, it is not likely that it will be practiced where there is a long-established system of employer-union agreement. Unless the employer is courting a fight with the union, he is not likely to attempt it. And wherever the National Labor Relations Act applies such favoritism is now illegal.

The Closed Shop and Enforcement of Union Discipline. The chief advantage that a closed-shop rule would bring, under these circumstances, is the greater ease in enforcing working rules that are not in the agreement and in enforcing internal union discipline, including the prompt payment of dues and assessments, upon those members who might otherwise prove recalcitrant or become delinquent. Where nearly all workers join the union as a matter of course, the closed-shop rule is regarded not so much as a means of "forcing them in" as of "keeping them in." And if the protection that union membership gives the individual in his particular interests is especially important — as in piecework trades or in trades in which the individual has important individual rights under a seniority rule — nearly all the workers not only join but take good care to remain in good standing. Under these conditions the closed-shop rule is regarded as not worth a fight if the employers are strongly opposed to it.

On the other hand, some unions make the closed shop a major objective. Where the men change frequently from one job to another, as in the building trades, the unions regard it as essential to the collection of dues and assessments and the maintenance of the union rules. As they put it, "The job is either a union job or it isn't; if it is, it must be one hundred per cent union." And many employers who deal with the unions in the building trades seem to regard the closed-shop rule as essential to "peace on the job."

The Closed Shop as an Organizing Device. It must be noted, too, that the closed shop has been used by some unions as an organizing device rather than as a defensive measure. As soon as the union has enrolled a sufficiently large proportion of the workers in a shop to threaten a strike with a reasonable chance of stopping operations, it demands a closed-shop agreement as a means of completing the organization of the shop and consolidating its position. When the closed shop is used in this way, it seems necessary to maintain it to prevent the loss of the shop through nonunion replacements or desertions, or both. Thus, the closed shop seems largely a product of uncertainty and struggle, as well as an instrument of union discipline.[5]

[5] The legal aspects of the strike to compel the discharge of nonunionists and of the closed-shop agreement are discussed in the next chapter.

FORMS OF ECONOMIC PRESSURE

THE STRIKE

The chief form of economic pressure used by unions to secure concessions from employers is the *strike*. The strike is a collective cessation of work with intent to return in a body to the same jobs after better terms have been forced from the employer by the concerted withdrawal of labor. If it is one hundred per cent effective it means the immediate cessation of all labor operations hitherto performed by the strikers. If the union includes other classes of workers than those for whom the demand is made, it is likely that the former as well as the latter will be called out on strike, thus enlarging the quantity of services that the employer must evaluate as a unit, in comparison with the union demands.

Stopping Operations Essential to Success. If the strike is to be made and kept one hundred per cent effective, not only must all the workers engaged upon that class of work in the establishment or establishments in which the strike is called join in the strike, but other workers capable of doing the work must refrain from taking the strikers' places. If the other potential replacements are themselves members of the same union, its problem is simplified. The economic struggle then becomes one of the relative economic endurance of the two sides. If the strike is local but the strikers are members of a national union, they are likely to receive financial support from the national union, provided the strike has the sanction of the national body.

If there are any workers in the establishment in which the strike is called who are employed on the class or classes of work "struck" and who are not members of the union, the strikers attempt to persuade them to join the strike. They also attempt to persuade any workers who might otherwise be induced to take the places of strikers — that is, to act as strikebreakers — to refrain from doing so. It is usual to station strikers, or strike sympathizers, around the plant for the purpose of persuading other workers not to go to work during the strike; this is known as "picketing." Unfortunately, when the strikers have been unable to persuade these others to join the strike or to refrain from strike-breaking, they have at times resorted to intimidation of these workers. Intimidation takes the pressure beyond the boundaries of peaceful economic coercion. It is not denied that physical intimidation may effect an economic result; the point is that it is not a legitimate form of economic pressure on either the other workers or the employer, however great the temptation may be to resort to it.

Sit-Down Strikes. During the winter and spring of 1936–1937, there was widespread use of what was called the "sit-down" strike. The sit-down method was a departure from the traditional method of picketing the place of employment from outside; the sit-down strikers occupied the employer's premises, in order to prevent further operation of the plant until the employer should come to terms with them. This sit down was, for the most part, the product of a campaign for organization. Workers who had been organized but a short time eagerly seized upon the sit down as a means of compelling the employers to recognize their union as the sole bargaining agency for the employees in the plant. After a few spectacular successes, the use of the sit down became almost epidemic. Workers hitherto unorganized, and even some who did not attempt a permanent organization, resorted to sit downs to secure all sorts of demands. Its most important use, however, was as a means of compelling the employer to deal with a newly organized union.

There is no doubt that, for workers only recently organized, the occupation of the plant was a more effective method of winning a strike than picketing from the outside. It was more effective as a means of keeping other workers from going to work, especially where there was a large group of workers opposed to the union. It gave the strikers a greater sense of control of the situation and so made it easier to keep up their morale. To be sure, the occupancy of the employer's premises against his will was undoubtedly illegal; but the sit-down strikers charged that the employers had violated the law first by refusing their demand for collective bargaining.[6] The civil authorities, too, were in many cases reluctant to use force to evict the strikers, and urged the employers to effect a peaceable settlement. There is no doubt that the method of seizure of the plant resulted, in many instances, in agreements

[6] See below, pp. 124–127.

that could not have been won by the simple withdrawal of their labor by the strikers.

The use of the sit-down technique is apparently on the wane, however. Resistance to it by the civil authorities has stiffened. Moreover, a number of leaders of older unions have declared against the sit-down strike. Their opposition is due in part to fear of restrictive legislation against unions if a method so patently illegal is persisted in. But it is also due in part to distrust of a method of collective action that can be so easily resorted to without prior authorization by the national union.

Economic Appraisal of the Strike. The effectiveness of the strike as a form of collective action has often been questioned. It has been contended that even if the strike is apparently successful in securing better terms than the employer would otherwise have given, the wage loss to the strikers exceeds the ultimate gain. The employment lost during a strike, however, is not necessarily a net loss. Some of the employment time lost may be made up after the strike is over; it may be merely an anticipation of seasonal idleness that would have occurred anyway.

Moreover, the loss incurred by the workers in a particular strike may be an investment in the sense that, by showing the employer the fighting power of the union, it may make it possible to get better terms later without a strike, through the use of the strike threat expressly or by implication. Few systems of collective bargaining have been established before the workers had proved their ability to conduct a formidable strike, or have been maintained without the occasional use of the strike. Whether the terms obtained by use of the strike or the strike threat have been offset by a reduction in the amount of employment available at those terms as compared with the amount that would have been available at lower terms, is part of the larger question of the economic effect of collective bargaining, discussed above.

THE BOYCOTT

Another form of economic pressure that has been utilized, but usually not until a strike has failed to put a stop to the employer's operations, is the boycott of his product. In a general sense, a *boycott* is an agreement not to deal with a person against whom those who enter into the agreement have a grievance. In labor disputes it is an agreement not to purchase from the "unfair" employer, as distinct from refusing to work for him. If the boycott is confined to the offending employer it is a *primary boycott*. But, unless the employer is selling directly to the consuming public, a boycott by workers cannot ordinarily be made effective except through a concerted refusal to buy from those who handle his products. When a boycott, or threat of boycott, is launched against those who would otherwise buy the offending employer's product, in order to coerce them to cease dealing with him, it is a *secondary boycott*. It is the secondary boycott, or even a more complicated form of boycott, that has usually figured in labor disputes. As its unlawfulness has been repeatedly affirmed by the courts, it is not much used today, at least not openly.

When the customer of the offending firm is likewise an employer, as in the case of a building contractor purchasing materials from a firm with whom a union is waging a struggle, the pressure on the customer to induce him to cease buying from the offending firm takes the form of a strike against the customer, or at least a refusal to work on products purchased by him from the offending firm. This is sometimes called a boycott also, although the lever against the customer is a strike, not a boycott. This, too, has generally been held unlawful.

The attempt to bring pressure to bear on an offending employer either through a secondary boycott, joined by trade unionists not engaged in the strike, or through refusal by trade unionists not engaged in the original strike to work on the products of the offending employer, represents an attempted enlargement of the collective action against the employer beyond the group whose terms of employment are directly at issue — namely, the employees of the offending employer. Although the courts have tended to restrict the use of collective action to those employed by the offending employer who is the original party to the dispute, there has recently been some legislation forbidding the use of injunctions against other workers in the same occupation or industry or in the same national union, who refuse to work on the products of the offending employer.[7]

[7] See below, pp. 134–135, 137–139.

This appears to strengthen the hand of national trade unionism.

THE LABEL

A positive — and legal — method of marshaling the purchasing choices of the union members and their sympathizers in support of the terms of employment asked by the union is the use of the *union label*. The label is intended to identify the products of those employers who have agreements with the particular union or unions using that label. Indirectly it is a means of diverting patronage from the employers who are not entitled to use it, but because it is not a "signal for a boycott" of a specified employer, and especially not for a secondary boycott, it does not fall under the ban of the law. Not all unions have labels. The label is used with greatest effectiveness, of course, by unions whose members are employed in making goods or rendering services for a market of which the wage-earning population is an important part; overalls are a good example of such a commodity.

ARBITRATION

Submission of the terms still in dispute between the union and the employer to a neutral person, or a board including one or more neutral persons, for a decision that is to bind both parties has often been proposed as a substitute for the strike. This is what is known as *arbitration*. The distinctive feature of arbitration is that it takes the final decision out of the hands of the disputants. This is why it is so often refused by unions, or by employers, when the dispute is an important one. Arbitration of the terms of a new contract is called *primary arbitration*. Arbitration of an issue arising out of the application of an existing collective agreement to a particular case — such as a protested discharge or the application of a wage clause to a particular individual or a particular class of work — is called *secondary arbitration*. It is much more acceptable than primary arbitration. Secondary arbitration involves submission to an outside judgment on a question involving only the interpretation or the application of a standard already agreed upon, not the fixing of new standards. The chance of an adverse decision in a particular case is often regarded as less objectionable than to let the matter drop or to press it to the extent of a strike. It is just because neither side is willing to surrender the chance of victory in a contest over new terms that primary arbitration is so difficult to secure.

The trade unions are not opposed to primary arbitration in the sense that they will never propose or accept it. But they wish to retain their freedom to choose what and when they will submit to the decision of an arbiter. Weak unions are more disposed to arbitrate, generally, than strong ones, just as an employer who believes he can defeat a strike is usually unwilling to accept arbitration if he fears that he may lose more through arbitration than through a strike. Unionists in a strong bargaining position have, for the most part, been skeptical of getting justice from arbiters whom the employers are willing to accept. They fear that the arbiters will not recognize the right of workers to advance their standards; that, in the matter of wages especially, the arbiters will tend to fix wages according to cost-of-living indices, or what is paid for similar work by other employers, thus denying the union's claim for an advance in real wages over existing standards. And for years the unions have opposed all proposals for compulsory arbitration — that is, legal compulsion to submit all disputed questions to the decisions of government boards and accept their decisions, a compulsion imposed upon the workers through the prohibition of strikes.

POLITICAL ACTION ON TERMS OF EMPLOYMENT

The Tradition of Opposition. Until very recently American labor organizations have opposed the fixing of such terms of employment as hours and wages by law. They have favored such protective legislation as safety laws, workmen's compensation for industrial accidents, and, in the last few years, compulsory unemployment compensation and old-age insurance. But for the main features of employment terms, especially for adult males, they opposed legal intervention. They preferred to strive for wider legal freedom in the use of collective economic pressure on the employer, whether by the strike or by the boycott. Right of way for collective economic pressure by independent unions (independent of the employer), rather than legal determination of hours and wages, has been the traditional trade-union program in this country. It is in accordance with this program that the unions have opposed compulsory arbitration, and still oppose it.

The Recent Shift to Legislation on Hours and Wages. In the past few years there has been a distinct shift toward favoring legislation to secure a reduction in the maximum work week, in order to increase the number employed. Along with this went support, by organized labor, of the wages as well as the hours features of the National Industrial Recovery Act of 1933. There was much complaint of the way the act was administered in these respects, but not of its avowed aims.

Since the demise of the Recovery Act, organized labor has continued to advocate federal legislation limiting the maximum hours of labor, such as "30-hour" bills. It has also continued to favor federal legislation for the fixing of legal minimum rates of wages, with the stipulation that these shall not be set below the rates fixed by collective bargaining for the classes of work in question and that government wage fixing shall not be used to supplant collective bargaining. As unionism spreads to industries and occupations hitherto unorganized or little organized, political action is likely to be increasingly favored by organized labor.

PART TWO

LABOR LEGISLATION

CHAPTER V

Legal Status of Collective Action by Labor

THE RIGHT TO ORGANIZE AND TO BARGAIN COLLECTIVELY

RECENT DEVELOPMENTS

FOR nearly a century the legal right of workers to organize and to act collectively in bargaining with their employer has been recognized in this country. Until recently, however, the workers' right was paralleled by an equal right on the employer's part to discharge a worker for joining a labor organization and to refuse to have any dealings with a labor organization not to his liking. Recently, the workers' right has been enlarged, so that they are now legally protected against retaliation by the employer for organizing activities and, more than that, they now have the positive right to bargain collectively with the employer regardless of the employer's preference in the matter.

Railway Labor Act of 1926. The recent change in the workers' rights commenced with federal legislation for the railroads and their interstate employees. The first statutory prohibition of employer interference with the employees' choice in the matter of organization for collective bargaining — at least the first that was held constitutional by the Supreme Court — was included in the Railway Labor Act of 1926. The prohibition was inserted in the act as a corollary of the requirement that the carriers and their employees shall attempt to agree upon terms of employment in conference between representatives authorized to act by the respective sides.[1] In order to insure to the workers freedom in choosing their bargaining agency, the statute adds that "representatives, for the purposes of this act, shall be designated by the respective parties . . . without interference, influence, or coercion exercised by either party over the self-organization or designation of representatives by the other." More specific prohibitions of employer interferences were added to the Railway Labor Act by amendment in 1934.[2] The amended act was upheld by the Supreme Court in March 1937.

The Anti-Injunction Act of 1932. The first important step toward extending to industry in general the right of workers to organize without employer interference

---

[1] The provisions of this act relating to the prevention or settlement of disputes over terms of employment are treated in the next chapter. The present chapter is concerned with railway labor legislation only as it affects the right to organize and to bargain collectively. It should be remembered in this connection that the National Industrial Recovery Act did not apply to the railroads and that the National Labor Relations Act does not apply to them.

[2] The amendments are treated in more detail below.

was taken in the so-called Norris-LaGuardia Act, the Anti-Injunction Act of 1932. This federal statute did not change the substance of the law; it dealt only with judicial processes, that is, with court orders and suits for damages. It was an act abridging the powers of the federal courts (below the Supreme Court) to issue injunctions in labor disputes or to hold the members of labor organizations liable for damages. The significant point is that this federal legislation contained the following declaration of public policy:

... though he [the worker] should be free to decline to associate with his fellows, it is necessary that he have full freedom of association, self-organization, and designation of representatives of his own choosing, to negotiate the terms and conditions of his employment, and that he shall be free from the interference, restraint, or coercion of employers of labor, or their agents, in the designation of such representatives or in self-organization or in other concerted activities for the purpose of collective bargaining or other mutual aid or protection.

The National Industrial Recovery Act of 1933. The National Industrial Recovery Act contained a requirement that all codes or agreements made in pursuance of the act should include prohibitions of employer "interference, restraint or coercion", of the kind forbidden by the Railway Labor Act of 1926 and condemned in the declaration of public policy in the Norris-LaGuardia Act. The prohibitions of employer interference contained in the National Industrial Recovery Act were, however, neither fully obeyed nor enforced. Discrimination against workers for union membership or activity, even to the point of discharge, was practiced with legal impunity.

National Labor Relations Act of 1935. The failure to secure the enforcement of the labor organization and collective bargaining clauses of the Recovery Act was the direct cause of the enactment of the National Labor Relations Act in July 1935. Although the National Labor Relations Act was from the first an independent measure, in the sense that it was intended to effect a permanent change in the substance of the law governing labor relations, irrespective of the continuance of the Recovery Act, the passage of the National Labor Relations Act was undoubtedly a result of the then defunct Recovery Act and the labor relations experience under it. The provisions of the new act were obviously designed to make the prohibitions contained in the Recovery Act not only permanent but more specific, and to secure their enforcement.

The National Labor Relations Act was passed in order to establish the right of the workers to organize and to bargain collectively without employer interference. Therefore, the act contains prohibitions directed only against the employers, outlawing practices that employers had formerly used to prevent workers from organizing and bargaining collectively. The act imposes no new obligations upon the workers, nor does it deprive them of any previous rights possessed under federal or state law.[3] The legality or illegality of acts

[3] At least, it does not deprive the majority of workers of any such rights; it does, however, reduce the rights of minority groups of workers in the matter of group bargaining with the employer. See below, pp. 127–130.

of coercion by organized workers, either against non-member workers or against employers, is not changed by the National Labor Relations Act. Nor does the act limit in any way the right to strike; this is one important difference between it and the Railway Labor Act.

In April 1937 the Supreme Court not only sustained the National Labor Relations Act but gave the act, in a series of decisions, wide application. The Court rejected the contention that the constitutional power of the federal government to regulate rights and procedures in employer-employee relations is confined to interstate transportation and other activities directly connected with buying and selling across state lines. The Court held that Congress has the constitutional power to prohibit acts that tend to cause labor disputes in manufacturing, when the manufacturing operations are so closely connected with the movement of raw materials and manufactured products in interstate commerce that the curtailment of the manufacturing operations by a strike would interrupt or obstruct the commerce. This point was sustained by a five-to-four decision. But the Court was unanimous in applying the act to a bus company engaged in interstate transportation. These decisions indicate, first, that the provisions of the act abridging the employer's rights are, on the whole, constitutional and, second, that the act has wide application to production as well as to commerce in the narrow sense.

State Legislation. Since the National Labor Relations Act has been upheld by the Supreme Court and given

such wide application to production, it is likely that
the act will be supplemented by similar state legislation
for employments to which the federal statute does not
apply. Indeed, such legislation has already been enacted in a few states. The topical analysis that follows is
based on the provisions of the two national acts — the
Railway Labor Act and the National Labor Relations
Act.

PROHIBITION OF EMPLOYER
INTERFERENCE

Discrimination Against Workers. The prohibition of
discrimination against workers for union membership
means that the employer may not use his "control of
the job" to influence a man not to join a union. The
employer may not make it a part of the employment
contract that the employee refrain from joining a union.
Nor may the employer discharge a worker, or discriminate against him in any other way, because he has
joined a union.

The first statutory prohibition (that was held constitutional) of such conduct on the employer's part was
contained in the Railway Labor Act of 1926. In the
1926 act the prohibition was implicit rather than explicit. When the Railway Labor Act was amended in
1934, specific prohibitions of employer interference or
discrimination were introduced. As amended, the act
not only forbids the employer to discriminate against
a worker for union membership, it also prohibits employer discrimination against a man because he is not

a member of a labor organization.[4] This would seem to preclude a closed-shop contract. However, the closed-shop contract has never been widely used on the railroads.

The National Labor Relations Act, also, forbids the employer to discriminate so as "to encourage or discourage membership in any labor organization."[5] The act, however, carries a proviso that this shall not be construed to preclude the employer from making a closed-shop agreement with an independent labor organization representing the majority of the workers in that unit. In other words, the employer may not discriminate either way unless and until a majority of his workers belong to an independent labor organization, and then that majority is free, so far as federal law is concerned, to bind the employer to an agreement to discriminate against anyone who is not a member of that organization. The National Labor Relations Act does not make a closed-shop contract lawful in any state in which such a contract is illegal under the state law.[6] It merely exempts the employer from any condemnation under this or any other federal statute if he agrees to a closed-shop contract and fulfills the contract.

[4] The act reads: ". . . it shall be unlawful for any carrier to interfere in any way with the organization of its employees . . . or to influence or coerce employees in an effort to induce them to join or remain or not to join or remain members of any labor organization."

[5] The act makes it an "unfair labor practice" for an employer "by discrimination in regard to hire or tenure of employment or any term or condition of employment to encourage or discourage membership in any labor organization."

[6] See below, pp. 133–134.

Company Unions Outlawed. The prohibition of employer interference with the workers' freedom to organize logically implies that the employer is prohibited from forcing a company union upon them, as the channel of dealing with him. Such was the interpretation put upon the Railway Labor Act of 1926 by the Supreme Court in 1930. The amended act of 1934 specifically forbids a carrier to give financial or other assistance to any "labor organization, labor representative, or other agency of collective bargaining."

The National Labor Relations Act prohibits the employer from financing any plan or association or organization through which the workers deal with him on terms of employment or even on grievances. The employer is forbidden to "dominate or interfere with the formation or administration of any labor organization or contribute financial or other support to it." And "labor organization" is so defined as to include any plan or association coming under the category of what are generally known as company unions. This usage of the term "labor organization" is somewhat revolutionary, but the target aimed at is perfectly clear. The question whether the workers might not prefer a company-financed channel for group dealing with the employer is, under the statute, beside the point.

THE RIGHT TO BARGAIN COLLECTIVELY

There is an important difference behind the circumstances that led to the statutory establishment of the positive right of the railroad workers to deal with the carriers, through labor organizations of the workers' own choosing, and the circumstances that led to the attempt to establish that same right through the National Labor Relations Act. In sharp contrast with the situation in industry, collective bargaining was the established practice on nearly all the railroads when the Railway Labor Act of 1926 was passed. This had been true, generally, since the days of government control during the World War. When the roads were returned to private operation, under the terms of the Transportation Act of 1920, there was laid upon both the carriers and the workers the statutory "duty" of attempting to settle their differences in conference between the duly authorized representatives of the respective sides. Although this duty had not been enforced by court order, it had by 1926 come to be generally recognized as the better way by the railroads, as well as by the workers. Both the roads and the workers' unions sponsored the 1926 statute which made this duty an enforceable obligation.

Moreover, the Railway Labor Act assumes the existence of agreements governing the terms of employment. It requires the side that desires a change in the terms to give notice, and it requires the other side to meet with the side desiring change within a specified period. The act also requires that both sides leave an opportunity for government intervention before resorting to hostile acts. Thus the employer knows that, if he does not attempt in good faith to reach an agreement in conference, government mediators and, perhaps, a special board of inquiry will strive to bring about an agreement.[7] In short, an agreement of some kind with the organized workers is difficult to avoid, if the workers are willing to come to terms, without courting the adverse judgment of the public.

The approach of the National Labor Relations Act, on the other hand, is negative or prohibitory, rather than affirmative. This approach is largely the result of the refusal of many employers to deal with unions during the Recovery Act period. The National Labor Relations Act makes refusal by the employer "to bargain collectively with the representatives of his employees", when the representatives are the choice of a majority, an "unfair labor practice"; it includes such refusal in the list of unfair labor practices forbidden to the employer. The term "representatives", by definition, includes a labor organization.

It is impossible to say how important this prohibition will be in promoting real collective bargaining. True collective bargaining relations cannot be brought about by prohibitions alone. There must be a will to agree, or at least a preference for agreement. An employer who is determined not to deal with an organization may be compelled by court order to go through the motions of negotiation; but only the workers, by threats to strike or other coercive means, can induce such an employer to come to an agreement with their organization. The extent to which this provision of the law will bring about the establishment of true collective-bargaining relations will depend upon the economic strength engendered, as a result of the law, by

[7] For further discussion, see below, pp. 143-145.

organization among the workers. In other words, the practical effect of the statutory change will come from its effect on the will of the workers to organize and to adhere to collective action.

MAJORITY RULE

The requirement that the employer shall deal with his employees collectively through their freely chosen representatives must be so defined as to make clear with what group or groups he must deal. Offhand, one would say that it is for the employees to define the group or groups — that the employer must accept whatever bargaining groups they resolve themselves into. But what if there is a conflict among the workers on the point? What if there are rival groups among the same class of workers — the "same class" in the sense that the terms of employment must, as a matter of practice, apply uniformly to all? Must the employer bargain with each group? Or, in case of conflicting claims to represent the workers, shall the employer decide with which set of representatives to deal? It is not only a matter of protecting the workers against being dealt for by representatives whom the majority do not want; it is also a matter of protecting the employer from being compelled to bargain with two rival organizations that have conflicting jurisdictional claims.

The problem has not been a very serious one on the railroads. Before the Railway Labor Act was passed, it was the general rule that, if there were more than one organization in a craft, the organization that had a majority should represent the craft on that road. When the Railway Labor Act was amended in 1934, this was written into it specifically.[8] In case of a dispute among the employees over who are the representatives of the majority, the National Mediation Board is authorized to investigate and determine who are the proper representatives.[9]

Here again, the pertinent provision of the National Labor Relations Act was the product of controversy. No issue of interpretation of the language of the clauses of the Recovery Act relating to collective bargaining was more fiercely debated than that of "majority rule", and on none were more conflicting interpretations handed down from high places. The practical stake was the right of the employer to continue to deal with a set of company-plan representatives when a majority of the workers wanted an outside union to represent them. The unions were generally in favor of majority rule, in order to consolidate their gains when they had the majority. They feared that the employer, by continuing to deal with a company union, would tend to discourage union membership. The majority-rule issue was thus largely a phase of the company-union issue.

The National Labor Relations Act establishes majority rule. Not only must the employer allow the majority to bargain collectively with him, but he is also excluded, in effect, from dealing with minority repre-

---

[8] The wording of the act is as follows: "The majority of any craft or class of employees shall have the right to determine who shall be the representative of the craft or class for the purposes of this act."

[9] The other duties of this board are discussed below, pp. 145–146. The jurisdiction of this board is confined to railroads and plane carriers. It has nothing to do with other industries.

sentatives.[10] Thus, the right to collective bargaining is, under this act, an exclusive right of the majority of the workers. No minority group may bargain collectively with an employer if there is a majority that wishes to bargain collectively. If there is a dispute over who are the representatives of the majority, the National Labor Relations Board, established by the act, may investigate and determine that question.[11] The Board, if it chooses, may hold an election for this purpose.

THE BARGAINING UNIT

it is group of employees.
or all subjects.

If majority rule is to be followed, it is necessary to determine what is to be the unit of employees, in the electoral sense, within which representatives are to be chosen for collective bargaining. Is it to be the craft, the railroad, the plant, or the whole industry? Before the recent legislation, the unit for collective bargaining was whatever the workers' union, by exerting economic pressure, was able to make it. But now that majority rule has been made a matter of law, the question of the bargaining unit within which the majority is to rule in group bargaining is also a matter for governmental determination.

The question of the bargaining unit has given little

[10] The specific language of the act on this point is as follows: "Representatives designated or selected for the purposes of collective bargaining by the majority of the employees in a unit appropriate for such purposes, shall be the exclusive representatives of all the employees in such unit for the purposes of collective bargaining in respect to rates of pay, wages, hours of employment, or other conditions of employment: *Provided,* That any individual employee or a group of employees shall have the right at any time to present grievances to their employer."

[11] The other duties of this board are discussed below, pp. 146–147. This board has nothing to do with the railroads.

trouble under the Railway Labor Act. Before the act was passed, practice had made the craft the base of organization on the railroads and the unit in choosing representatives for collective bargaining. There is no issue of industrial unionism versus craft unionism on the railroads. In the amended act of 1934, as indicated above, craft bargaining is coupled with majority rule.

Under the National Labor Relations Act, however, the determination of the appropriate unit within which the majority is to have exclusive collective bargaining rights is likely to prove much more troublesome. The act leaves the determination of the bargaining unit to the future. And it entrusts the decision to the National Labor Relations Board.[12] The act thus imposes upon a government agency the duty of deciding whether a majority of a smaller group must yield in collective bargaining to the majority of a larger unit, if there is such a majority. It is one thing to exclude from collective bargaining a minority of a craft or class, of which the majority has chosen a different organization; it is quite another thing to rule out a majority of a particular craft that is a minority in the plant as a whole. With the rivalry now going on between craft unions and industrial unions for membership and for recognition by employers, the administration by the board of this provision of the act is likely to prove both difficult and embarrassing.

[12] Following is the wording of the act on this point: "The Board shall decide in each case whether, in order to insure to employees the full benefit of their right to self-organization and to collective bargaining, and otherwise to effectuate the policies of this Act, the unit appropriate for the purposes of collective bargaining shall be the employer unit, craft unit, plant unit, or subdivision thereof."

LEGAL RESTRICTIONS ON COERCION IN LABOR DISPUTES

Lack of Uniformity. Legal restriction on coercion in labor disputes is marked in the United States by great confusion. The respective rights of workers and employers rest, for the most part, on the common law; which is to say, in effect, upon the courts' interpretations of the common law — and there are forty-eight different sets of state courts. Besides, the common law may be modified by statutes in the various states, which constitute another source of diversity in the law. Thus, whether a particular action is held lawful or unlawful may depend upon the state in which it occurs. Certain actions of labor combinations are also within the circle of restraints of interstate trade forbidden by the federal anti-trust acts and enforced by the federal courts.

Some types of conduct resorted to in labor disputes are against the criminal law as well as against the civil law. For example, physical violence against persons attempting to work during a strike is not only an invasion of the civil rights of those persons to seek and take employment and of the employer to hire them, but it is also a criminal act. That violence against persons or property should be unlawful at both civil and criminal law is taken for granted, whether it grows out of a labor dispute or not. The real issues as to what should be the respective legal rights of the parties in a labor struggle are concerned with coercion in the economic sphere, apart from violence or physical intimidation, and chiefly with coercion through refusal to work or refusal to buy.

THE STRIKE

Purpose. Whether or not a strike, peacefully conducted, is lawful depends upon the purpose of the strike. The courts vary somewhat in the purposes that they hold lawful, but in general they hold that a strike for better terms of employment for the striking workers is lawful.[13] Any damage that results to the employer's business because of the strike is held to be incidental to the pursuit by the workers of their own legitimate interest — the infliction of damage is not their *primary* purpose and gives the employer no basis for legal action. The right of workers to strike, however, is confined within this limit; namely, to advance or protect *their own interest.* Thus, there is no inalienable right to strike regardless of the purpose of the strike. A strike is a *concerted* or *combined* action against the employer, and although any individual may legally quit under any circumstances that do not involve a violation of the contract of employment he has entered into, the strike must have a legal justification to be legal, and that justification is the promotion of the strikers' own legitimate interests.

But how far does their legitimate interest extend? That it covers the advancement or defense of their own direct terms of employment is unquestioned. Beyond

[13] For discussion of the restrictions on strikes in the interest of the general public, see below, Chapter VI.

that, there is some confusion in the decisions of the courts. Most courts have held that purposes that only indirectly advance the strikers' interest, if at all, are outside the pale. Such purposes include an attempt to force the discharge of a nonunionist, an attempt to prevent an employer from using nonunion materials such as building materials made by nonunion labor, or an attempt to assist unionists striking against another employer by calling a "sympathetic" strike. Moreover, if the purpose of a strike would make it unlawful, the threat to call such a strike is also unlawful.

The strike to secure the discharge of a nonunionist has been held unlawful by most courts that have passed on the question. The principle invoked is the general one that any person has a right to sell his labor (or his goods) to any person who will buy it (or them) without the exercise of coercion by a third person to restrain the second person from the purchase. The strike to compel the employer to discharge a nonunionist is held to be that kind of unlawful interference with the nonunionist's right to work. What the court sees is a combination against an individual to deprive him of his right to work. The court refuses to accept the contention that the strikers are not acting maliciously against the nonunion man but are only trying to increase the effectiveness of their combined action in advancing or defending their own terms of employment; the injury to the nonunion man outweighs, in the eyes of the court, any indirect benefit to the union members.

Where the strike to compel the discharge of a nonunionist is held unlawful, the strike for a closed-shop agreement is usually held unlawful also. However, a closed-shop agreement voluntarily entered into by the employer is held lawful in some states. As the employer is exercising his legal right not to hire non-unionists, presumably because he expects to get better results by employing unionists exclusively, the non-unionist is not being deprived by the union of any right he would otherwise have. Some courts have even issued injunctions against the violation of a closed-shop agreement by the employer through the employment of non-unionists, holding that this course was a violation of a contract entered into for a sufficient consideration.

The strike against the use of nonunion materials by an employer against whom the workers have no other grievance has likewise been held unlawful by many courts. It is held to be an invasion of the right of the producer of the materials to sell his goods to anyone who will buy them, free from coercion by third parties. If the strike is against the use of materials or equipment sold by a producer located in a different state from that in which the strike in question occurs, the strike is held to constitute a restraint of the producing employer's interstate trade and thus forbidden by the federal anti-trust acts. The fact that the men refusing to work on the "unfair" material are members of the same national union that is carrying on a struggle with the nonunion producer of the materials or equipment does not, it is held, justify the restraint of interstate trade. The practical force of these decisions has been weakened, however, by the Norris-LaGuardia Act of 1932, which prohibits the issue of injunctions by the federal courts against such refusals to work on the part of workers in the same trade, industry, or national union.

"Sympathetic" strikes, that is, strikes to aid other striking workers, are generally held illegal. If a strike is really a sympathetic one, it is by definition not one to advance the strikers' own interest but a strike to enlarge the pressure on an employer against whom other workers are striking. However, the fact that the sympathetic strikers make no demands for themselves at the moment does not necessarily mean that they do not expect ultimately to improve their own position by what the courts may regard as a sympathetic strike. All the unions in the building trades, for example, frequently call their men off a building when one union has "struck the job", because each union wants the support of the others if and when it has to strike over a grievance of its own. There is a difference between this kind of a sympathetic strike and a strike of many unrelated trades to help the milk drivers, the street-car men, or the longshoremen. However, it is common to lump them all and hold all of them illegal.

Methods. It is obvious that the purpose of a strike, however legitimate, cannot make legitimate the use of violence in the course of the strike. The same is true of physical intimidation. But what constitutes physical intimidation? For example, the conveying of information to those seeking employment in, or actually employed in, a place that has been "struck", and the attempt to persuade them not to work there, are usually held to be legal. When do such practices become transformed into intimidation? This is the real issue in the lawfulness or unlawfulness of picketing by strikers or their sympathizers. "Peaceful picketing", which some judges have declared a contradiction in terms, is generally held lawful; but intimidation is obviously unlawful.

May picketing be proscribed in advance on the assumption that it will inevitably lead to unlawful acts? In practice, it frequently has been prohibited, by the terms of an injunction; and whatever is forbidden by an injunction order is unlawful until the injunction is lifted. The Norris-LaGuardia Act forbids the federal courts to issue injunctions against "giving publicity to the existence of, or the facts involved in, any labor dispute, whether by advertising, speaking, patrolling, or by any other method not involving fraud or violence." But the courts still have to decide what "involves fraud or violence."

In recent years there has been a growing movement against the use of professional strikebreakers — men who do not take the strikers' places with intent to remain in them at the terms refused by the strikers, but who are employed only for the duration of the strike and then pass on to another strike scene. It is contended that professional strikebreakers are used to prevent peaceful picketing and to provoke violence and disorder with the object of defeating the strike. Some of them, according to the evidence, have records that are anything but peaceful. In June 1936 a federal statute was enacted prohibiting the transportation of strikebreakers or guards across state lines with intent to employ them to obstruct or interfere with peaceful picketing during a labor dispute.

THE BOYCOTT

The Primary Boycott. The legality of a primary boycott against an offending employer by his employees has been questioned at times, but ordinarily the legality of the primary boycott only becomes an important issue when those sympathizing with the employer's workers join in the boycott. Such a primary boycott, even when extended by sympathizers, is of little practical effect unless the offending employer is selling his product directly to the consuming public.

The Secondary Boycott. It is the secondary boycott that is important in labor disputes. The secondary boycott involves coercion of a third party, such as a retailer selling the offending employer's product.[14] The boycotters threaten to cease dealings with the third party unless he ceases to deal with the offending employer. This secondary boycott was long ago held illegal, and in most states it is still illegal.

INJUNCTIONS AND SUITS FOR DAMAGES

A distinction must be made between the substantive law, which defines what is lawful or unlawful, and the court procedures available for remedial action or even for the prevention of threatened acts presumed to be unlawful. The traditional procedure against an offend-

[14] The refusal to work on materials purchased from an offending employer has also been called a secondary boycott by some courts.

ing party or parties has been an action for damages, instituted after the injury has been inflicted. If the action of the offending person or persons has also been criminal, there may be prosecution at criminal law as well. The damage suit, however, has not been used much in labor disputes. There has been much more frequent recourse to what may be called preventive procedure, as contrasted with the action for damages, or even prosecution at criminal law. This preventive procedure is that of injunction — an order from a court to a person, or persons, to refrain from doing certain things that threaten unlawful damage to the one seeking the order, and, perhaps, to do certain things by way of correction.

The use of the injunction in labor disputes has been long and bitterly attacked by labor organizations, and there has been considerable legislation in recent years curtailing the issuance of injunctions. Organized labor's opposition to the injunction has been based in part upon the abuse of this form of procedure, but it is also based largely on a belief that the substantive law that it has been used to enforce is also unfair and should not be enforceable by any form of procedure. The Norris-LaGuardia Act of 1932, which was strongly favored by organized labor, not only imposed much stricter regulations with respect to procedure, but forbade the federal courts to issue injunctions at all against the doing of certain things in a labor dispute. Several states, also, have adopted similar restrictions on the issuance of injunctions. That the injunction is not regarded as evil in itself is evidenced by the fact that in recent years labor organizations have not infrequently resorted to injunctions against employers — or even against other unions.

The limitations imposed upon the use of the injunction have aroused new interest in the use of the damage suit to secure redress for injury inflicted during a labor dispute. This focusing of attention upon the law with respect to the recovery of damages has also been stimulated by the granting of new rights to organized workers under the National Labor Relations Act, by the recent expansion of labor organization, and by the frequent resort to unlawful acts in the strikes that have accompanied the extension of organization.

May damages be recovered from the union itself for injury suffered through unlawful acts by the union officers or members? The answer varies with the jurisdiction. Under the federal anti-trust acts a union may be sued for damages in the federal courts. But in some states a union cannot be sued in its own name. To what extent can the individual members of a union be held liable for unlawful damage inflicted as a result of orders given by the union officers? Again, the law differs among the states and the federal jurisdiction (under limitations imposed by the Norris-LaGuardia Act). In brief, the law with respect to the recovery of damages for injury suffered in the course of a labor dispute is neither clear nor uniform.[15]

[15] This applies also to the recovery of damages for violation, by either side, of a collective agreement.

Government Intervention in Labor Disputes

TYPES OF INTERVENTION

Mediation. The intervention of government agencies in labor disputes, for the prevention or termination of strikes or lockouts, may or may not involve the use of the coercive powers of government on one or both of the parties. Mediation, the simplest form of intervention by a government agency, is presumably free from any attempt to coerce either party to agree to any terms or to end the strike or lockout. The mediators simply tender their good offices in attempting to find a basis of agreement between the parties. The characteristic of true mediation is that, if it fails to bring about a settlement, it leaves both parties as free as it found them. High officials of government have at times practically forced one of the disputing parties to accept unsatisfactory terms by threatening, implicitly at least, some sort of reprisal or public condemnation. Pressure of this kind is not within the scope of pure mediation, however.

Voluntary Arbitration. If the mediating agency fails to secure a direct agreement between the parties on terms, it usually urges them to submit the matters still in dispute to arbitration. If the parties are free to reject arbitration, which means, of course, that there will be no arbitration unless both sides consent to it, the arbitration, if accepted, is voluntary arbitration. It is "voluntary" because it is entered into voluntarily. The law may give the proceedings of the arbitrators judicial standing, with authority to put witnesses under oath, and the award may be made legally binding, but if the parties are free to reject arbitration in the first place and go on with the strike or lockout, it is still voluntary arbitration. It is common for voluntary arbitration laws to designate some government agency, usually the mediating agency if there is one, to select the neutral arbitrators for the parties who have agreed to enter arbitration under the law, in the usual event that the parties cannot themselves agree on the neutral arbitrators.

Compulsory Investigation. The third type of intervention, and the first that involves any passing of judgment regardless of the wishes of the parties, is known as compulsory investigation. This means the holding of a hearing, with or without the power to compel testimony under oath, and the publication of the findings of fact and, perhaps, the recommended terms of settlement. The parties are compelled to allow the investigation of the merits of the case and the publication of the findings and recommendations, even though this may "prejudice the case" of one or both with the public. There is no legal compulsion to accept any terms, or to refrain from hostilities; the only pressure is that of public opinion.

Compulsory Waiting Period. A fourth type of intervention couples with compulsory investigation a compulsory waiting period during which the parties must refrain from coercive acts. This is to allow time for the investigation to be held and the findings or recommendations of the investigators to be considered. After the waiting period is over, the parties are free to strike or lockout if they wish. There is thus no compulsion on terms, merely an enforced delay on strikes or lockouts. A compulsory waiting period should also involve prohibition of any change in the terms of employment by the employer to the disadvantage of the workers, until after the expiration of a specified period. If the employer may legally reduce wages or increase hours before the waiting period is over, he can force the workers either to accept his terms or to resort to what may be held to be an illegal strike. As a matter of fact, there are not many lockouts in the narrow sense of closing the plant to compel the workers to accept the employer's terms; the employer has merely to change the terms and let the workers decide whether to accept them or strike. The reciprocal of forbidding strikes is the prohibition of changes by the employer in the terms of employment.

Compulsory Arbitration. The final type of intervention, compulsory arbitration, involves the prohibition of strikes and lockouts at any time. Under compulsory arbitration an award is handed down and both parties must adhere to that award unless they both agree to some other terms. Compulsory arbitration implies the existence of a government agency of arbitration that has essentially the powers of a court, in order to arrive at the facts at issue. Compulsory arbitration does not exist in the United States. A Kansas law of 1920, which set up what was essentially a system of compulsory arbitration, was held unconstitutional by the United States Supreme Court on the ground that it violated the employer's freedom of contract as to wages and hours. This statute was not confined to industries affected with a public interest, like public utilities.

INTERVENTION BY STATE OFFICIALS

Most states make some provision for mediation and assistance in voluntary arbitration by a government agency. In some states the agency is a permanent board, usually made up of representatives of employers, labor, and the public. In other states these duties are added to the regular duties of some state official or officials. Many states also provide for compulsory investigation in some types of disputes. In one state, Colorado, a compulsory waiting period is combined with compulsory investigation but this statute applies only to industries affected with a public interest.

FEDERAL INTERVENTION

Railroads. Railroad employment is the only one that has a history of intervention under a special federal

statute. Continuous statutory provision for federal intervention in labor disputes on the railroads goes back
to 1888. The present Railway Labor Act provides a
machinery for mediation and voluntary arbitration,
plus a provision for the appointment of a special board
of investigation if and when an "emergency" is created
by the failure of voluntary methods. If an emergency
board is appointed, both sides must refrain from
coercive measures to secure a change in the terms of
employment until after a specified period.

The governmental coercion in this system of intervention is applied to procedure, not to terms of employment. As pointed out above, the law assumes that
there are agreements covering the terms of employment. If a change in terms is desired, notice of specified
duration must be given. During the notice period the
parties are required to confer together and attempt to
agree on new terms. The carriers are forbidden to
change the terms, except by agreement with the workers, until after opportunity has been allowed for mediation by the government agency. If the mediators
fail to secure a direct agreement or an agreement to
accept arbitration, and if an emergency board is appointed, the carriers may not change the terms until
after the expiration of the "emergency period" of sixty
days. During the emergency period the workers are
also forbidden, in effect, to strike. Presumably they
must refrain from strikes during the notice period required for conference and mediation. This plan of
intervention, established in the 1926 Railway Labor
Act, was retained in the amended Railway Labor Act

of 1934. It has, on the whole, operated very successfully.[1]

The mediation agency for the railroads is a permanent National Mediation Board of three members. The board mediates but it does not arbitrate or investigate. If there is to be a voluntary arbitration under the act, the board assists the parties, when necessary, to form a special board for that arbitration. If there is to be an emergency board for investigation, the President appoints a special board for that particular dispute.

The intervention plan just described applies to disputes over the terms of a new contract. For disputes over the interpretation or application of existing agreements—that is, for the settlement of particular grievances — there is a similar requirement of notice and conference. However, the 1934 amendments to the act provided a separate agency — the National Adjustment Board — for handling secondary disputes that cannot be settled otherwise. Although there is nominally but one Adjustment Board, it has four separate divisions, one for each of four separate groupings of crafts, and each of the four divisions operates independently of the others.[2] This board is made up of an equal number of representatives of the carriers and the labor organizations, but in case of deadlock a neutral referee must be called in so that a decision can be reached. If the members of the divisional board do not agree promptly on a referee, the National Board

[1] In April 1936 Congress extended the coverage of the act to common carriers by air and carriers transporting air mail.

[2] An amending act of April 1936 authorized the establishment of an adjustment board for air transport, when deemed necessary, by the National Mediation Board.

of Mediation must appoint one. If the decision is against the carrier, the workers may obtain a court order to enforce it, should the carrier refuse to comply with the decision.

General. There is no special federal agency for intervention in labor disputes, apart from railroad and air transportation, except the "Conciliation Service" of the United States Department of Labor. This service was established in 1913. It is a mediation service only. There is no statutory provision for voluntary arbitration. The fact that the mediators are connected with the Department of Labor makes many employers wary of them, as they fear that the mediators are necessarily "on the side of the unions."

The lack of any federal machinery for compulsory investigation has at times been painfully apparent. How far the federal government can constitutionally go in this direction is still a question. It would seem, however, that legislation for compulsory investigation, and even a compulsory waiting period, would be constitutional in those employments to which the National Labor Relations Act applies.

The National Labor Relations Act makes no provision for the settlement of labor disputes in the ordinary sense. It sets up a machinery for the prevention of unfair labor practices by the employer. Its primary purpose is the elimination of certain causes of labor disputes by taking those issues out of the field of economic strength and putting them into the field of law. The National Labor Relations Board set up by the National Labor Relations Act is a quasi-judicial body for the enforcement of legal rights; it has no mediatory functions with respect to terms of employment. In this it is radically different from the National Mediation Board for the railroads. And the basis of the National Labor Relations Act differs so far from that of the Railway Labor Act that it provides that "Nothing in this Act shall be construed so as to interfere with or impede or diminish in any way the right to strike." If the National Labor Relations Act is successful in increasing the number of independent labor organizations that follow the method of collective bargaining, as now appears likely, it may well lead to an increase in the number of strikes over terms of employment, at least in the next few years.

CHAPTER VII

Public Regulation of the Terms of Employment

THE BASES OF PUBLIC REGULATION

ECONOMIC AND ETHICAL BASES

THE resort to legal regulation of the terms of employment indicates the unwillingness of the public to accept any longer the results of individual bargaining, and also a conviction that collective bargaining will either not be used or, if used, will not prove effective in bringing about the minimum standards desired. Legislation on terms of employment means the abandonment of reliance on freedom of bargaining, whether individual or collective.

What are the economic possibilities of improving working conditions and other terms of employment by law, without throwing some of the workers concerned out of employment? The answer depends, of course, upon the degree to which the existing terms

fall short of what the employer would give these workers rather than not get their labor. Experience indicates
that there is often such a gap, especially in the case
of women and unskilled male workers. For these,
generally, the only alternative to legislation has been
individual bargaining. The likelihood that individual
bargaining does not give terms as good as could be
secured if there were collective action by the workers
has been discussed above.[1] But legislation may get
more for the workers than they could get for themselves through collective action, since under the method
of legislation there is no dependence upon the voluntary
adherence of all the workers to the program and no
(legal) possibility of the employer giving employment on worse terms.

However, labor legislation rests on a broader basis
than the economic possibility of enforcing the highest
terms that can be obtained for those already employed.
The body politic has a duty to prevent the continuance
of terms of employment that are unjust or of conditions
that are injurious to the health of employees or dangerous to their morals. This may require the enforcement of standards of employment that will result in
the exclusion from employment of some who would
otherwise be employed. It is better public policy to
raise to a decent standard the terms for those to be
employed, and to meet in some other way the problem of those excluded, than to allow unregulated individual bargaining to depress the terms of employment unduly for all. In some cases the state may

[1] Pp. 83–94

deliberately exclude persons from employment in what is deemed to be their own interest as well as the public interest; as, for example, children, or adults suffering from physical disqualifications that make them peculiarly liable to injury through accident or occupational disease. The exclusion of young people or of women from certain employments may also be based on moral grounds.

The case for legislation does not rest on an assumption that all, or even most employers, are opposed to the observance of higher standards. Legislation may be necessary to prevent those employers, perhaps a minority, who are willing to depress the terms of employment in order to get or hold sales, from engaging in this "unfair" kind of competition with those employers who would prefer to conduct their business on a higher plane. Indeed, some employers have at times favored legislation as the only practicable means of ending the resort to lowering labor terms as a means of competing for sales. The enforcement of certain minimum standards through legal action means that the competition must be conducted on at least that minimum level of labor terms.

CONSTITUTIONAL BARRIERS

The movement for regulatory legislation on employment terms has had to face, in this country, not only the argument that it is economically unwise as well as unfair to individual employers and employees, but also two definite constitutional limitations on labor legislation. The first of these is the limitation on in-

terference with the freedom of contract of employers
and adult workers, imposed upon the Congress by the
Fifth Amendment, and upon state legislatures by their
own constitutions and by the Fourteenth Amendment
to the Constitution of the United States. This does
not apply to the legislative fixing of standards for
direct employment of labor by government units or for
work done under contract by private employers for
a government unit. The other limitation is that imposed upon federal action by the fact that our federal
government is one of delegated powers; the federal
government may not act in matters within the powers
held to be reserved to the states.

It is recognized that the states have the power to
regulate working conditions and other terms of employment, where such regulation is necessary to prevent
fraud or injury to the health, safety, or morals of the
workers. The federal government has similar power
with respect to workers engaged in interstate commerce. But the problem is: How far may labor legislation go without interfering with the freedom of contract between employers and their employees? This
problem has bothered the state courts and the United
States Supreme Court for half a century. The decisions
have not always been consistent; this is true even of
the decisions of the Supreme Court. But, generally
speaking, the trend has been toward permitting an
increased regulation of physical conditions and even
of hours of labor. The regulation of wages of men in
private employments, however, other than transportation and public utilities, has generally been held un-

constitutional. It was not until 1937 that the Supreme Court of the United States declared the regulation of women's wages constitutional.

Direct regulation of the terms of employment by the federal government, as contrasted with regulation by the states, has been held unconstitutional except in interstate transportation. The Supreme Court has declared that the power of Congress to regulate commerce does not extend to direct regulation of the terms of employment in production carried on within the states.[2] So far, that power has been held to be reserved to the states. This constitutional limitation has kept the state, rather than the country at large, the unit of legal regulation of employment terms, even though the market for the product is frequently far wider than one state.

The Supreme Court has recently held constitutional an act of Congress prohibiting the shipment of prison-made goods into a state that prohibits the sale within the state of goods made in prisons. On the basis of this decision, it is assumed that Congress may constitutionally protect a state from the competition, within its own borders, of goods produced in states with lower labor requirements. But this would not protect the state with higher requirements from such competition when it is trying to sell its products in states with lower standards than its own. The fact that the fixing of standards would still be a matter for the individual state to determine would leave a practical difficulty in the way of raising labor standards.

[2] The National Labor Relations Act does not attempt the regulation of the terms of employment.

DIRECT SAFETY AND HEALTH MEASURES

Specific regulations for the protection of workers from bodily injury, or injury to health, constitute the earliest type of effective labor legislation in the United States, and the type most extensive in content. The guarding of dangerous machinery, the use of protective devices against dangerous gases, protection against the hazards of fire and of explosion, protection against extremes of temperature, protection against improper ventilation, will suggest the subject matter of such regulations. The actual regulations would fill many volumes. Very many of them are rules made by administrative bodies authorized by legislatures to apply standards laid down in more general terms by statute; as, for example, the safety regulations prescribed for the railroads by the Interstate Commerce Commission.

This is direct safety and health legislation, as distinguished from some other types of labor legislation that have also been thought necessary for the protection of the health and safety of the workers, such as laws reducing the hours of labor, and "full crew" laws for the railroads. Because they are direct safety and health measures they have not been considered serious invasions of property rights or of freedom of contract, as have wages laws and even some hours laws. They affect the physical condition of employment rather than those terms of employment that have been regarded as directly subject to bargaining. There has always been a general legal obligation upon the employer to furnish a safe work-place and safe tools and other instruments of production, and proper safeguards for the handling of the materials of production. The constitutional right of the state to reduce this general obligation to specific requirements has been little questioned. So far as the worker's freedom of contract is concerned, it has been repeatedly recognized that the state may constitutionally deprive the worker of the right to work under unsafe or unhealthful conditions, whether his willingness to do so be due to economic pressure or to his own ignorance, indifference, or recklessness. This constitutional right of the state extends even to the prohibition of the employment in certain occupations of persons especially liable to injury in them.

It is by no means intended to imply that safety and health regulations have been extended to cover all measures proved to be technically feasible for the prevention or reduction of the recognized causes of accident or disease operating in places of employment. The cost of the preventive measures is still an important obstacle to making them obligatory, in spite of the general acceptance of the principle that money costs should not outweigh the cost in human safety and health. Moreover, many workers are omitted from the coverage of some of the laws. The administrative difficulty in enforcing protective legislation of this kind upon a large number of small employers, as well as the political difficulty of getting it through the legislature, account for many exemptions. For example, there is almost a dearth of protective legislation of this kind, as well as of other kinds, for agricultural labor.

CHILD LABOR

STATE LEGISLATION

The question of child labor is more than a labor question; it is a part of the general question of child welfare. There is no state in the union that does not prohibit the employment of children below some specified age, at least in some type of work. Most states have imposed some minimum educational qualification for leaving school for work, and in some states the employed child must attend school part of the time.

The prohibition of the labor of children under specified ages in certain employments is not the only form of child-labor legislation. The hours that children are permitted to work are more strictly limited than those of women. For children under sixteen, where employment below this age is not prohibited, the eight-hour limit is almost universal. In some state laws the hours limit is lower for girls than for boys in the same age grouping.

Child-labor legislation by the states, as distinct from the federal government, has not been held back by constitutional barriers. The child has no freedom of contract; the issue is between the rights of the parent and the guardianship of the state, and the courts have leaned toward the latter in this as in the matter of compulsory education. For many years the arguments for and the argument against more stringent age requirements have both been based, generally, on what is alleged to be best for the development of the child, physically, mentally, and morally. Little has been heard in recent years of the "crippling-of-industry" argument against the prohibition of child labor. On the other hand, the inexpediency of allowing children to compete with adults for employment has been especially stressed in the recent years of widespread unemployment.

FEDERAL LEGISLATION

Constitutional Difficulties. The constitutional difficulty in child-labor legislation is that of state versus federal jurisdiction. It was in the sphere of child-labor legislation that Congress first ran into the constitutional barrier against national labor legislation. In 1916 Congress passed a National Child Labor Act. The impetus for the passage of that act came from the contention that interstate competition under widely varying state standards, or almost total lack of legal standards in some states, was preventing the advance of their standards by the more progressive states. To limit this sort of competition, the terms of the federal act excluded from interstate commerce products on which children below certain ages had been employed.

In 1918 the Supreme Court, by a five-to-four decision, held the act unconstitutional as beyond the scope of the federal power to regulate commerce. It was held to be an invasion of the reserved rights of the states to prohibit or regulate the use of child labor within their own respective borders. The court did not hold the standards in the federal act "unreasonable"; the point was that Congress lacked the constitutional power to enforce these standards on the producers of any state by excluding their products from interstate commerce if they did not comply with them. An attempt in 1919 to secure approximately the same result by imposing a federal tax on employers using child labor in violation of the standards specified was also held unconstitutional, in 1922, this time with only one of the nine judges dissenting. The so-called "tax", the court held, was not really a tax but a penalty for the violation of statutory prohibitions or regulations that Congress had no right to impose on producers in the states.

Proposed Constitutional Amendment. The result of these two decisions was the adoption by Congress and submission to the states, in 1924, of the only proposed amendment to the Constitution to give Congress power to legislate on employment conditions that has yet been submitted to the states. The proposed amendment would give Congress power to limit, prohibit, or regulate the labor of persons under eighteen. Much opposition was offered to it on the ground that it might be interpreted to give Congress authority over other activities of persons under eighteen than merely wage employment. Only a few states ratified the amendment prior to 1929 and more than a quarter had acted adversely on it.[3]

[3] Ratification by three fourths of the states is necessary for adoption.

The depression gave a new stimulus to the movement against child labor. Most of the "codes of fair competition" approved under the National Industrial Recovery Act included a prohibition of the employment of children under sixteen (the minimum age under the National Child Labor Act of 1916 was fourteen). This aided the renewed drive for the adoption of the proposed child-labor amendment. By March 1937, twenty-eight states had ratified it, including some that had formerly rejected it. However, ratification was then defeated in several states, largely because of the contention that the proposed amendment could be used to impose national control of the youth of the country. This check to the ratification of the proposed amendment and the recent decisions of the Supreme Court sustaining a broader interpretation of the powers of Congress under the commerce clause of the Constitution have led to a renewal of the attempt to meet the problem of interstate competition by excluding child-labor products from interstate commerce.[4]

HOURS OF LABOR

The regulation of the hours of labor of minors has already been discussed in connection with child labor. When we turn to the regulation of the hours of labor of adults, we find that the primary basis of maximum-

[4] A provision of this kind was included in the Black-Connery Bill, the so-called Wages and Hours Bill, which was under consideration by Congress when the regular 1937 session adjourned.

hours legislation has been the necessity of safeguarding the workers from injury to health and the increased liability to accident brought on by long hours. Whatever other reasons the advocates of such legislation, or the legislators themselves, may have had for reducing the hours of labor by law, the necessity of such legislation for the protection of the health and safety of the workers was kept in the forefront; it was only on this ground, apparently, that the constitutionality of such a limitation of freedom of contract could be sustained.

Since 1930 much more has been heard of the necessity of reducing the hours of labor by law in order to increase the number employed. Indeed, this was the basis of the maximum-hours regulation attempted under the National Industrial Recovery Act. But that act was declared unconstitutional as exceeding the scope of federal jurisdiction. Moreover, the constitutionality of state legislation to effect the same purpose is still doubtful. We return, therefore, to the consideration of hours regulation based on health and safety grounds.

MAXIMUM–HOURS LAWS FOR WOMEN

The regulation of the hours of labor has been carried much farther for women than for men. Because women are much weaker physically than men and because injury to women is presumed to have a more adverse effect on the race, it has been easier to get maximum-hours laws for women from the legislatures and to secure affirmation of their constitutionality from the courts. Another factor that has influenced the legislatures, and has been accepted by courts, is the inferior bargaining power of working women.

Nearly every state in the union has placed some legal limitation on the hours of labor of women, at least in some occupations. The employments usually covered are those in "manufacturing, mechanical, and mercantile" establishments. Some laws cover hotels, restaurants, etc., as well. Domestic service is not included. Although the majority of the states do not permit more than nine hours a day, less than a third have reached the eight-hour standard and not all of these impose the corollary of the forty-eight hour week. In some states, exceptions from the general maximum are allowed for certain employments; as, for example, work in canneries.

A number of states limit the specified hours within which the permitted number of hours may be worked, in order to prohibit night work. The main ground for the prohibition of night work is health protection, although protection from dangers to morals is also advanced as a reason.

MAXIMUM-HOURS LAWS FOR MEN

The regulation of the hours of men has been restricted, for the most part, to a small number of occupations that are deemed especially hazardous. Transportation and mining head the list; for interstate carriers, coastwise vessels, and American vessels in foreign trade, the regulations are imposed by the federal government. Hours in tunnel construction, saw and planing mills, cement mills, and in a few other types of establishments, are also regulated in some states. Two states have a ten-hour maximum for manufacturing, with overtime permitted in emergencies. A few states limit individual workers to six days' work in seven, with exceptions for watchmen and similar occupations.

The constitutionality of hours laws for men, under the Fourteenth Amendment, has had a checkered history. As early as 1898 the United States Supreme Court upheld a Utah statute fixing an eight-hour maximum for miners. Seven years later the same Court, by a five-to-four decision, held invalid a New York ten-hour law for bakers. Twelve years later, in 1917, it upheld a general ten-hour law for manufacturing in Oregon, a decision that presumably overruled the decision in the New York bakers' case.

The decision in the Oregon ten-hour law case was not followed by any widespread extension of hours legislation for men. The decision came after the ten-hour day had already been generally established, except in some "continuous-operation" industries, like the steel industry, by voluntary action. Organized labor was, on the whole, opposed to the extension of maximum-hours legislation for adult males, holding that collective bargaining was the best method of reducing their hours of labor. Many unions had already attained an eight-hour day and were looking forward to the forty-four hour week or even the forty-hour week. Any legal maximum that would be upheld by the courts on health and safety grounds might well be higher than that which the unions hoped soon to secure by collective bargaining, and they feared that the legal maximum might be assumed by the public to be a fair minimum also. The movement for the five-day week in the post-war decade showed that the hours question, for men at least, had generally passed beyond the health and safety stage.

Today the main reason advanced for maximum-hours legislation is the reabsorption of the unemployed. So far, the constitutionality of legal compulsion to reduce the number of hours for this purpose has not been established. Moreover, any proposal to reduce the working week, by legislation, considerably below the number of hours generally in vogue, raises the further question of whether a reduction in weekly wages is also to be prohibited. Such a prohibition would involve an interference with freedom of contract, with respect to wages, that has not yet passed the constitutional test.[5]

THE REGULATION OF WAGES

Wages may be regulated by law directly, or they may be regulated indirectly through compulsory arbitration. As pointed out above, the fixing of legally

[5] For the regulation of hours, along with wages, under the National Industrial Recovery Act, and under the Coal Conservation Act — both of which were held unconstitutional —, see below, pp. 170, 172–173.

The Black-Connery Bill, which was under consideration by Congress at the time of the adjournment of the regular session of 1937, proposed to exclude from interstate commerce the products made under substandard hours and wages. The bill, as it was passed by the Senate in July 1937, would permit the fixing of a maximum of forty hours a week. This was the most common figure for the normal work week under the Recovery Act codes.

binding wages through compulsory arbitration under a state act, in general employments as distinct from transportation and public utilities, was held by the Supreme Court of the United States to be in violation of the Fourteenth Amendment.[6] It may be that compulsory arbitration as to wages in intrastate transportation and in public utilities under state jurisdiction is constitutional. The issue has not been presented. However, the Supreme Court has declared that Congress has the power to pass a compulsory arbitration law for the interstate railroads, and it upheld the constitutionality of the Adamson Act,[7] which prohibited the payment of less for eight hours than for the number of hours then being worked, pending an investigation and report by a commission. This may serve as a precedent for state legislation for compulsory arbitration in intrastate transportation and in public utilities. The same public interest that makes constitutional the regulation of the rates charged by these enterprises may also make constitutional the fixing of wages by compulsory arbitration in order to prevent the interruption of the service.

The fixing of minimum wages by direct wage legislation has had as its purpose, of course, the prevention of the payment of wages considered too low, rather than the prevention of inconvenience to the public through strikes or lockouts in an essential service. Postponing for later consideration the wage legislation of a "recovery" nature, we shall consider first the state

[6] See pp. 142–143.
[7] This act was passed in September 1916 to avert a nationwide strike in the engine and train service.

minimum-wage legislation for women. These acts cover minors also, but the main purpose of the legislation is the establishment of minimum wages for adult women, and we shall restrict our discussion to that aspect of it.

MINIMUM-WAGE LAWS FOR WOMEN

History. From 1913 to 1923 minimum-wage laws were passed by a dozen states, and one was enacted by Congress for the District of Columbia.[8] Most of these laws called for the fixing of the minimum wage at the cost of healthful and decent subsistence for a woman living alone. In 1917, the United States Supreme Court, by an even split of four to four, allowed the decision of the Oregon Supreme Court to stand — that the minimum-wage law of that state was not an unconstitutional invasion of the freedom of contract. Six years later the Supreme Court held unconstitutional the District of Columbia minimum-wage law, of the same type as the Oregon law, on the ground that it was a violation of the freedom of contract guaranteed by the Fifth Amendment. As this meant that the state laws were in contravention of the same language in the Fourteenth Amendment, the decision ended this phase of state minimum-wage legislation.

Even had there been no constitutional check, it is doubtful if there would have been much spread of minimum-wage legislation in the period of prosperity following the 1923 decision. But the wage cut-

[8] This does not include the Massachusetts law; the minimum-wage "decrees" in that state were not legally binding.

ting that went on after 1930, which appears to have been especially heavy in the wages of the lowest paid groups, brought on a movement to put an end by law to sweatshop wages for women. The sponsors of the new legislation, in the hope of escaping the constitutional reef on which the earlier laws had been wrecked, avoided the "living-wage" standard and asked for a wage based on "the fair and reasonable value of the service." Minimum wages were not to be fixed, however, unless the wages in the occupation were *both* (1) less than the value of the service and (2) less than a living wage; it was not the purpose of the legislation to secure wages equal to the value of the service for all working women but only for those whose wages were below a living level.

This new type of minimum-wage act — the "minimum fair-wage" type — was adopted in 1933 by seven states. It is significant that these states included six predominantly industrial states, not one of which had been included in the earlier group; namely, New Hampshire, Connecticut, New York, New Jersey, Ohio, and Illinois. Massachusetts enacted a similar statute in 1934 and Rhode Island in 1936. Meanwhile, the advent of the President's Re-employment Agreement in the summer of 1933, with its minimum-wage provisions, and the later adoption of the separate industrial codes, undoubtedly held back the issuance of wage orders under the 1933 state legislation. Then, in June 1936, this type of act was also condemned, as in violation of the Fourteenth Amendment, by the Supreme Court of the United States in a five-to-four decision.

Ten months later, however, the Supreme Court, again by a five-to-four decision, refused to follow the earlier decision in the District of Columbia case and upheld the constitutionality of the minimum-wage law of the State of Washington. The Washington law is one of the old-type laws, but this latest decision of the Supreme Court establishes the constitutionality of the new-type laws as well. Since the decision of the Supreme Court, in March 1937, there has been renewed activity in the regulation of minimum wages for women under state laws.

Economic Effects. The experience with state minimum-wage laws in this country has not been extensive enough to furnish any very important inductive conclusions as to the possibilities of raising women's wages generally by this method of coercive action, without appreciably reducing the number employed. Not one of the leading industrial states attempted to fix legal minimum wages before 1933, and mandatory orders have been issued for only a small number of occupations under the new-type laws. Certainly, the wage fixing that has occurred has not resulted in much unemployment, nor has it resulted in the reduction of higher wages to the minimum figure, so far as the available data show. Favorable experience with minimum-wage fixing in a localized service industry like the laundry industry does not, however, prove the feasibility of raising wages generally through minimum-wage fixing under state laws in an industry like the cotton textile industry with a wide area of competitive production.

The economic possibilities of raising women's wages by state minimum-wage legislation, without reducing the number employed, remains, therefore, largely in the sphere of *a priori* reasoning. And here we must distinguish between the possibility of raising wages that are below those paid for similar work in the same or a comparable occupation and the possibility of raising women's wages generally to the cost of healthful and decent living for a woman living alone. It would seem likely that, in most occupations, a minimum-wage law could raise wages to what the "best" employers are already paying without reducing appreciably the number employed. It could at least raise all to the level that would be paid under conditions of informed two-sided competition. And in view of what is known of the effects upon women's wages of the kind of competition we have had, it would seem that there are many gaps here that might be closed by a minimum-wage law.

In considering the possibility of raising women's wages generally to the cost-of-living-alone level, we must remember that the wages structure in women's employments has not been built on a minimum price of labor equal to the cost of living alone. Many, if not most, women who seek employment are members of a family group; the current cost to the family of healthful and decent living for such a woman is less than it would be if she were living alone. The supply of women's labor available for less than the cost of living for a woman living alone has kept the wages of women much below that level in numerous occupations scattered through many states. It is by no means certain that a legal minimum wage considerably higher than the wages now paid would not attract new, and more efficient, applicants for jobs in some occupations and result in the displacement by new workers of some women now employed, as well as in a reduction in the total number employed.

The extent to which wages could be raised in a particular occupation without reducing the number of women employed depends upon a number of factors. The most important are the following: the proportion of the wages of this class of labor to the total cost of production; the effect of higher wages on the efficiency of the workers; the technical feasibility of substituting other methods for this labor, and the cost of these other methods; the degree of competition among the employers in the sale of the product; and the elasticity or inelasticity of the demand for the product. The mere enumeration of these factors indicates the complexity of the problem, even where the action takes place entirely within one state. In this country there is, in many occupations, the added complication of interstate competition. But whether the possibilities be great or small, the establishment of wage boards for low-wage occupations, with authority to fix legal minimum rates of wages up to a cost-of-living-alone level, should aid rather than retard a solution of the problem of women's wages, provided the boards do not push wages up so fast and so far as to throw a large number of women out of employment when there is no other employment open to them on better terms.

REGULATION OF WAGES OF MEN

However great the desirability of minimum-wage legislation for women, it leaves untouched the central problem, which is the low wages received by so many adult males. If it is a living wage that we seek to establish, it is the wages of the adult male that must be our chief concern. It is the adult male to whom we normally look for the support of the family. No concept of a living wage is adequate that is not based on the assumption of family living as the normal situation and on the further assumption that the family is to be supported from the wages of one adult male.

In spite of the overwhelming importance of the wage levels for adult males, there was no direct regulation of the wages of men in private employments in this country prior to the coming of the Recovery Act. Such minimum-wage legislation as had been attempted by the states had not, as pointed out above, included men. There was a general assumption that the constitutionality of wage legislation for men was less likely to be upheld than that of wage laws for women. In addition, there was the opposition of organized labor to the fixing of men's wages by law, an opposition even stronger than that to maximum-hours laws, and for the same reasons. The effect of legal minimum-wage rates on what could be secured by collective bargaining was feared even more than was the effect of maximum-hours laws on the further reduction of hours by collective bargaining.

MINIMUM–WAGE FIXING UNDER THE NATIONAL INDUSTRIAL RECOVERY ACT

Purpose. The primary purpose of the minimum-wage provision of the National Industrial Recovery Act was "to increase purchasing power." It was closely related to the provision for fixing maximum hours. The act did not specify that hours were to be reduced, but it was well understood that the purpose of the hours provision was a reduction in hours in order to increase the number employed. If this were not to result in a reduction in the weekly wages of those already employed, their hourly wages would have to be increased. Consequently the program called for the fixing of minimum wages as well as maximum hours. Every code or agreement given the force of law under the act was to include maximum hours of labor and minimum rates of pay.

It must not be overlooked, however, that the Recovery Act contained authorization for the fixing of minimum-wage rates on a "reform" as well as a "recovery" basis. One of the purposes mentioned in the act was "to improve the standards of labor." Moreover, the codes were to be "codes of fair competition", and "fair competition" was construed to mean competition based on a reasonable minimum of wages. There is no doubt that the principle of fixing minimum wages as a "floor" for competition was widely accepted at the time and that it still has wide support.

It must be recognized that in the fixing of minimum rates for adult males no attempt was made to bring all wages up to the standard of a living wage on a family basis. Forty cents an hour for a forty-hour week is, in most communities, far short of a living wage for a man and a wife and two or three minor children. The minimum rates fixed for women came much closer to the "living wage for a woman-living-alone" standard. But in the case of males the gap between actual wages and the family living-wage basis was so large in so many employments that it was beyond the scope of an emergency wage-raising measure to attempt to close it.

The Differentials. For the most part, the minimum-wage rates fixed in the codes were set for the lowest paid groups alone. Only in a small number of codes were specific minimum rates set for the more highly paid occupations in the industry, and these were nearly all relatively well-organized industries in which the unions were able to secure recognition in the code of the differential rates already established for the more skilled groups by collective bargaining. In a few codes, as in the master code for the construction industry, it was stipulated that the rates to be established by collective bargaining should be the code minimum rates for the respective occupations. But most of the codes left the rates for the more skilled groups to some such general phrase as "equitable differentials shall be retained" or "there shall be an equitable readjustment" of wages already above the specified minimum to meet the reduction in hours.

Differentials in the minimum rates for the lowest

paid were frequently allowed on the basis of sex, region, and size of city. Lower minimum rates for women than for men were common. Of the geographic differentials, the most common was that between the rates for the South and those for the North. Another type of place differential was that between the rates for less populous places and those for the larger cities; the former, of course, were lower.

The geographic differentials reflect an assumption that differences in wages growing out of differences in local conditions were too strongly entrenched to be completely dislodged. No doubt this left some employers with a competitive advantage, in the form of lower wage rates, over other employers in the same industry. How important this was it is difficult to tell. The lower wage rates in certain sections of the country were affected by the composition of the labor force and its living standards, as well as by the lower cost of living in the narrower sense. The experience under the Recovery Act with the problem of fixing minimum-wage rates on a national, or at least an industry-wide, basis served to illustrate the complexities of the problem, even apart from the complications introduced by the competition between industries.

WAGE REGULATION UNDER THE
GUFFEY ACT

The passage of the Coal Conservation Act, the so-called Guffey Act, in August 1935, was the direct result of the elimination of the bituminous coal code by the Supreme Court decision invalidating the Recovery Act. That decision came at a time (May 1935) when the operators and the union were attempting to agree on terms for the renewal of the Appalachian Agreement. This agreement had been made originally at the time of the adoption of the code, and its wages terms had been incorporated in the code. The agreement had expired April 1, 1935, but had been extended to permit further negotiation. The parties were deadlocked and a nationwide bituminous coal strike was threatening when the Guffey Act was passed.

The outstanding characteristic of the Guffey Act, with respect to its wages provisions, was the fact that the wages agreed to by collective bargaining, between employers representing two thirds of the tonnage and representatives of the majority of the workers, were to be the legal minimum rates for the respective districts. In the case of hours, the maximum hours permitted were to be those set for the industry as a whole by similar representative bargaining. The legal standards were thus to be those arrived at by collective bargaining. This and the circumstances under which the act was passed indicate that it was a law to secure industrial peace as well as stabilization of prices and wages in the industry. It was not a minimum-wage act in the ordinary sense. The act was declared unconstitutional by the Supreme Court in May 1936.[9]

[9] The Black-Connery Bill, as passed by the Senate in July 1937 (see above, p. 162, note 5), would permit the fixing of minimum-wage rates, by a national board, for the production of goods admitted to interstate commerce. However, the board would not be allowed to fix the minimum rate above forty cents an hour, and provision was made for geographical differentials as well as interindustry differentials.

PART THREE

SOCIAL
SECURITY

CHAPTER VIII

The Problem of Economic Insecurity

TODAY most working people are totally dependent upon the contents of pay envelopes for their livelihood; yet pay envelopes, like railway timetables, are subject to change without notice. No worker is certain what his next week's earnings will be. The family income may be reduced by any one of many misfortunes. The breadwinner may get sick. He may be laid off or employed only part time. He may be injured, perhaps for life. He may even die. All these hazards threaten the security of every wage earner's family.

Increased Risks. With extreme specialization and mechanization most of these hazards have increased. Machinery has tended to increase the number of industrial accidents, the amount of industrial disease, and, at times, the amount of unemployment. A new invention may make a worker's previous training worthless, reducing the earnings of a skilled craftsman to those of a common laborer. Also, workmen are likely to be retired at an earlier age in mechanized industries, thus reducing the length of their working lives.

Extreme division of labor leads to interdependence and to instability. With specialization and exchange, employers are dependent upon cash markets over which they may have very little control. Changes in the weather, the fashions, or consumers' taste, may bring about a change in an employer's demand for the services of workers. Employment also changes with fluctuations in the general rate of spending. If people spend less, fewer workers will be employed. As employment is a by-product of money making, whenever business for any reason becomes unprofitable, workers are laid off. Yet, in a highly specialized economy, the worker's family is usually dependent, for its subsistence, solely upon his job. His job may be so specialized that he is untrained for other types of work.

Modern industry undergoes rapid changes that increase the worker's insecurity. Businesses migrate from the North to the South or from the East to the West, leaving behind stranded communities. The increased use of oil and electricity for fuel throws a shadow across the future of many coal miners' families. Not only did the automobile displace the horse and buggy, but it has contributed to the eighteen per cent decline in the number of railroad employees from 1920 to 1929.

What all this means is that workers today are exposed to a variety of hazards that make their incomes very unsteady. To some extent these economic hazards are inherent in a money economy that is highly specialized and highly mechanized. In large measure our economic system, rather than the individual worker, is responsible for this instability in earnings.

WORKERS' INSECURITY

Accidents and Sickness. The yearly record of accident and sickness among workers serves to illustrate how these risks reduce the earnings of workers. In 1935, for example, about 1.4 million employees were injured while working. Their actual and future wage losses were estimated at 470 million dollars.[1] The loss of earnings resulting from sickness is even greater. In a year like 1935, wage earners in families receiving incomes under $2,500 suffered a loss through sickness of twenty-five to thirty dollars a year per worker.[2]

In part, these health risks result from the physical conditions surrounding the job. Fatal accidents, for example, are frequent in mining, and coal mining in the United States is more dangerous than in Europe. Much sickness and disease is either directly or indirectly due to the nature of the worker's employment. He may work in an unhealthy atmosphere or with poisonous materials, like mercury and lead. The testimony of a social worker before a Congressional committee recently revealed that of 2,000 miners hired to drill a tunnel in West Virginia, 476 had died of silicosis

[1] *Accident Facts* (1936 edition), published by The National Safety Council, Inc., Chicago, p. 54. The U.S. Bureau of Labor Statistics has estimated the total annual cost of industrial accidents in the United States as five billion dollars.

[2] Falk, I. S., *Security and Sickness* (Garden City, 1936), pp. 13-15

and about 1,500 more were doomed to death from the same disease, which is caused by breathing an atmosphere loaded with fine particles of silica dust.

Unemployment. The risk of unemployment is responsible for the largest loss of earnings. Studies of unemployment since 1900 seem to indicate that, on the average, eight per cent of all workers are unemployed, at an estimated loss of about four billion dollars a year. During depressions as much as twenty or thirty per cent of the working force may be idle, while in prosperous periods the figure may fall to four or five per cent, which means that even in the 1920's at least one million workers were always seeking work.

Workers may be unemployed for various reasons. Some are out of work for short periods of time when shifting from one employer to another or from one occupation to another line of work. Such transferring or turnover of labor is occurring constantly for personal or economic reasons. The worker may dislike his job or the boss may dislike his work. Also some businesses are expanding while others are going bankrupt; employees must adjust accordingly. Casual laborers who take odd jobs are usually seeking work between jobs. It is estimated that even in good times over 3,000,000 workers each year are "separated" from industrial jobs and are, therefore, at least temporarily unemployed.

Some unemployment is connected with the seasonal character of certain industries and is, therefore, classified as seasonal unemployment. Employment in agricultural areas reaches a peak during the harvest period.

In off-season periods agricultural laborers may be looking in vain for a job. Certain kinds of construction work cannot be done in winter weather, so that skilled building workers, although receiving high hourly wage rates, fail to earn such large yearly incomes.

Unemployment is also caused by the business cycle. In periods of depression many more hands are idle and larger expenditures for unemployment relief are required. The average worker in the course of his forty-five working years will pass through eight or ten depressions.

Finally, technological unemployment is a threat to the wage incomes of many workers. Workers may lose their jobs by the introduction of a new machine or a new technique for doing their work. The introduction of the new invention may, of course, bring a saving to consumers by lowering the cost of producing the product and hence its selling price. It is possible that the reduction in price may be sufficient to permit consumers to increase their purchases of that product or some other products enough to cause such an increase in the quantity of goods sold that all the workers displaced by the machine will be hired to help produce that additional amount of goods. Such a course of events is possible but, in some instances, improbable. With monopolistic or semi-monopolistic control of supply under oligopoly or monopolistic competition, it may not be so profitable for producers to reduce the price after installing the new machine, perhaps because the demand for that particular product is relatively inelastic. If prices are not reduced and the rate of spending remains the same, the same quantity of goods will be sold as before. But with the new technique fewer workers are needed to produce that quantity of goods and, temporarily at least, the workers displaced by the new machine will be looking for jobs. For this reason, technological unemployment has sometimes been referred to as price-inflexible unemployment.

However, unemployment is not easy to classify or to define. Some people may seem physically unable to do a good day's work. Are these so-called "unemployables" to be included as unemployed? Some people refuse to work unless they are offered the "right" kind of a job at a "decent" rate of pay. Are they unemployed? All sorts of problems arise when one attempts to count the unemployed.

Despite such problems, it is clear that most unemployment, whether seasonal, cyclical, or technological, is not the fault of the worker. Usually he is not to blame because he loses his job and his income. If he works in one line of business he is more likely to be laid off than if he works in another line.

Although in prosperous times the economic losses from unemployment run into billions of dollars — probably over two billion dollars in 1929 — during depressions such losses are counted in tens of billions of dollars. According to official estimates, the total compensation to employees fell from 51.5 billion dollars in 1929 to 29.4 billion dollars in 1933, a drop of forty-three per cent in four years.[3] Making allowance for

---

[3] *National Income in the United States, 1929–1935,* United States Department of Commerce, Washington, 1936.

changes in the cost of living for wage earners, this meant a twenty-five per cent decline in the real income of employees as a group.

But the burden of this employment shortage was not evenly distributed among all workers. While in electric and gas utilities, in trade, in recreation and amusement, and in personal service industries the number of employees declined about twenty-five per cent from 1929 to 1933, employment decreased almost fifty per cent in the metal industries and almost sixty per cent in the construction industry.[4] Figures for the percentage of all trade-union members who were employed in the spring of 1933 tell the same story. Only thirty per cent of the union building workers and only fifty per cent of the union metal workers were then employed, while in all other trades taken together, eighty per cent of the union membership was employed.

These figures indicate that employees in those branches of business that are close to the consumer are less subject to the risk of unemployment or underemployment. Fluctuations in employment are much greater in the so-called producers' goods industries which manufacture capital equipment. This is largely because the consumers' goods industries curtail their purchases of equipment during depressions.

Old Age and Nonaccidental Death. The economic losses resulting from illness, injury, or unemployment of wage earners have been indicated. It is more difficult to estimate the loss of family earnings that results

[4] *Ibid.*

when the breadwinner's working days come to an end either because of death from some nonindustrial cause, or because his advanced age disqualifies him for regular employment. Industry wants young and active workers, yet the average age of the American population is constantly increasing. In 1937 one out of fourteen persons in this country was sixty-five years of age or older. By 1990, it is estimated, one person in seven will have reached sixty-five. According to estimates, sixty-five per cent of the 7,800,000 people sixty-five years of age or over in 1937 were wholly dependent upon friends, relatives, or upon public or private charity.

PROTECTION AGAINST INSECURITY

How are these hazards of accident, illness, unemployment, old age, and early death to be met? How are wage earners to be protected from fluctuations in their earnings that are caused by forces largely beyond the control of any worker? Who is to pay for the losses resulting from these risks that in part are inherent in our economic system? To these questions, social insurance is one of the answers.

In the past such losses have been met by a variety of methods. They have been met by the worker and his family; in some cases they have been partially met by benefit plans operated either by the worker's trade union or his employer; to some extent they have been met by public and private charity; and finally, in the case of industrial accidents, the losses have been met by workmen's compensation or industrial-accident insurance on a compulsory basis. The adequacy of these various methods will now be considered.

The Worker and His Family. A few figures for incomes during the prosperous year of 1929 will make clear how difficult it is for the families of workers to shoulder the losses resulting from illness, injury, death, unemployment, or superannuation of the breadwinner. The Brookings Institute estimates that eighty-four per cent of all employed people earned less than $2,000 in 1929. Since some families have more than one working member, sixty per cent of all families had an income below $2,000. From 1929 to 1933 the average earnings of employed wage earners dropped from about $1,470 to around $1,100.

A wage earner's family must meet the losses from economic misfortune either by using up its savings, or by running into debt, or by reducing its standard of living. Most of the families with incomes under $2,000 save very little, even if one includes in savings such items as purchases of insurance, securities, or real estate. On such a basis, it is estimated that the non-farm families with incomes between $1,000 and $2,000 saved, on the average, but fifty-four dollars per family in the prosperous year, 1929. If families with incomes under $1,000 are included, this net saving is turned into a net debt per family averaging fifty dollars for all families with incomes under $2,000.

Private Insurance. The private insurance carried by wage earners is largely the industrial type. Industrial insurance is much more costly than ordinary insurance, partly because the premiums are collected at the home of the policyholder each week by an agent. In 1930 there were over 75,000,000 industrial policies in force. Though this type of insurance accounts for three fourths of all life insurance policies, the face value of industrial policies does not average much above two hundred dollars. Such policies, therefore, afford practically no protection to the wage earner's family. In fact, so difficult is it for workers to carry even that small amount of life insurance that about ninety per cent of all industrial policies are surrendered for cash, or are allowed to lapse through failure to pay premiums at some time before the policy matures or the policyholder dies.

From these figures it is evident that wage earners now are not protected by private insurance policies from the economic hazards here discussed, nor are their incomes adequate to pay the premiums that would be necessary to carry insurance protection against each of these hazards. They are not even able to carry two- or three-hundred-dollar burial insurance policies.

Trade-Union Benefit Plans. A few trade unions have established plans for old-age benefits, sickness benefits, disability benefits, or unemployment benefits for their members. However, these plans covered no more than one per cent of the working population in 1931 and in most instances they were not financially sound. In that year trade unions were dispensing a total of about forty million dollars for all types of benefits, with death benefits accounting for almost half of this total. Less than 100,000 workers were covered in 1931 by unemployment-benefit plans established either by trade unions or jointly by trade unions and private companies.

Company Benefit Plans. Although more extensive than trade-union plans, company benefit plans have covered but a small percentage of the working population. Furthermore, companies in competitive lines of business must make such plans pay for themselves. It is claimed that they do so, for the most part, by increasing the worker's efficiency, reducing labor turnover, and forestalling labor troubles. Workmen may be less ready to strike, quit, or join a union if such action will deprive them of a pension in their old age. Also, the worker usually fails to get any pension if he is fired, or if the company goes out of business or simply abandons the plan.

It is estimated that some six million employees were covered in 1931 by group life insurance policies, which are sold to establishments employing fifty or more persons. The employer pays at least a part of the premiums. If allowance is made for salaried positions, the average death benefit for wage earners under group insurance would probably be below $1,000.

The other type of company welfare program of significance is the payment of pensions to retired workers. In 1931 about 400 companies had some sort of retirement plan, and that year some 130,000 pensioners were receiving about 100 million dollars under such plans. The pensioners are so few in number because one usually must be with a firm at least twenty years before he is eligible for a pension, and less than ten per cent of all factory workers are with one firm that long. Furthermore, in 1932 only "about eight per cent of the employees in company pension plans were covered by plans in which the guarantees were both actuarially and financially sound."[5]

In 1931 about 50,000 employees of fifteen companies were covered by company unemployment-benefit plans, although two thirds of them were in a plan that had been suspended. An authority says: "The general policy of the companies has been to concentrate unemployment on those not entitled to relief under the plan, thus keeping eligible workers employed and reducing claims for benefits."[6] In the same year a few companies had plans for sickness benefits and dismissal compensation, but these plans covered very few wage earners.

It is evident from this recitation of facts and figures that, at best, trade-union and company benefit programs have afforded some protection to a very limited number of workers against only two economic hazards, superannuation and death. Private benefit programs to provide protection against the risk of unemployment have not covered one per cent of the working population. As a means of offsetting the losses of earnings, amounting to billions of dollars, that arise from the hazards here discussed, such company and trade-union programs have been of practically no significance. Consequently, most of the burden of these losses that has not been shouldered by the worker and

[5] Latimer, Murray W., *Industrial Pension System in the United States and Canada* (1932), p. 876
[6] Stewart, Bryce, *Unemployment Benefits in the United States* (1930), p. 169

his family has been carried by public and private welfare organizations.

Public and Private Relief. In the first half of 1935, over four million able workers and their families were receiving public relief because they could not land a job. At that time over one seventh of the country's population was receiving public relief, and one out of every two persons over sixty-five years of age was dependent upon others for his or her support.

When business was booming in the decade of the 1920's, the number of persons dependent upon public and private charity was steadily increasing. During that decade the expenditures for relief of the poor and needy in their own homes just about doubled, and public funds were responsible for an increasing share of the burden. By 1929, it is estimated, relief organizations were spending 85 million dollars for aid to the unemployed, the aged, the sick, and the disabled. About three fourths of the funds for relief were then coming from taxes and one fourth from private donations.

From 1929 to the end of 1934, relief expenditures nearly doubled each year, yet relief expenditures in 1933 and 1934 amounted to only six and twelve per cent, respectively, of the estimated loss in wages from total unemployment in those years. By 1935, public expenditures for relief amounted to well over two billion dollars, while private funds then accounted for but two per cent of all relief expenditures. About four fifths of the families on the relief rolls were there through lack of employment and the other fifth contained no member who was able to accept a full-time job, because of either sickness, age, physical disability, or family cares. Full-time re-employment would, therefore, have solved the problem for about eighty per cent of the relief cases.

The real issues in this whole problem of wage earners' insecurity are: Who is to meet the loss in earnings occasioned by these hazards that are inherent in our economic system? And what plan or procedure should be followed if those who suffer from these hazards are to be given some assistance?

Partly a Tax Problem. The first question is in large measure a matter of taxation. Most workers cannot save enough money to meet such losses themselves. Even in good times, their earnings are insufficient to purchase private life insurance. It is also evident that private benefit plans, whether trade-union or company programs, have not afforded most wage earners adequate protection against these economic hazards. Consequently, when a family's earnings drop towards zero, its resources and credit are soon used up and an application blank for public assistance is filled out. The family is then supported, at least in part, by tax funds. Even in normal times private charitable institutions have played only a minor role.

If the poor and needy are supported by local tax funds, property-tax payers foot most of the relief bills. If they are supported by federal funds, income-tax payers bear a large part of the relief cost. The source of the funds plays an important part in the issue of federal versus local relief. In either case, however, the source of the funds to foot the bill is in no way directly related to responsibility for the risks that gave rise to the need.

Responsibility for Risks. It has been suggested that a tax on employers in some way related to the risk might cause a reduction in the risk and, therefore, the losses; and to the extent that such a reduction failed to take place, the consumer of the product should pay for the costs of producing that product, including the human costs. For example, the consumer of coal would pay for the extra risk to the miner's life and limb from such underground work.

In many instances, lower money costs are only possible by increasing human costs. The speeding up of machinery may increase the accident rate, injure the health of the worker, and shorten his working life. Should not this increased risk to workers somehow be included in the money costs, when it is the employer who decides the speed at which machinery shall run? Is not a charge for the depreciation of the labor element in production just as proper as a charge for depreciation of capital equipment? The introduction of a new invention may separate a number of workers from their jobs, at least for a time, and may reduce their lifetime earnings considerably. The workers had nothing to do with the invention or introduction of the new machine. Should not the loss of workers' earnings, at least until they find another job, be included in the cost of installing the new machine? Why should the workers and property-tax payers bear the full cost of unemployment and other economic hazards of modern industry?

If the costs of production represented by industrial accidents, premature superannuation, and industrial unemployment fall upon the workers and the taxpayers and not upon the particular industries concerned, that encourages such industries to use methods of production and to pursue production policies that may cause a large number of layoffs and accidents and tend to shorten the working lives of employees. In part such industrial hazards cannot be eliminated. Some occupations are inherently more dangerous and more unhealthy than others. Despite employers' efforts, the risk of unemployment will be greater in capital goods industries and in lines of business subject to seasonal demand. As consumers' tastes change, some industries expand and others decline. If the consumer is to enjoy the privilege of shifting workers into and out of jobs as his fancy changes, should he not pay the cost involved in the exercise of that privilege? Because of extreme specialization, the consumer gets more for his money. Should he not, therefore, pay for the unemployment that periodically occurs when a reduction in his expenditures causes a decline in demand and a breakdown in the process of exchange?

Need for Government Action. Experience indicates that workers, employers, and consumers will not voluntarily pay in full for these industrial risks nor reduce them in cases where such reduction is possible. It would hardly be profitable for one employer to protect his workers against the hazards of injury, sickness, unemployment, death, and superannuation, unless his competitors likewise did so. In the past, private and voluntary action has failed to meet even a minor portion of the problem. Some sort of compulsion has proved necessary, and only the government can exert that compulsion. It does so through taxation. The taxes should be levied on a national scale, otherwise employers in one locality will suffer in interstate competition with employers in another locality where no taxes are levied on employers to meet such risks.

The government could, of course, try to tax employers, employees, and consumers with some regard to responsibility for the risk, though the responsibility of each might be very difficult to determine in all cases. The tax would certainly have to be levied before the loss of earnings occurred, for employers and employees might be unable to pay all the tax if it was levied only as workers were injured, laid off, or retired. Taxes for unemployment would have to be levied in good times, for a tax adjusted to changes in employment would be so steep in a depression that many firms would be bankrupt. The government would, therefore, accumulate these tax funds in advance to meet the losses in earnings when they occurred.

SOCIAL INSURANCE

The second of the above-mentioned issues in the problem of economic insecurity will now be considered, namely: What procedure should be followed in granting assistance to those suffering such economic losses?

Contrast of Social Insurance with Relief. The government could use the money collected by taxes for unemployment or other hazards to pay the costs of poor relief. In that case, a sick, injured, old, or unemployed worker would be eligible for assistance from tax funds only when he was down and out. A relief applicant must prove to a home investigator that all his economic resources have been used up — that he is a pauper — before relief will be granted. By the time he is penniless, the worker may have lost his morale and his self-respect. Relief is necessary assistance for the poor. It is not related to the worker's previous earnings, but is proportioned according to his family's need, measured by the number of mouths.

The government could follow another procedure. It could consider the taxes collected as contributions to a reserve to meet the risks of accident, illness, unemployment, or premature old age. Then, when a worker suffered from one of these hazards, benefits would be paid to him automatically as a matter of contractual right, just as a widow or a disabled policyholder receives benefits from a private insurance company. The benefits would be fixed in advance and would not be dependent upon the recipient's economic resources, nor would they vary with the condition of the locality's budget. Insurance is sure and carries no stigma of relief. There would be no home investigation by a case worker to make certain that the family was in dire need before weekly benefit payments were received. The worker would not first be ground down to destitution; his self-respect would be preserved. The worker's benefits would also be related to his previous earnings and, therefore, to his customary standard of living. This is the method of social insurance.

Contrast of Social with Private Insurance. Social insurance benefits, like private insurance benefits, are based on previous contributions into a general fund. The chief difference between social insurance and private insurance is that the government usually compels the payment of contributions to social insurance. It does so by levying taxes. By compulsion the government forces people, who otherwise would not do so, to contribute to insurance against certain risks. Private insurance companies cannot compel people to buy insurance. Social insurance is primarily for the benefit of wage earners whose incomes are not sufficient for them to provide protection against the major economic hazards that lead to destitution and dependency.

Social insurance cannot prevent these hazards from causing tremendous losses in earnings each year. To some extent such hazards are inherent in our system of industrial production and could be materially reduced only by radically changing the system or by returning to a simpler type of economy such as existed at the heyday of the medieval gilds. Since the risks arise out of a social situation from which society in general benefits, it is argued that the losses should be distributed over a wider group than those directly affected, the workers. That has to be done, since these hazards to earning power occur so frequently that insurance against them is much more costly than the various kinds of property insurance. Working-class incomes are far too small to bear the full burden of such expensive insurance.

In order to conserve social insurance funds so that they will not be exhausted, the benefits payable from them are limited in one or more of several ways. After the loss of earnings begins, there may be a short waiting period before the payment of benefits commences. Benefits are usually much less than the full loss in earnings and are only payable upon proof that the worker did not incur the loss in order to get the benefit. Frequently, the total sum that any one worker can receive in benefits is limited. Some of these limiting devices are practiced also in the field of private insurance. Limiting the benefits to fifty or sixty per cent of the worker's normal weekly earnings tends to eliminate the danger that may arise in administering relief; namely, that for the lowest paid workers the relief standards are equal to or above the recipient's customary standard of living.

Diffusion of Risk. Insurance is, of course, the provident and businesslike method of meeting risks too large for any individual to bear singlehanded. Insurance applies the idea that there is safety in numbers, and usually the larger the number, the greater the safety. The more people there are in an insurance organization the less likelihood there is that a number of deaths, fires, or accidents will bankrupt the insurance scheme. A fire insurance company with all its policyholders in San Francisco would have been bankrupt by the San Francisco fire. As it was, the policyholders got what their policies promised, because the losses resulting from the fire were distributed among policyholders all over the country. Insurance is based on spreading an average loss over a large group. Each individual in the group contributes a small amount to a common fund, knowing that, if he suffers a part of the average loss in any one year, he will receive the promised benefits.

Administrative Costs. Large numbers in an insurance organization also reduce the administrative costs for each dollar distributed in benefits. The cost of administering social insurance programs should be somewhat less than the cost of administering relief, because social insurance does not involve repeated home investigations to establish and assess the family's various needs. Experience with workmen's compensation in this country shows that insurance under state-administered programs is usually somewhat cheaper than insurance with private companies.

Action on Social Insurance in the United States. European countries had compulsory accident, unemployment, and old-age insurance twenty or more years before such types of social insurance were adopted in this country. Though many European countries had compulsory health insurance before the World War, we as yet have no such legislation.

Why have we always been far behind Europe in adopting social insurance measures? There are a number of reasons. Agriculture has played an important role in our economy in the past, and the Industrial Revolution occurred here relatively late. American thought has been colored by the pioneer and frontier spirit which opposes any such compulsory action on the part of the government. Some people have called social insurance a scheme for sharing the wealth. That argument can be used against practically all taxation. Few, if any, taxpayers benefit from government services by exactly the amount they are taxed; therefore, such taxes as school taxes are wealth sharing.

Not only were there possible constitutional difficulties, both federal and state, to be overcome in order to establish social insurance in this country, but there has been no political party that represented primarily the workingman's interest, such as a labor party or a strong socialist party. Bismarck is reputed to have inaugurated a program of social insurance in Germany to weaken rising Socialism in that country. Organized labor in this country has opposed some types of compulsory social insurance until a few years before laws were actually passed establishing such programs. This was especially true of unemployment insurance.

It is significant that the real impetus to social insurance has been federal encouragement and that social insurance programs have been started under progressive administrations in Washington. President Theodore Roosevelt, by his vigorous messages to Congress urging industrial accident-compensation laws, was instrumental in the passage of such laws in thirty states from 1910 to 1915. President Franklin D. Roosevelt was largely responsible for the Federal Social Security Act, passed in August 1935. This Act established a national old-age insurance system; it encouraged, by imposing a special tax, the establishment of state plans for unemployment compensation; and it provided for federal grants-in-aid to approved state plans for (1) old-age relief, (2) care of dependent and crippled children, (3) assistance to the blind, (4) maternal and child health, and (5) public health services. The provisions of the Social Security Act relating to unemployment compensation and to old-age insurance and assistance will be treated in detail in the following chapters.

CHAPTER IX

Compensation for Industrial Accidents and Unemployment

BECAUSE there are a number of similarities between state accident-compensation laws and state unemployment-compensation laws, they will be treated in the same chapter. Though such similarities exist, the nature of the risk in each case is entirely different. Accidents do not result from the same causes that bring about unemployment. Industrial accidents result from conditions *within* the plant; unemployment is a result of conditions *outside* the plant. The latter is in large measure a cyclical phenomenon. Therefore, any similarities with industrial accident compensation should not be emphasized too strongly in discussing programs to compensate workers for unemployment. As we shall see later on, there has been some tendency to exaggerate these similarities.

INDUSTRIAL ACCIDENT COMPEN-SATION

Industrial Casualties. Something was said in the previous chapter about the losses from industrial accidents. One is surprised to learn that the casualties in industry at home during the World War exceeded our casualties in France. Some industrial accidents could be prevented by safety devices and care, but some accidents will happen regardless of precautionary measures, when workers must use powerful, complex, and dangerous machinery.

The Common Law. There was not the same danger of accident two centuries ago, when the journeyman worked in a shop in the master's home. Yet our common law on accidents got its color from such small-shop conditions. It is based on the idea of personal fault and negligence on the part of the master, the worker, or his fellow workmen. In order to collect damages, the worker had to sue his employer for them.

Certain judicial decisions about 1840 established a wall of special defenses around the employer that made it very difficult for an injured employee to win a damage suit. The employer could escape liability for damages by pleading and proving any or all three of the following: (1) that the worker knew the risks of injury in that shop and, in accepting the job, assumed the ordinary risks connected with it; (2) that he also knew and accepted the risk of injury from neg-

ligence or carelessness on the part of his fellow workers; (3) that the worker was in some degree careless
or negligent in connection with the accident, regardless of the guilt of the employer. The result was that
the employee, to win a suit, had to show that the injury was caused by the employer's failure to use ordinary care while he himself had exercised such care.

By a series of statutes enacted after 1885, one or more
of these three special employer's defenses were abolished in various states, and the worker's chance to collect damages from the employer was improved. The
injured employee had to prove, however, that his
employer was negligent. This, in many cases, was
difficult to do. His fellow workmen and the foreman
would hesitate to testify against the employer for fear
that they would be discharged. For the same reason,
the injured worker himself was often afraid to sue. If
he brought suit, the case might drag on for two to six
years before finally being settled — many serious accident cases did. Few workers could afford such lengthy
litigation. Ambulance-chasing lawyers took their cases
on contingent fees running to fifty per cent or more
of the damages awarded by the jury. The whole system was extremely wasteful. Some employers took out
private insurance, but less than one third of their
premium payments reached the injured workmen;
costs of litigation absorbed a large part of the premiums.

*The Movement for Industrial Accident Compensa-
tion.* In the 1890's a number of European countries
passed compulsory accident-compensation acts to elim-

inate this wasteful method of damage suits. By 1910 practically all workers in European countries were covered by such laws. In 1898 both the United States and the New York Labor Bureaus made elaborate studies of European experience with industrial accident compensation, but the idea didn't "take" until the federal government enacted the first law in 1908 covering all its civil employees.

Some people argued that industrial accident compensation was unnecessary since the United States Steel Corporation and the International Harvester Company had established voluntary schemes, and other firms would soon follow suit. A state, it was also said, could not enact such a law without penalizing firms within its borders in competition with companies in states having no accident-compensation law. Some people even maintained that such laws would undermine the morals of workers by encouraging them to injure themselves for the compensation, though all laws forbid compensation in cases of willful injury. The course of events and the arguments used were very much the same later in the case of unemployment compensation by state law.

The first compulsory laws enacted in 1910 were declared unconstitutional by state supreme courts. As a result an "elective" law was devised, which gave the employer and employee a choice. They could either choose the new method of accident compensation or the old damage-suit method. But if the employer rejected compensation, he was deprived of the three special employer's defenses in case of suit. If the worker rejected compensation and chose to sue, the employer's three special defenses were restored. Consequently, almost everyone elected to come under compensation.

Not only was the elective law upheld by the United States Supreme Court, but in 1917 the Court also upheld a compulsory compensation law that made the employers in certain businesses pay a pay-roll tax to insure their workers in a state-administered compensation fund. These laws were sustained as within the police power of the state. Between 1910 and 1915, thirty states enacted workmen's compensation laws, and by 1937, forty-six states had such acts. Because of the constitutional developments, most states have the elective type of law, although fifteen states now have compulsory laws.

Advantages of Compensation Method. Automatic compensation is a much better way to handle accident cases than legal suit to establish the employer's liability for damages. In the first place, it saves the social waste of lengthy litigation. This is a saving to both employer and employee. The United States Supreme Court was especially impressed by this argument. Moreover, damage suits are not conducive to good employer-employee relations.

Secondly, compensation assures the injured worker of prompt medical attention. Under the damage-suit method, his earnings cease at the very time he needs medical attention, and he may lack adequate funds. Assurance of prompt and fairly adequate medical attention is another social gain that is also to the employer's interest, since the injured worker is likely to be back sooner, ready and able to work. Thirdly, the worker gets his compensation when he needs it most — during the period he is unable to work — rather than many years after the accident occurred. Fourthly, both the cost to the employer and the compensation to the employee are definite and certain. They do not vary with the sympathies of the jury or the employer's financial condition. Lastly, accident compensation tends to place the emphasis on accident prevention, where it belongs.

No longer is "Whose fault is it?" an important issue. The question of the fault has, for the most part, been forgotten. Workmen's compensation has, to all intents and purposes, become straight accident insurance. People recognize that some accidents will happen regardless of preventive measures and that, therefore, the worker should be protected from that risk by insurance. In the matter of accidents, industry's responsibility for its victims has been established. The costs of carrying industrial accident insurance have become a part of the costs of production and, as such, have presumably been passed on to the consumer of the product.

Purpose of Compensation. It is clear that accident compensation has been used, and upheld by the Supreme Court, as a device for meeting a social need at the least social cost. Indeed, industrial accident compensation in general covers only one third of the wage loss and medical cost; two thirds of the money costs of work injuries in this country still rest upon the worker. Some argue that the proportion of this cost borne by industry is too small to encourage sufficient safety measures and that the accident rate in American industry, for that reason, is relatively high. However that may be, the fact that the death benefits under accident compensation vary with the number of dependent children surviving shows that the purpose is to meet a social problem.

State Laws. The state laws are very divergent with respect to coverage, contributions, administration, and benefits. There is no single type of law that seems to have won wide favor.

It is estimated that about seventy per cent of all employees are covered by compensation in the forty-six states with accident compensation laws. No act covers all workers within the state although the New Jersey law includes about ninety-nine per cent of them. Three groups almost universally excluded are agricultural workers, casual workers, and domestic servants. Evasion of the law by employers is not infrequent, and oftentimes workers are ignorant of their compensation rights.

The cost of compensation is usually placed upon employers. In a few states, workers' wages are also taxed, to meet part of the cost of medical care only. The early emphasis on "fault" has largely been responsible for putting the burden on employers under elective laws. Emphasis on accident prevention has also played a part. The notion is that, with the entire cost placed on employers, it may pay them to take measures to reduce the number of accidents in their plants.

The cost of compensation, and therefore the employer's premium, varies from industry to industry and from state to state. In states with liberal benefits for injuries, the cost to the employer is greater than in states with less liberal laws. Within the same state the premium will vary according to the risk of accident in that line of business and in that particular establishment. This so-called merit rating of firms is partly based on their past accident experience and partly on the conditions surrounding the work in that particular plant. It is difficult to determine to what extent merit rating has operated to decrease accidents, because in many cases the consequent decrease or increase in the premium rate charged the employer would be too small to have much effect on his business decisions. This is especially true when an employer's experience rating is based on a period of years, say the last five years, instead of the past year or two.

The administrative features of state laws vary considerably. The majority of employers take out accident insurance for their employees with mutual or stock insurance companies under private management. Many states permit employers, usually large concerns, to carry their own accident risks and to pay compensation to their own employees. Under such "self-insurance", the company usually puts up securities to cover future compensation claims. Seventeen states have state insurance funds or state-operated insurance. In eight of these states, the employer can take out accident compensation only with the state fund; in the other nine the state insurance scheme competes with private insurance companies for the business.

Various reports and investigations indicate that the exclusive state-fund method of administration has proved to be the least expensive way of handling accident compensation.[1] An exclusive state fund is more economical because it eliminates large agents' commissions, spreads overhead costs over more customers, and distributes losses over a wider group. In most states without state funds, the private insurance companies refuse to insure certain lines of business and certain employers considered poor risks. Consequently, many employees are left without that protection. Recently a number of private companies underwriting industrial-accident insurance have become insolvent.

Benefit provisions are not the same in any two states. Most state laws provide a waiting period between the date of the injury and the date benefits begin. This waiting period excludes persons with short-time injuries lasting from three days to two weeks (depending on the state) from receiving money benefits for wage loss, though they do receive medical benefits. The weekly money benefit is usually based on a percentage of the normal weekly wage, ranging between forty and seventy per cent. Most acts limit the total weekly compensation for wage loss to a maximum of fifteen or twenty dollars a week, and also limit the money benefit to a certain number of weeks. Less than one half of the state laws provide for compensation for life in case the worker is totally disabled for life and less than one fourth of the laws provide for compen-

[1] See Dodd, Walter F., *Administration of Workmen's Compensation* (New York: 1936), pp. 557–58. The cost of administering workmen's compensation under exclusive state-fund plans averages about fifteen per cent of contributions, which is much less than the cost to the state under the old damage-suit method.

sation for life if the worker is partially disabled for life. All states provide for some medical care, but only eight states allow full medical benefits for the entire duration of disability.

Because of the various limitations on benefits in state laws, the injured worker has to bear more than one half of the direct money cost of work injuries in the most liberal states and three fourths of such costs in less liberal states. On the average, workers disabled partially or totally for the rest of their lives only receive partial support during one third of the period that they suffer the disability. Nevertheless, it is estimated that compensation laws disburse from two to three times the amount spent by all private charities in the United States.[2]

Since compensation seldom continues for the full duration of the disability, there has been a movement on foot, aided by federal grants to the states since 1920, to retrain and rehabilitate injured workers so that they may be able again to contribute in some measure to their own support.

UNEMPLOYMENT COMPENSATION

In the previous chapter it was pointed out that a certain amount of unemployment, even in prosperous

[2] Epstein, Abraham, *Insecurity, a Challenge to America* (New York, 1936), p. 606. According to an estimate, the total compensation paid in 1930 to injured workers was $240,000,000, plus an additional $72,000,000 paid for medical and hospital treatment. This total expenditure of $312,000,000 was incurred in 1930 because of 2,107,000 injuries among 19,683,500 covered workers. See Dodd, *op. cit.*, p. 697.

times, seems to be a feature of an economic system highly specialized, highly mechanized, and motivated by the lure of profits. Though some unemployment seems normal nowadays, one cannot predict the amount of unemployment with the same degree of accuracy that the total number of serious accidents can be forecast. For this reason and because unemployment causes much greater losses in earnings, no unemployment insurance plan guarantees the payment of benefits to unemployed workers for more than a relatively short period of time, say fifteen or twenty weeks. This is one of the reasons why unemployment compensation will not eliminate all unemployment relief.

The question of fault has not played the same role in the matter of unemployment compensation that it has played in accident compensation. The employer is not legally liable for the unemployment of his former workers. Legally, no one is to blame when a worker cannot find a job or can obtain only part-time employment. An individual worker or an individual employer can do little to decrease the total amount of unemployment. If it were profitable to hire more workers, presumably employers would do so. An employer in the construction industry or some capital goods industry is not to blame because the demand for his product falls off so much during depressions.

It may be possible for some employers in seasonal industries to spread out their total annual employment more evenly over the year, but no individual producer can increase demand in general or cause people to spend their money more rapidly. Unemployment is tied up with a decline in demand, and no individual alone is responsible for that. For this reason, one should not expect much reduction in unemployment on the basis of any particular features of an unemployment-compensation law. Merit rating of employers is much more likely to reduce accidents than to reduce the total amount of unemployment. In fact, merit rating may cause employers to stabilize their employment at lower levels. But before discussing the features of state unemployment-compensation plans in detail, something should be said about the development of unemployment compensation both here and abroad.

Development of Unemployment Compensation. The first unemployment-compensation law enacted in this country was the Wisconsin Unemployment Reserve Act. Enacted in the spring of 1932, it became compulsory on July 1, 1934, for the employments covered. In some respects, it is unfortunate that the Wisconsin law was the first American act. It is patterned more closely after American accident-compensation acts than after European systems of unemployment insurance. Like our accident-compensation laws, it provides for contributions only from employers and borrows the merit-rating feature from accident compensation. This encourages the notion that an employer is as much to blame for unemployment as he is for industrial accidents, and that the remedy for unemployment is for each employer to stabilize his employment — as though that would increase total employment in all lines of industry.

The Wisconsin law disregards foreign precedents and experience. None of the foreign laws contains provisions for merit rating and employees always contribute to the system. The European systems of unemployment compensation are of two types, trade-union funds and compulsory insurance in a state fund. In the trade-union type, the union administers the system and pays benefits from the contributions of its members together with subsidies from the municipal and, perhaps, the national government. This system of trade-union benefits for unemployment started in Ghent, Belgium, in 1901 and today exists in ten European countries on a nationwide scale. The employer, of course, does not contribute directly in the trade-union type of system.

The first country to adopt a compulsory unemployment-insurance law was Great Britain in 1911. Since then seven European countries have adopted such laws. These laws, in general, follow the British example. Usually the cost is divided between the employees, employers, and the state, with the first two contributing equal amounts and the state either contributing one third or somewhat less than the employers or the employees. Most European laws, unlike our state laws, adjust the unemployed worker's weekly benefit to the size of his family. In many of the European compulsory schemes, benefits can be drawn for a longer number of weeks than under our state laws. This is partly because most of our state laws provide for contributions from employers only.

Federal Legislation. The existence of the Wisconsin law had considerable influence upon the provisions of the Federal Social Security Act dealing with unemployment compensation. The Wisconsin law had been in operation over a year when the federal act was passed in August 1935. The federal act does not set up a system of unemployment insurance at all, but simply makes it easier for the states to do so. The federal government levies a uniform pay-roll tax of three per cent on all employers and allows a credit, up to ninety per cent of this federal tax, for pay-roll taxes paid by employers into a state unemployment-compensation fund. For example, a federal tax of $3,000 would be levied on an employer with an annual pay roll of $100,000. If the state had a pay-roll tax of 2.7 per cent for unemployment compensation under a plan approved by the Social Security Board, this employer could deduct his state tax of $2,700 from his federal tax of $3,000, so that he would pay the federal government only $300, or ten per cent of the federal tax levy. In other words, after a state passes an approved unemployment-compensation law, employers in that state, instead of paying the entire federal tax, pay only ten per cent of the federal pay-roll tax into the federal Treasury, and pay the rest into the state fund for unemployment benefits to eligible workers residing in the state.

By imposing a uniform tax upon all employers in the country and permitting this ninety per cent credit, the Social Security Act removed the major obstacle to state action on unemployment compensation. That obstacle was the reluctance to levy state taxes for unemployment compensation on producers within the state for fear that it would hinder them in competition with employers in other states not levying such a tax. This fear was partly responsible for the merit-rating provisions in the Wisconsin act which permit an employer's contributions to fall to zero under certain circumstances. With a uniform federal tax, all employers in the country are affected substantially the same, whether or not their state passes an unemployment-compensation law.

In order to secure federal approval for the state plan so that the employer can credit his state pay-roll tax against ninety per cent of the federal tax, the state law must meet certain standards. These standards for state laws include the following provisions with regard to labor standards and use of funds:

1. No worker shall be denied benefits if he refuses a new job where there is a labor dispute, where he would be required to join a company union or refrain from joining a trade union, or where the wages, hours, or conditions of work are substantially less favorable than for similar work in that locality.

2. All benefits shall be paid through public employment offices unless the Social Security Board grants permission to other agencies.

3. All funds raised from state taxes for unemployment compensation shall be deposited in the United States Treasury and such funds must be used solely to pay benefits to unemployed workers.

These same standards must be met by state laws if the state is to receive federal subsidies for the administration of its law. The funds for such federal subsidies are to come from the remaining ten per cent of the federal pay-roll tax that is not subject to credit for taxes paid into state funds under approved state laws.

The second provision listed on page 214 affords a constant test of the unemployed worker's willingness to work. He must report at a clearinghouse for jobs each week in order to receive his benefit. Any new job can be offered to him at that time. In this way the payment of benefits is related to the more important task of obtaining jobs for the unemployed.

The third provision is to afford maximum safety for the unemployment-reserve funds as well as to safeguard the country's financial structure. Normally the reserve funds will be invested by the United States Treasury in federal bonds. The demands on these reserve funds will fluctuate considerably, being heaviest when business slackens. Some central unit must be responsible for investing all the state reserve funds, which in good times will amount to a total of two or three billion dollars, and for liquidating the investments to meet large benefit payments in bad times. Without some central control, our financial institutions and markets would be upset by large surplus funds for investment in good times and sudden sales of securities in bad times. If the securities in which these funds are invested were thrown upon the market for liquidation during a depression, that would probably cause increased deflation. Also, the handling of the reserve should be co-ordinated with the activities and policies of the federal reserve authorities. This requirement that all state funds for paying benefits be deposited in the federal Treasury prevents private insurance companies from playing the part in unemployment compensation that they have played in accident compensation.

The federal law contains practically no restrictions on the types of state laws that can be approved. Laws of the Wisconsin type, or laws patterned after the European compulsory type, may receive approval. Approved laws may also include provisions for guaranteed employment, somewhat similar to provisions for self-insurance in accident-compensation laws, whereby an employer who can guarantee his employees forty weeks of employment each year is exempt from the federal pay-roll tax.[3] Of course, the federal act forces the states to finance a large part of their unemployment benefits from pay-roll taxes. So far, no state has levied any other type of tax for that purpose.

The federal authorities took the attitude that the states should have a wide latitude with respect to the type of law they may adopt. This would permit experimentation with various procedures in order to discover what provisions are most practical for conditions in this country. Consequently, the forty-eight state laws that have received federal approval are almost as varied as are the state accident-compensa-

---

[3] The employer must guarantee forty weeks of thirty hours each week for a twelve-month period. He must have built up a reserve of 7.5 per cent of his average pay roll as security for his guarantee.

tion laws. These forty-eight laws cover over twenty million employees.

Pooled Fund versus Employer Reserve. One fundamental difference among the various state unemployment-compensation laws in this country is whether, as in private insurance, all contributions are pooled in a single general fund, or the state law sets up a separate fund or reserve for each and every company or employer in the state. A system permitting separate employer reserves means thousands of segregated company reserves, with the unemployed worker's benefits depending solely on the condition of his particular employer's reserve. Only the Wisconsin law provides straight company or employer reserves. The laws of three states (Kentucky, Indiana, and Vermont) provide for a mixture of the two types, with employers either electing one of the two or contributing to both an employer reserve and a general pool. The other forty-four states have pooled-fund plans.

One can get a notion of what this distinction involves by assuming that private insurance reserves were divided into thousands of separate parts, each part reserved for a group of persons as small as eight in number. Under such circumstances, if any single group suffered severe losses from accident, fire, theft, or death, the insurance company would be unable to fulfill the promises contained in the policies of persons in that group. The group's reserve would be too small to do so. Such a segregation of reserves would mean smaller and more irregular benefits for policyholders in groups most severely affected by the particular risk.

Thus, under an employer-reserve plan of unemployment compensation, unemployed workers in lines of business like building, metals, and capital goods industries, which are severely affected by depressions, would receive smaller benefits and less adequate protection.

So certain is it that many of the segregated employer reserves will become exhausted early in a depression that the Wisconsin law provides for reduced benefits as an employer's reserve begins to vanish, in which case the unemployed worker never receives his full benefits. By concentrating the worker's risk, the employer-reserve plan tends to intensify his misfortunes, for both his job and his unemployment compensation depend upon the business fortunes of a single employer, who may be hiring as few as eight workers.

Many employers, especially those in industries that are close to the consumer and therefore are less affected by depressions, prefer the employer-reserve plan. The employer-reserve plan tends to tie workers in such industries more closely to the company since they are more certain of full benefits if they work for a more stable firm like a large newspaper, a bank, a life insurance company, or some public utility. Also the employer-reserve plan assures the employer of automatic merit rating, for his tax rate depends entirely on the condition of his reserve account.

Merit Rating. Of the forty-four states with single, pooled funds, thirty-five disregard European precedents by providing for merit rating of employers. The laws of the other nine states, including New York and Pennsylvania, contain no definite provision for merit rating, although some do provide for an investigation to determine the advisability of such a provision. The Supreme Court decision in the New York case seems to indicate that laws without merit rating do not contravene the federal Constitution. Under the Social Security Act, the ninety per cent of the federal tax on employers that is subject to credit for state taxes may be reduced in accordance with the merit-rating provisions in state laws. Consequently, if an employer's state tax rate is reduced to zero by merit rating, he would only pay a federal tax of .3 per cent (one tenth of three per cent) of his pay roll.

Merit rating in unemployment-compensation laws differs from merit rating under accident compensation in that it is based entirely upon the employer's past experience. An employer's merit rating is determined by comparing his past tax contributions with the benefits paid to his workers. The more his total contributions over a period have exceeded such benefits, the better is his rating and the lower is his tax rate. Thus, an employer's rating does not depend upon the number of workers he lays off, but upon the number he lays off who fail to find steady work within a week or two and who, therefore, draw benefits. For this reason, an employer's merit rating is partly a matter of luck and will tend to be good in prosperous times even though he lays off many workers, because they will soon obtain other jobs. Furthermore, the reward of rate reduction will go to those employers fortunate enough to produce necessary consumers' goods which enjoy a stable market.

Merit rating has been advocated as a device for reducing unemployment. Its proponents believe that business men themselves are partly responsible for the large volume of unemployment and that the enactment of laws imposing penalty taxes on unstable businesses will prevent much unemployment. Such government regulation of business they consider praiseworthy.

Is the employer who maintains his working force at a fixed figure, year in and year out, benefiting society to such an extent that he deserves to be rewarded by a reduction in his unemployment tax up to ninety per cent? It is well to remember that stabilization of employment, especially after a depression, may mean stabilization of unemployment as well. Firms that would hire workers for a period of time may hesitate to do so if they are subject to higher taxes whenever they fail to furnish such new workers with permanent jobs. Rather than pay higher "demerit" taxes on an enlarged labor force, employers will be inclined to keep their working forces at a minimum. Since the working population of the country normally expands at the rate of about one per cent a year, it would seem as though the highest reward should go to employers who, by expanding their employment at least five per cent over a five-year period, help to absorb the nation's labor supply.

Furthermore, experience has demonstrated that the stabilization of one business may cause fluctuations in another industry and may even increase the amount of unemployment in a locality. Suppose the two firms in the same locality have peaks and valleys of employment that so dovetail that there is no unemployment. If one of these two firms should proceed to stabilize its employment throughout the year, a larger labor force would be required at times in that locality, and at other times part of the labor force would be unemployed. Which firm would be responsible for that unemployment and should be penalized for causing it?

Under merit rating, the employer's tax will fluctuate with changes in business conditions over which he has very little control. A business man is not personally to blame if the market for his product declines and he is forced to curtail operations. Differentiated tax rates on employers will not abolish the business cycle, nor put a stop to new inventions, nor control consumer demand for different commodities. Merit rating will tend to reduce an employer's tax in good times, as though he were responsible for prosperity, and to increase his tax during depressions, when his business is doing badly and he is least able to stand a tax increase. Usually taxes are related to the taxpayer's ability to pay; merit rating tends to make the employer's tax vary according to his inability to pay. Higher penalty taxes during a depression may force some concerns in difficult straits to give up the ghost entirely.

Many state laws provide for merit rating in only one direction — downward. By reducing the contributions of some employers without corresponding "demerit" tax increases for other employers, merit rating tends to operate as a fund-depleting device. The writing of such

tax-reducing provisions into state laws may make a
number of state unemployment funds insolvent during
severe depressions, thus depriving unemployed workers
of their promised benefits. It has been suggested that
states should be required to offset "merit" reductions by
corresponding "demerit" increases, so that merit-rating
provisions do not threaten state funds with bankruptcy.

Low merit rates in some states tend to force the
legislatures of other states to provide similar tax reductions in order to prevent firms within their boundaries from suffering in interstate competition or from
migrating to a low-rate state. In eight states the employer's tax may be reduced to zero. In an economy
constantly upset by new inventions, mergers, changes
in style and taste, or by changes in the rate of spending,
it would seem as though the employees of no employer
are so certain of future employment that his tax rate
should be reduced to zero. Past experience may be a
poor guide for rating employers, especially when, as
in a few states, only the last three or five years — not
even a complete business cycle — are used as the basis
for merit rating.

In this connection the experience of Great Britain is
enlightening. When the British unemployment insurance law was originally projected, the industries
that had especially low percentages of unemployment
were coal mining with 1.3 per cent, textiles with three
per cent, and boots and shoes with three per cent. These
industries wished to be excluded from the general unemployment insurance act so that they could set up
special schemes of their own. Yet a few years later

these same industries were among the most depressed of British trades.

Tax differentials of two or three per cent of pay roll will not amount to more than one per cent of the production costs of many employers. For such employers, penalty taxes under merit rating may prove too small to cause much change in business practices, in which case the added cost of calculating every employer's merit rating each year would seem to be a waste of money.

On the other hand, a uniform tax on all employers would not stimulate them to try to keep their workers from drawing benefits to the same extent that merit rating would. Some employers can reduce seasonal fluctuations in their operations, which, under certain circumstances, may reduce seasonal unemployment and result in a real social saving. An equal tax on all employers also would not allocate the cost of unemployment to each industry and firm so that the consumer of the product would have to pay that cost along with the other costs of production. It is argued that the only justification for pay-roll taxes to finance unemployment compensation, rather than graduated income taxes, is to make the public, whose buying habits produce fluctuating employment in particular industries, pay for the resulting cost of unemployment.

Some proponents of merit rating also assert that to require employers in a stable industry to contribute to the support of workers who have been laid off by establishments in a fluctuating industry is unfair. But taxes are usually levied upon those best able to pay them. And if the unemployed were not supported by benefits under unemployment compensation, they would be supported on relief. The stable industries would be taxed to pay the cost of their relief, so why not for the cost of their compensation?

Coverage. Most state laws follow the federal tax in the matter of coverage. The federal tax is levied on the pay rolls of employers of eight or more persons, but exempts employees in the following classes: agricultural workers, domestic servants, government employees, and employees of nonprofit institutions. The reasons for such exemptions are partly political, partly legal, and partly administrative. A number of state laws apply to employers of less than eight. The federal tax covers about fifty per cent of all gainfully employed persons in the country.

Contributions. Because the federal pay-roll tax of three per cent is levied on employers only, all state laws levy a pay-roll tax on employers, usually 2.7 per cent unless reduced by merit rating, in order to obtain the full ninety per cent tax offset provided in the federal law. Also the notion behind merit rating — that employers are responsible for unemployment and will reduce unemployment if penalized enough by higher taxes — seems to demand that the full burden be imposed upon employers. Only eight states provide for employee contributions in addition to the employer's tax. None of the American laws, except that for the District of Columbia, provides for government contributions as is the case in Europe.

Whether employees should contribute is a much debated question. It is argued that some employee contribution is more equitable, helps to maintain the self-respect of the worker drawing benefits, and is necessary to give workers adequate benefits in states with high unemployment records. On the other side, it is pointed out that the employees are not responsible for unemployment and even under the most liberal state law will still bear much more than half the wage loss from unemployment. After a waiting period, the unemployed worker can draw only fifty per cent of his normal weekly wage for fifteen or sixteen weeks in a year. Some also argue that a part of the employer's tax is shifted to the employee anyway.

That brings up the question of shifting and incidence of taxation.[4] Under conditions of monopoly or semi-monopoly, the employer may bear part of the tax. But under conditions of pure competition, the employer's tax will tend to be shifted either forward to the consumer through higher prices or backward to the employees through lower wages. This will be true to the extent that the tax bears equally on all employers. If there is merit rating, it may be more difficult for the full burden of the tax to be shifted to labor or to consumers. Of course, the tax tends to raise the price of labor to the employer — especially one who has to pay a "demerit" tax — so that he may try to conserve on labor, thereby decreasing his demand for labor and perhaps causing more unemployment or lower wage rates.

Benefits. The benefit provisions vary from state to

[4] For a discussion of tax shifting see Luthringer, G. F., Chandler, L. V., and Cline, D. C., *Money, Credit, and Finance* (1938), Chapter XIV.

state, since the federal law contains no requirements as to the amount or duration of benefits. In general, state laws provide weekly benefits of fifty per cent of normal weekly wages, after a waiting period of three or four weeks in any one year. The maximum weekly benefit is usually fifteen dollars. Unlike accident compensation, the length of the benefit period depends upon the length of previous employment and earnings, but is seldom more than sixteen weeks in any one year. Such limits to benefit payments are necessary to maintain the solvency of the fund. The steady inflow of contributions into the fund, even during a depression, is also very important in assuring full benefits. Of course, benefits depend on the rate of contributions and only those employees covered by the state pay-roll tax are eligible for benefits.

The provisions relating the rate of benefit to weekly wages act as an incentive to workers to earn higher wages, and those relating the duration of benefits to previous employment are an incentive to workers to establish good work records. If a worker quits or is discharged for misconduct, he is barred from benefits for a time at least, and usually no benefits are paid to workers on strike. Furthermore, no benefits are paid to workers who refuse to accept "suitable employment" for which they are reasonably fitted and which is not too far from their residences.

This matter of suitable employment raises some question as to the effect of unemployment compensation on the bargaining power of labor. Fear that this provision would break down labor standards was one of the reasons organized labor in America formerly opposed unemployment-compensation laws. Actually it would seem that such laws will tend to support wage rates, especially if suitable employment is interpreted rather narrowly.

Unemployment results from a failure to make a sale of labor services, and failure to make such a sale is sometimes due to the price demanded for the services. In this respect unemployment compensation differs from accident compensation. Any measure that supports an unemployed worker so that he is not forced to accept work at any price strengthens the worker's bargaining power. On the question of the wisdom of adopting measures that tend to support wage rates during a depression there are differences of opinion. Employers often object to unemployment-compensation schemes on this ground rather than on the score that they are taxed two or three per cent of pay roll. However, there may be a gain to society if a skilled worker, say a carpenter, is not forced by depressional unemployment to accept an unskilled job from which he may never return to his former skilled work.

Criticism of the Federal Act. Some experts say that a national system of unemployment compensation or a plan of federal subsidies to state systems is preferable to the tax-credit or offset method provided in the Social Security Act, whereby employers receive credit up to ninety per cent of their federal tax for similar taxes paid under a state law. The offset method was selected partly because it was considered more certain to be held constitutional. The provisions of the Social

Security Act dealing with unemployment compensation
have been upheld by the Supreme Court, but a dissenting opinion indicates that the subsidy or federal grants-
in-aid method would have been approved by more of
the Supreme Court justices. The subsidy method would
not have necessitated duplicate federal and state taxes
and tax organizations, and it would have permitted the
levying of various types of taxes other than pay-roll
taxes to finance unemployment compensation.

It is also claimed that the Social Security Act fails to
set up adequate standards for state laws and cannot do
so because of the difficulties, including constitutional
ones, of trying to control state actions by the tax-offset
method. The act sets up no standards for the selection
of staffs of state administrations and, consequently, in
a majority of the states such appointments have not
been made strictly on a merit or civil-service basis. To
what extent poor personnel is responsible for the several
weeks' delay in the payment of some unemployment
benefits is difficult to say.

According to some estimates, administrative costs
may run to twelve or fifteen per cent of total contributions in many states that provide for merit rating
and have administrative staffs largely appointed on a
political basis. In England, the cost of administering
unemployment insurance has been about eight per cent
of total contributions.

Under the federal act, states with approved laws may
pay benefits as small and for as short a period as they
wish. With separate state systems, it would seem that a
state, having double the rate of unemployment that

another state has, should either have a tax rate twice as high to pay the same benefits, or, with the same tax rate, its benefits should average half as large as those in the state with the better unemployment record. Actually, states with the poorest unemployment records levy the same tax and offer about the same benefits as states with the best unemployment records. Consequently, a number of experts are predicting insolvency for many state unemployment-compensation plans. In granting funds to states under a federal subsidy system, allowances could be made for such differences in rates of unemployment.

Since the federal act puts no limits to the amounts that states can offer in benefits to eligible unemployed workers, the states are competing with one another in generosity. Some states have recently reduced tax rates, or increased benefits, or done both. Reduction of contribution rates and increases in benefits helped to make the British Unemployment Insurance system technically insolvent after 1920. Merit rating to zero in some states is putting other states under pressure to reduce the pay-roll taxes on their industries, though such a reduction may impair the solvency of the state fund. The federal act, by permitting merit rating even to zero, has not eliminated all fear that a state may place itself in a position of economic disadvantage if it levys a pay-roll tax sufficient to assure full payment of benefits as large as most states now promise their unemployed.

A national system would spread the losses from unemployment more widely and, therefore, would give more protection to the workers, especially in small and one-industry states. It would also meet a problem that state laws fail to meet — that of migratory workers who fail to qualify under any state law, and of workers who move from one state to another, becoming unemployed in the second state before they have established an employment record there to qualify for full benefits. It would also eliminate the need for forty-eight separate state administrations, some of which are too small for efficient operation. The trend in social insurance abroad has been from local and state schemes to a national system.

No Cure-All. Whatever the system or area of administration, an unemployment insurance system will not eliminate unemployment, nor will it completely relieve those who suffer from unemployment. It is only one of the lines of attack upon the problem. It does not aid workers excluded from the coverage of the state laws. It will not assist a man who has been unable to build up a previous work record in order to qualify for benefits, nor does it give further assistance to one who has exhausted his sixteen-weeks-a-year benefit. It is designed to compensate only employable persons who are able and willing to work and who are unemployed through no fault of their own. For these reasons, it will not eliminate unemployment relief and poor relief. It only cushions the impact of unemployment on the worker.

Immediate registration of unemployed workers at public employment exchanges will give a more accurate measure of the extent and trend of unemployment in various lines of business at any time. Such registration of the unemployed will be helpful in guiding workers and in planning programs of public work. Public works and work-relief programs, if they do not simply displace normal public activities and regular employees by emergency work and workers, as has so frequently been the case, may help to reduce the amount of unemployment. Some believe that, by control of the investment of unemployment-compensation funds, bank reserves and the money supply may be regulated so that the price level will be kept more stable. Also, assurance of unemployment benefits when unemployed may make people less hesitant to spend in times of slump. Had New Jersey's unemployment-compensation law been passed some years before the 1930–1933 depression, it is estimated that 180 million dollars would have been paid in unemployment benefits to New Jersey workers from the end of 1929 to the end of 1933, or more than three times the amount of public money spent for emergency relief.

CHAPTER X

Security for Old Age

The Problem of Superannuation. The chapter on economic insecurity indicated that workers are suffering from the ever-widening gap between the date of displacement from industry and the date of their death. While our industrial methods more and more put a premium on young and adjustable workers, the average age of our working population continues to increase. Consequently, the period of "economic old age", when a worker can no longer earn his keep, is lengthening.

A century ago the average span of life in America was but thirty-nine years. At present it is almost sixty years. Our birth rate is also declining. Consequently, the average age of our population has been increasing and will continue to do so for some time. As in Europe, where the average age is higher than here, more and more economic activity will be directed to meet the needs and tastes of middle-aged and older people.

As a people we are gradually growing older and

older. Whereas in 1870 but one out of every thirty-four persons in this country was sixty-five years of age or over, in 1935 one person out of every fourteen had attained the sixty-fifth year, and it is estimated that by 1990 one out of every seven persons in this country will be sixty-five or over. Men who reach sixty-five still have, on the average, eleven or twelve years of life before them.

At the same time that the span of life is reaching the sixties or seventies, the age limit of gainful employment for those laid off and looking for a job is ebbing back into the fifties and even the forties. In hiring new workers many firms now have an age deadline of around forty-five.[1] Industry is looking for young workers who can stand the pace of modern production and can adapt themselves to new techniques. Therefore, a middle-aged worker who loses his job because of a slump in business, a new machine, or a shift in industry, may have difficulty in locating another. The problem of premature superannuation or permanent unemployment in middle age has become a pressing one.

Recovery has not meant pre-depression earnings for many middle-aged workers, some of whom lost their lifetime savings in the depression of the early 1930's. Hence the demand for Townsend plans and state old-age pensions.

In former days, many old folks could support them-

---

[1] Studies of some 220 American factories and the manufacturing plants in New York State revealed that in 1929 and 1930 almost one third of them had fixed maximum hiring age limits, commonly forty-five. Plants without such fixed age limits in practice hired few workers over fifty years of age.

selves late in life because they were independent enterprisers, such as farmers, shopkeepers, and the like.
On the farm or in small villages, age meant only a
continuation of one's occupation at a slower speed.
The independent enterpriser can produce goods at his
own pace, but a laborer in a large plant must keep
up with the others. Moreover, contrary to the rule in
professional and white-collar work, the peak of the
average industrial worker's earning power is reached
in early middle life. The depression aggravated this
tendency for the earnings of many workers to decline
rapidly in the latter part of their lives.

The President's Committee on Economic Security
estimated that in 1935 at least one half of the seven
and a half million people over sixty-five were not self-
supporting — about 900,000 of them were receiving
emergency relief or old-age assistance and 150,000 more
were receiving industrial or trade-union pensions. A
study by the Social Security Board showed that in 1937
almost three out of four persons sixty-five or over were
dependent wholly or partially upon others for support.

The discussion of company benefit plans in the chapter on economic insecurity showed that company old-
age pension plans, even before the depression, were
supplying benefits to relatively few people and were
restricted in their scope by the drive for profits. The
limit to benefits under such plans is, Will they pay
the company? As indicated in that chapter, the burden
of old-age dependency has fallen, and will continue to
fall, on the public purse.

OLD-AGE ASSISTANCE

Prior to Social Security Act. In 1934, twenty-eight states had free pension or old-age relief laws, and about 200,000 pensioners were receiving an average monthly grant of $16.50 under such laws, with the grants varying widely from state to state. The first of these state assistance laws had been passed in 1923. The rapid increase in state laws after 1923 indicates the political pressure that the aged were putting upon state legislatures.

The assistance under these laws is based on personal need, with the taxpayer meeting the entire cost. In order to qualify for one of these gratuitous pensions, a long period of residence within the state was required. Because of financial difficulties, especially during the depression, many of these laws either were not functioning or pensions were being reduced below a proper minimum. Most of the needy aged were being cared for as unemployment relief clients.

Under the Social Security Act. In order to improve the state laws and to get the needy aged off the unemployment relief rolls, the Federal Social Security Act provides for a subsidy to approved state old-age assistance plans. The federal government matches state grants on a fifty-fifty basis up to fifteen dollars of federal money per pensioner. No special taxes are levied by the Social Security Act to provide the funds necessary to meet the federal share of the cost of such old-age relief.

In 1937 five sixths of the states had approved plans.

In those states some 1,300,000 aged were receiving monthly grants averaging almost nineteen dollars per recipient. Under most state plans it is possible for a man and his wife, if both are in need, to receive a maximum of thirty dollars each, or together sixty dollars a month. In five states, pensions have been averaging over twenty-five dollars a month. From state to state and within the same state there has been a wide range in the size of grants as well as the proportion of persons over sixty-five receiving old-age assistance. This divergence in grants to the needy aged has in part been due to state and local politics.

The cost to the federal government and the states of such old-age assistance will surely rise in the future, but just how much is hard to say. The experience of Canada and European countries with old-age assistance grants indicates that they increase steadily in amount as the number of aged persons increases and the employing age recedes. Also, assistance becomes more respectable as more people are forced to accept it. Estimates indicate that the total cost might reach two or two and a half billion dollars a year by 1980. That would be a sizeable sum to meet from federal and state budgets.

Reduction in Assistance by Old-Age Insurance. The President's Committee on Economic Security, which was commissioned to draft a plan to cover the whole problem of security, decided that some social insurance scheme was necessary to lighten this prospective burden on the general taxpayer and to prevent old-age dependency rather than relieving it after it had occurred. The committee proposed that future candidates for old-age assistance, along with their employers, be required to contribute to a national scheme for old-age annuities, which would provide monthly benefits of a certain sum from age sixty-five until death. This was the sort of scheme that a number of private concerns had adopted in trying to safeguard their employees from dependency and poverty after retirement. Since 1920 the federal government had also been following the method of compulsory insurance for retirement and invalidity, with all federal employees under civil service included and with the employees and the government both contributing.

Such a contributory system of old-age annuities, covering over fifty per cent of the working population, would, according to the committee's estimates, reduce the old-age assistance burden on the general taxpayer by 1980 to less than forty per cent of the amount it would reach by that date if such a contributory system were not started. Of course old-age assistance would still be necessary for that part of the working population not covered by the contributory scheme. This estimated reduction of sixty per cent in the burden on general taxpayers helps to explain why many wealthy persons supported the proposal for a contributory system of annuities for retired workers. Such annuities could only be provided by taxation — in this case equal taxes on the employer and the employee. It was recognized that private insurance companies could not hope to sell annuities to low-paid workers on an individual commercial basis. The federal contributory system has not decreased the number of pension plans or old-age insurance carried by private firms — many employers are supplementing the federal benefits — and it has helped employers with unsound pension plans and those without any such plans out of their difficulties. With the federal scheme in operation, they will be less subject to criticism when they retire an old worker and advance a younger man to fill his shoes.

Whatever the financial procedure adopted, however, these retired workers must be supported from the goods produced and the services rendered by the rest of the population. That is true whether the worker receives the funds for his support in the form of an assistance grant, after an investigation that smacks of poor law procedure, or whether he receives it in the form of a monthly annuity payment, after years of contributions. In the one case the funds come from the pockets of the general taxpayers, in the other case from the pockets of the workers and their employers. The employers may be able to shift their half of the tax burden to consumers of their products. But no financial manipulation can eliminate the burden itself or cover up the fact that retired workers are consuming but not producing. More will be said on this score later on.

OLD-AGE INSURANCE

Old-Age Annuities Abroad. Even before the World War, but especially after that event, many European countries established compulsory old-age insurance or annuity systems as the most satisfactory way of providing for the support of retired wage earners and their dependents. By 1930, seventeen European and several Latin American countries had adopted such measures.

These compulsory schemes usually apply to lower paid employees in manufacturing, although persons exempted from the compulsory plan are permitted to come in on a voluntary basis. In most of these plans the employers and the insured workers contribute, with the state supplementing their contributions by a subsidy. In practically all of these compulsory schemes, the monthly annuity payment varies with the former wage level of the worker and the length of time he has contributed before retirement at, say, age sixty-five. The monthly payments until death are, in general, about fifty per cent of the worker's average weekly wage.

Under the Social Security Act. The compulsory old-age insurance plan established by the Social Security Act follows these foreign plans rather closely with two exceptions. Under our scheme the federal government does not contribute a subsidy from general tax funds, so that a huge reserve must be built up, as is the case when such matters are handled by private insurance companies. Furthermore, private insurance companies helped to block a proposal that would have permitted the purchase of old-age annuities, up to fifty dollars per person, from the government on a cost basis, after sixty-five. Such a voluntary annuity plan would have reduced the expenditures for old-age assistance and aided the general taxpayer.

The Social Security Act sets up a national system of old-age insurance. This is the only part of the social security program that does not require state participation and state legislation. The operation of forty-eight separate systems of old-age insurance would involve all sorts of administrative difficulties, would be unduly costly, and would undoubtedly result in failure in certain states. An old-age insurance system is based on estimates of age distribution in the future. Shifts in industry from one state to another would upset such estimates. An efflux of young people or an influx of old persons would alter the age distribution within the state. Such migration of old folks as that to Southern California and Florida recently would eventually wreck a state old-age insurance system.

A national system is more convenient and economical. Interstate changes of residence would require the transfer of individual credits for past contributions from one state to another. With widely differing state plans, more complications would result. As the administration of old-age insurance is relatively simple and routine in nature, it is more adapted to large scale operation than is unemployment compensation. When the federal system of old-age insurance is in full swing, the administrative expenses each year will, it is estimated, amount to but five per cent of the annual contributions. The constitutionality of the old-age insurance provisions of the Social Security Act was upheld by the Supreme Court in May 1937.

Coverage. The national old-age insurance scheme covers over twenty-seven million workers or nearly sixty per cent of the working population of the country. Most of the employments exempt from the unemployment insurance tax are also excluded from the compulsory old-age program and for the same reasons: non-profit organizations at the request of their representatives, farm and domestic employments because of the administrative difficulties involved in collecting such a tax. However, establishments hiring one or more persons are subject to the old-age tax, though the unemployment insurance tax only includes employers of eight or more. Railroad employees are covered by a separate retirement system of old-age annuities established by Congress in 1937.

Contributions. Two different taxes are levied to finance old-age insurance: a tax on the pay rolls of employers and a tax on the wages of employees. However, there is no employer or employee tax on that part of any worker's wages from one employer that is in excess of $3,000 a year. These two taxes, the employer's on pay rolls and the employee's on wages, start at one per cent each in 1937, and increase by one half of one per cent every three years until they reach three per cent each in 1949. After 1949 the total combined tax rate remains at six per cent. By 1950 the estimated receipts from these old-age taxes will be about 1.9 billions of dollars. For constitutional reasons the proceeds of these taxes go right into the general funds of the Treasury.

Benefits. Benefit payments commence in 1942 and are related to the worker's previous earnings which were subject to the tax. Relating the benefit payments to contributions tends to spur workers to achieve good wage and employment records. The conditions for receiving benefits are: that the worker's earnings sub-

ject to the tax have reached a total of $2,000, that he
has reached age sixty-five, and that he has retired from
gainful employment. Benefits will normally take the
form of annuities paying a fixed sum each month to
retired workers for the rest of their lives. The life ex-
pectancy of a man sixty-five years old is eleven or twelve
years; for a woman it is fifteen years.

In case the beneficiary should die before age sixty-
five, his estate will receive three and a half per cent of
his total wages subject to the tax. If he should die
after age sixty-five but before receiving monthly
annuity payments equal to three and a half per cent
of his total wages since 1936, his estate will receive
the difference. Therefore, employees subject to the act
are sure of a return amounting to at least three and a
half per cent of all wages taxed.

In general the monthly benefit payments will be
about one half of the average monthly earnings of the
worker during the period he was covered by the act.
However, the benefit schedule favors the lower paid
workers and those who enter the system relatively late
in working life and will retire in the near future.

The bias of the benefit schedule in favor of lower
paid workers and those now along in years may be il-
lustrated by the following examples. A worker with a
monthly salary of $100, who enters the system at age
fifty-five, will get a monthly benefit over three times
as large under the federal system as he could buy from
a private insurance company for the same money. But
a worker with a monthly salary of $250 would be better
off before age thirty-five, if his taxes and his employer's

taxes could be used to purchase an annuity for him from a private company; at an entrance age of fifty-five, the federal system would pay him twice as much from age sixty-five until death as he would get for the same money from a private company.[2]

The federal act, therefore, not only compels the purchase of annuities for support in old age, but also tends to redistribute income in favor of the older and the lower paid workers to the comparative disadvantage of younger and higher paid employees. As we shall see, higher taxes to accumulate a huge reserve is the method whereby the younger workers and their employers, especially after 1948, are forced to carry an extra heavy load: the cost of their own old age, part of the cost of supporting covered workers who are now too near retirement age to pay in full for their benefits, and, as general taxpayers, part of the cost for old-age assistance to aged persons who are in need.

Despite this bias in favor of those retiring soon after 1942, when benefit payments begin, the average benefits paid will not be large. It is figured that the average pension in 1945 will be only nineteen dollars a month and in 1955 only twenty-five dollars a month; for 1965 the figure is thirty-three dollars a month; and for 1980

[2] Epstein, Abraham, *Insecurity, a Challenge to America* (New York, 1936), p. 765. The benefit schedule favors those soon to retire to such an extent that some persons along in years have tried to have their friends or relatives hire them and pay them a total of, say, $2,000 in wages over a five-year period. The total old-age taxes on $2,000, even at three per cent, would only be sixty dollars, whereas such a worker retiring at age sixty-five would receive a benefit of ten dollars a month. If he lived the average of eleven years after reaching age sixty-five, he would receive a total of $1,320 in benefits for the sixty dollars he and his employer paid in taxes. In case of death, benefits to the extent of three and a half per cent of his total wages taxed ($2,000), or seventy dollars, would be paid to his estate.

it is forty-six dollars a month. Therefore, the benefit payments, during the first ten or fifteen years that the federal system makes such payments, will not be so large as the gratuitous pensions now being granted in a number of states, where such old-age assistance grants average twenty-five dollars or more per recipient and still higher per couple.

Larger gratuitous pensions than "earned" pensions may make the federal old-age insurance system unpopular, especially if gratuitous state assistance is given so freely and generously that an old couple may receive fifty or sixty dollars a month. Under the federal contributory plan a worker earning $2,000 a year would have to work and pay taxes for thirty-five years before he or she would be eligible for a benefit of sixty dollars a month after age sixty-five. State old-age assistance has been expanding so rapidly — in half of the states with approved plans more than one out of every four persons sixty-five or over have been receiving such assistance — that proposals have been made to begin benefit payments under the federal contributory program before 1942 and to increase such payments during the next decade or two so that the federal program will not be overshadowed and discredited by state old-age assistance.

Although the average benefit under the contributory program may be but forty-six dollars a month in 1980, the total benefit payments at that time will run at a rate of 3.5 billion dollars a year, according to the estimates. As so many private concerns with retirement plans have learned, this pension business soon runs into big money.

Reserves. Because contributions begin long before benefits are paid, there is a gap between total contributions and total benefits when an insurance scheme is just starting or is expanding. During 1935 the total premium income of the 340 life insurance companies doing business in the United States was 3.7 billion dollars and total payments to policyholders amounted to 2.5 billion dollars. Most of the difference between these two figures went into invested reserves of the companies, which amounted to more than 20 billion dollars in 1935. If the sales of life insurance policies should so drop off that these 340 companies paid out more in death benefits than they received in premiums, part of this 20-billion-dollar reserve would be used to make up the difference. If a life insurance company's sales of new policies ceased, then its reserve would vanish as the last policyholder died and his estate received the promised death benefit.

In contrast to private insurance, most foreign old-age insurance systems do not provide for the accumulation of such huge reserves. They operate mostly on the so-called "pay-as-you-go" basis. Since the state compels people to contribute by levying a tax on them, there need be no fear that contributions will cease under a social insurance scheme. As long as the total wages upon which the tax is levied do not decline over a long period of time, the premium income will more than cover the outgo in the form of benefits to retiring workers, and there is no need for a large reserve. If the tax is collected, the workers are sure of their benefits, unless the benefit payments are too large.

Most foreign systems are subsidized by the state to permit larger benefits.

The compulsory old-age insurance system set up by the Social Security Act follows the financial pattern of private or voluntary insurance rather than foreign social insurance precedents. For this reason alone, a large reserve must be accumulated. But the federal program contemplates a reserve much larger than would be necessary if each policy paid its own way. Interest on the large reserve is to assist in paying for the higher "unearned" pensions for those now well along in years who will retire shortly after 1942. They and their employers will not have contributed a sum sufficient to pay for the monthly benefits the annuitants will receive.

The President's Committee on Economic Security proposed that the federal government pay the cost of these unearned benefits by a subsidy from general tax funds, since the compulsory insurance system will save funds for the general taxpayers in the years to come by the amount that it reduces old-age relief. If that were done the reserve would be reduced considerably. However, the Treasury wanted the system to be sound financially, which meant self-supporting. Of course, the Townsend Plan of two hundred dollars a month for all over sixty was to be self-supporting in the sense that taxes were to be levied to finance the benefit payments. The federal old-age insurance system could only be made self-supporting in this sense by raising the tax rate on pay rolls, which means the younger workers and their employers, rather than federal income-

and excise-tax payers, must meet the cost of unearned
benefits for those who retire during the first decade
or two after 1942. By so sparing income-tax payers at
the expense of workers earning $3,000 a year or less,
the federal government favored those in the higher income brackets.

Because the old-age taxes on pay rolls rise to six
per cent in 1949, total contributions will exceed benefit
payments until 1980. During the first ten years, less than
ten cents out of every dollar of such taxes will be paid
out in benefits, the other ninety cents being used to
build up the huge reserve, which, it is contemplated,
will reach about fifteen billion dollars in 1950, about
thirty billion dollars in 1960, and about fifty billion
dollars in 1980, remaining near that figure thereafter.
By 1980 over one third of the funds for pension
benefits are to come from interest on this huge reserve
and the rest from the taxes on employers and employees
(see the figure on page 248).

This matter of reserves raises some interesting economic questions. How is the reserve to be invested?
How will it affect federal spending and the money
supply? Does it lighten the burden of the next generation?

The excess of tax income over benefit payments is
to be appropriated by Congress each year to the reserve
fund. This fund is to be invested by the federal Treasury in federal bonds or the bonds of federal agencies,
so as to yield at least three per cent interest. The
Treasury may either buy up outstanding federal bonds
or it may issue new government bonds to the reserve,

thus increasing the federal debt and probably federal expenditures.

Since the old-age reserve of 45 or 50 billion dollars is not to be held in the form of commodities or cash,

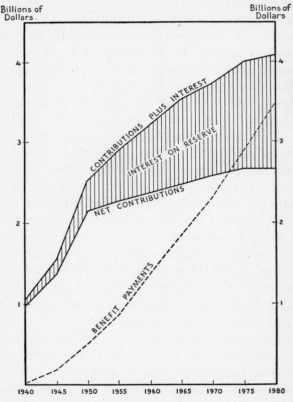

ESTIMATED INCOME AND DISBURSEMENTS UNDER
FEDERAL OLD-AGE BENEFITS PROGRAM BY FIVE-
YEAR INTERVALS, 1940–1980.

but is to be invested in federal bonds, the federal debt will always have to be at least as large as the old-age reserve. The law seems to make a large federal debt mandatory, requiring an increase in the present federal debt and precluding a debt-reduction program. In this way, the old-age reserve may disturb federal finances. Whenever the old-age reserve brings about an increase in the federal debt, the government must either find a way to spend the funds received from the reserve in exchange for the debt or it must reduce other federal taxes. Therefore, such a large old-age reserve may well mean a forced increase in federal spending. There will be pressure to have the government engage directly or indirectly in profit-making enterprises in order that this increased government spending will bring a return of three per cent to pay the interest on the additional federal debt. Otherwise, taxpayers will have to pay the interest charges on the additional debt and the old-age program may, in reality, be receiving a federal subsidy at the taxpayers' expense.

The only good reason for accumulating a huge reserve in federal debt is so that the interest on the debt will help to meet the mounting benefit payments. If the government does not spend the money in such a way that the nation's productive power, and therefore the national income, is increased by the amount of the interest payments, the reserve has failed to perform its economic function and there is little excuse for its existence. It will prove difficult for the government to invest (spend) the reserve in a way that will cause a significant increase in the real income (goods and services) of the nation, which is necessary if the burden on future generations for support of the aged is to be lightened by reason of the reserve fund. Workers and their employers will really be providing for the workers' old age only if investment of the old-age reserve increases the country's capital equipment so that a larger amount of useful goods is available in the future.

Now let us look ahead to 1980, when the reserve has reached its height and our retirement benefits come due. Then, we old folks will collect monthly benefits to the tune of 3.5 billion dollars a year. Probably all of that 3.5 billion will be spent for consumption. Why invest at age sixty-five, when you are assured of benefits for life? What we then consume, of course, the youth of 1980 cannot eat, wear, or enjoy. Whether we have really provided for our idle old age, or are consuming at the expense of the rest of the citizens in 1980, will depend on how the federal government previously spent the taxes levied on our wages. If they were spent in a way that enlarged the national product in 1980 by the amount we then consume, we have really paid for our old age. If not, the burden of our old age rests, as it has in the past, upon those who will, in 1980, be under sixty-five.

After considering this whole question of old-age reserves for six years, a Swedish commission of experts recommended that Sweden abandon the full-reserve principle. The commission pointed out that a large reserve makes the old-age program very rigid and inflexible, so that adjustments cannot readily be made to changes in the price level, the standard of living, or the rate of industrial progress. In the past there has not been a marked degree of stability in the price level. An extreme inflation like that in post-war Germany would, of course, wipe out the entire old-age reserve.

As the chart on page 248 indicates, the reserve is to be accumulated by levying higher taxes and paying smaller benefits during the next few decades than would be necessary if only a small contingency reserve were accumulated to balance tax income and benefit payments during depression periods, when tax revenues decline somewhat. It has been suggested, therefore, that the accumulation of the huge reserve could be prevented either by checking the increase in the taxes on employers and employees, or by increasing the benefit payments during the next couple of decades, or by a combination of these two methods, so that each year most of the income from the pay-roll taxes will be disbursed as benefits to retired workers. Lower tax rates would avoid an overcharging of younger workers and their employers, and also would moderate the tendency for pay-roll taxes to decrease employment. Increased benefit payments would help to check the rapid expansion and extension of state old-age assistance, and would help to prevent the federal contributory program from being discredited by more generous grants under state assistance programs.

There is some thought of trying to iron out business cycles through the investment of the reserve funds. This might be attempted either by regulating the rate and

SUMMARY CHART OF SOCIAL SECURITY MEASURES

	Administration	Coverage	Contributions	Benefits
Industrial Accident Compensation	state administration entirely	varies with state law	employer's premium varies with state law and merit rating	weekly money and medical benefits, varying from state to state
Unemployment Compensation, under Social Security Act	state administration, encouraged by 90% federal tax credit and federal subsidy for administrative costs	varies with state law; federal tax on employers of 8 or more	federal pay-roll tax of 3% on employers, with deductions allowed up to 90% for state unemployment taxes on pay rolls	weekly when unemployed, varying from state to state
Old-Age Assistance under Social Security Act	state administration, with federal subsidy up to $15 per recipient under approved state plans	needy over 65, after investigation	no special federal taxes to finance subsidy	monthly in money, varying widely with recipient's needs and local administration
Old-Age Insurance, under Social Security Act	federal administration entirely	employees in establishments hiring one or more	federal tax on employer and employee on wages up to $3,000 a year (tax is 3% on each after 1948)	fixed monthly sum till death after reaching age 65 and retirement

direction of their investment or by using them to control the money supply and the price level. During a boom some of this tax money, instead of being invested in federal bonds, might be hoarded in the Treasury or deposited in the federal reserve banks to reduce member-bank reserves as a means of restricting bank loans, if such steps seemed necessary to prevent a rise in the price level. Although depressions and unemployment may be mitigated by the investment of these funds or the payment of benefits, it should be pointed out that high pay-roll taxes on employers will cause them to conserve on labor as much as possible, thus tending to increase so-called technological unemployment.[3]

Summary of Social Insurance Measures. The provisions of the various social security programs that have been discussed in this and the previous chapter are presented schematically in the diagram on the opposite page.

[3] See McIsaac and Smith, *Introduction to Economic Analysis* (1937), pp. 240–259.

CHAPTER XI

Relief and Public Works

UNEMPLOYMENT compensation is not a complete substitute for unemployment relief. As indicated in the section on unemployment compensation, relief will be needed by unemployed workers in occupations not covered by compensation, and relief may also be necessary for workers who are covered but have exhausted their rights to unemployment benefits.[1] In many cases, unemployed workers will draw all the benefits that the compensation law provides for them long before they return to regular employment.

During depressions the unemployed who have exhausted their benefit rights may become so numerous that there will be public pressure to relax the eligibility rules and to extend both the duration of benefits and the coverage of the state compensation laws. Such relaxation of the rules might bankrupt the state plans; it would also interfere with the character of unemployment compensation as a payment related to pre-

[1] See pp. 230–231.

vious work records. Both these results may be avoided
if some provision is made for a program of unemployment relief — separate from unemployment compensation as such, but closely co-ordinated with it. A supplementary relief plan to provide for workers whose
periods of enforced idleness extend beyond the limits
of state compensation laws presumably would be but
part of a larger relief plan that would include workers, not covered by compensation, who lose their
means of support and are in need of public assistance.
The problem of relief is, of course, wider than the
problem of unemployment. This discussion will be
confined to the relief of able-bodied workers whose
families are in need because they cannot obtain a
job.

RELIEF

What sort of a relief program should be adopted?
Should the program be administered and financed by
the locality, the state, or the federal government?
Should the relief be given in the form of a cash hand-
out (the "dole"), or should it be in the form of wages
for work (employment relief)? If relief is to be given
in the form of public employment, should a program
of work relief be pursued, or should the program be
confined to public works built by contract? These are
some of the many questions that arise in considering
methods for relieving those who suffer from unemployment. And, of course, reserving the construction

of public works for depression periods has even been suggested as a method of eliminating some depressional unemployment.

LOCAL VERSUS STATE OR FEDERAL RELIEF

In this country, relief generally has been the responsibility of the local units of government — the villages, the cities, and the counties. During the depression in the early 1930's, however, relief costs were so huge, and many local units were in such financial straits, that the states and the federal government had to assist the localities with their relief responsibilities.[2] The question arises from this recent experience: Is the locality the appropriate unit for administering and financing relief?

So far as administration is concerned, the answer depends primarily upon the size of the local unit and the character of the local personnel. Some local units of government are too small to achieve the economies of specialization and large purchases, and local personnel is frequently selected on a political rather than a merit basis. Certain authorities have suggested that the county is the best unit of administration for all areas except cities of 30,000 or more inhabitants. But is a city, or even a county, the most appropriate unit to levy the taxes to meet relief costs?

Local units of government rely primarily upon property taxes for their revenues. Therefore, a large

---

[2] Cf. Luthringer, Chandler, and Cline, *Money, Credit, and Finance* (1938), pp. 348–350, 352–356.

volume of unemployment in any locality will mean high relief costs and higher taxes on local real estate. Such higher taxes will not only depress local real estate values but will also increase the costs of doing business in the locality. With high taxes on buildings, new industries are not likely to be located in that area, nor will businesses already located there be apt to improve or expand their properties, inasmuch as the high taxes would apply to any improvements. On the contrary, the owners of business establishments in the locality will tend to let their buildings and equipment depreciate, or have them torn down, in order to reduce their tax assessment and hence their local tax bill. Such measures will tend to decrease the amount of employment in the locality and to increase relief costs. The circle is complete: high relief costs mean higher property taxes; higher property taxes curtail local business operations; curtailed business spells more unemployment and larger relief burdens. This vicious circle is likely to occur wherever large relief costs are financed entirely by local taxes.

The circle can be broken if either the state or the federal government assumes a portion of the relief costs and thereby spreads the tax burden over a wider area. The larger government units can equalize the financial burden by assisting especially those municipalities with the heaviest relief loads. Also, these larger units of government, by levying profit or income taxes, can place the tax burden on those best able to pay. Cities and counties cover too little territory to use such taxes.

Profit and net income taxes do not cause local production and employment to decline. Since the tax is a percentage of the profit made, there is no incentive to curtail business operations or capital improvements in order to reduce taxes. If no profit is made, no tax is paid. For this reason, profit and net income taxes do not force businesses into bankruptcy. The property tax, however, may do so, since the same tax is levied on a firm no matter how large its profit or its loss may be.

If relief is to be administered locally, some financial assistance to the localities by state or federal grants-in-aid for relief would seem necessary during severe depressions. Some persons who advocate local administration of relief really want relief to be financed locally as well, since federal aid is likely to mean higher federal income taxes. They argue that the locality should take care of its own unemployed. But surely a particular locality is not responsible for a business depression, nor is it to blame if such a depression effects local industry very severely. Furthermore, workers on the local relief rolls may have been employed by firms that are outside the boundaries of the local unit of government and, therefore, are not subject to the taxes it levies. In such cases, the local taxing unit cannot tax the firms that are immediately responsible for its large relief expenditures.

WORK RELIEF

Another issue in unemployment relief concerns the method of giving relief. Should relief take the form of a dole or the form of wages for work on relief projects?

In defense of public employment as a relief measure, it is argued that such employment preserves the morale and work habits of the unemployed, tests their willingness to work, and utilizes idle labor and capital resources that otherwise would be wasted. The claim is that work relief, by conserving human values and improving public property, results in an ultimate saving to the community — in short, that it benefits the relief clients in particular and the community in general.

It is true that labor unused is lost forever, though that is not true of material resources. It is, therefore, possible to waste materials on relief projects, if the projects are poorly planned and constructed, or if they are of little value to the community. It is even possible to waste or spoil human resources in the sense that skilled workmen, such as watchmakers, may be worse at their trade after laboring on a relief project, or that the work standards and habits of relief employees may be adversely affected by relief jobs on which the supervision is lax, the operating efficiency is low, and "soldiering" is rife.

Nature of Work Relief. It is well to bear in mind the characteristics of work relief and how it differs from normal work. Relief workers are hired because they are impoverished and not because of their ability or qualifications for the job. They are usually discharged only when they no longer need relief; and, if they no longer are in need, they will be discharged no matter how well they do the work. Also, the normal incentives to do better work, such as advancement in rank and pay, are usually absent in work relief. A good work-relief record is of little value in advancing one's economic position. There is, therefore, little incentive for a relief client to do a good day's work.

Work relief is usually done by "force account" [3] rather than under private contract. By operating and supervising work-relief activities, the relief authorities control the personnel on each relief project, so that they may determine from week to week the exact amount of relief to be furnished to each client in the form of wages for work. Also, materials and machinery are sparingly used on relief projects, since wages to relief clients must comprise most (usually about eighty per cent) of the total expenditures on the project.

Work relief must be done on public property. It must not be work that is only of special advantage to particular property owners. Another customary requirement is that the relief projects shall consist of work that otherwise would not be done — purely "made work." If normal municipal work is performed by the relief employees, there is a tendency for relief workers to displace regular municipal employees. Such displacement of regulars by reliefers is especially likely to occur during a depression, when normal public expenditures are being reduced so that local budgets can be balanced. If relief workers pave the streets, shovel the snow, and collect the garbage, the city fathers are

---

[3] Force account means construction by the government unit itself rather than having the project done by letting contracts to private firms.

very likely to reduce the municipal appropriation for street paving, snow removal, and garbage collection.

It has been the experience both here and abroad that substitution of relief employees for regular municipal workmen occurs on a wide scale whenever a large work-relief program is undertaken.[4] Especially is such substitution likely to occur when the state or federal governments subsidize work relief up to one hundred per cent of the total cost of the project. Such state and federal subsidies permit municipal officials to do normal municipal work in the name of relief at much less expense to the local budget. In this way, work relief relieves municipal budgets. The payment of lower wages to relief workers than to regular workers also tends to put a premium on doing normal work as relief projects. It is partly for this reason that labor unions frequently forbid any member to work at his trade on a relief project, though they will permit a member to perform relief work that is not a part of his trade. The unions fear that, if normal work is done as relief work at relief wages, there will be a corresponding reduction in the regular work for their members.

Under the rules and regulations of the Federal Emergency Relief Administration, work relief was to

---

[4] From a detailed study, the Governor's Commission on Unemployment Relief in New York State concluded that, with a very large program of work relief, "it can scarcely be expected that substitution may be avoided." See *Work Relief in the State of New York: A Review of Its Characteristics, Functioning, and Value* (New York, August 10, 1936), p. 97. The Commission cites many instances in which civil-service employees were replaced by relief workers or workers were transferred from regular pay rolls to relief pay rolls.

be confined to work "apart from normal governmental enterprises and not such as would have been carried out in due course regardless of an emergency" — work not considered important enough to perform even in prosperous times. However, it proved impossible to restrict relief work to extraordinary jobs, such as "manicuring" the sides of highways and beautifying parks, when more necessary, normal municipal functions were being abandoned either because the municipality was short of funds or because the taxpayers had demanded a reduction in municipal expenditures.

The Economics of Work Relief. Whether work relief is more economical than direct relief (the dole) is a much-mooted question. The federal relief authorities have claimed that relief employment is the soundest method of providing relief. Some state relief authorities, however, have maintained that "any conditional mixing of work and public relief is both socially and economically unsound." In 1932 the Director of Emergency Relief in New Jersey stated that "the great bulk of public made work is not a public economy as against direct relief" and that any increase in public work might better be executed in the normal way (as public works under private contract) than as relief work. Experience with work relief in England, Germany, and Canada has also led to the general opinion that public employment is not the best method of giving relief to unemployed workers.

The truth is that a categorical answer cannot be given to the question: Is work relief economical? The answer will depend upon the particular local circumstances.

Before a work-relief program is adopted in a locality, at least five factors should be considered.

In the first place, there is the additional expense involved in giving wage relief rather than direct relief. This includes the nonrelief costs of planning and supervising the project, of transporting the workers, of supplying them with equipment and materials to construct the project, and of compensating them for serious injuries. The cost of caring for a family by work relief is generally from thirty to sixty per cent more than it would cost to provide for the family to the same degree by direct relief.[5]

In the second place, relief work is not performed with normal operating efficiency. The workers are hired because they are in need, and not because they are especially fitted for the job. The normal incentives for better work are lacking. Hand, rather than machine, methods are used where possible, so that most of the money will be paid as wages to relief clients. Much of the work must be done in winter, when the weather is unfavorable for construction work, because it is then that relief rolls reach their peak. These are some of the reasons why the average efficiency on relief projects throughout the country seems not to have been above fifty per cent of normal operating efficiency.

These two factors of efficiency and additional cost are basic. Work relief can hardly be economical if the work

[5] From a study of 3,750 relief cases in 1934, the Governor's Commission in New York found that, under comparable circumstances, the cost of work relief exceeded the cost of direct relief by eighty-two per cent.

done is not worth at least the added cost of work relief over direct relief.[6]

A third factor is the effect of work relief on the morale, skills, and work habits of relief clients. Advocates of work relief claim that it conserves the labor resources of the community. This they believe to be true even though work relief may result in some regular workers losing their jobs to relief employees.

During the 1930–1933 depression almost every occupation and profession was represented by those on the relief rolls — from deep-sea divers and stool pigeons for the police, to chemists with college degrees and former $50,000-a-year executives. In large cities only a small percentage of the relief clients in ordinary times earned their living by outdoor work, yet almost eighty per cent of all relief employment in urban areas in the East was of the unskilled, manual variety. It hardly preserves skills or morale to put a minister to work with a pick and shovel, a chemical engineer with a rake, or an architect with an ax. Federal relief officials

[6] Suppose that, according to estimates, it would cost seventy per cent more to have relief clients work on a particular project than to care for their families by direct relief. Suppose also that the expected efficiency of relief workers on this project was forty per cent of normal. Under such conditions, the same amount of relief could be given either for 100,000 dollars as direct relief or for 170,000 dollars as work relief — a difference of 70,000 dollars. For every 170,000 dollars spent on work relief, the community would, at forty per cent operating efficiency, receive a return of 68,000 dollars worth of work. The added cost of wage relief, over direct relief, in this case would be 70,000 dollars and the return to the community would be but 68,000 dollars. It would, therefore, be more economical to do the work by contract or as regular public works and to take care of the relief clients by direct relief. Of course, if the operating efficiency under work relief were well above forty per cent of normal or if the added cost of work relief were below seventy per cent, it would be more economical to do the job as a relief project.

frankly admitted that at least one fifth of the relief clients had skills and trainings that could not be utilized within the confines of the WPA program of work relief. And on top of that, trade unions usually will not permit their members to utilize their skills on normal and necessary municipal work done under the guise of relief work at relief wage rates.

Whether relief will have an adverse or beneficial effect on relief clients will depend, therefore, upon the quality of supervision on the job, the attitude of relief clients toward the work, and the nature of the project — whether it is worthwhile work that utilizes the particular skills of relief clients in the locality.

The fourth factor to consider is the value of the completed project to the community. Is the project the most useful one that could then be performed in the locality? That is not likely to be the case if the project is "made work" or if it conforms to a federal requirement restricting relief projects to work that would not be done even in prosperous times. There is no economy in doing needless work or even in building half-rate projects — half-rate when judged by the immediate and ultimate need for them.

Finally, in determining whether work relief is economical, allowance must be made for any displacement of more efficient employees by relief workmen, less capable and untrained for the work. Whenever such displacement occurs, the labor turnover and the loss involved in training raw recruits for new jobs represents a real social cost. It was to avoid such displacement that the federal authorities during the depression of the early 1930's tried in vain to restrict work relief to extraordinary jobs — to work that would not be done in normal times. There is, however, no solution to the dilemma: if the project includes normal municipal work, displacement is likely to occur; if it consists entirely of abnormal work, it will be of relatively little value to the community.

Actually what is most needed during a depression, especially by the unemployed, is more food, clothing, and other products rather than more public improvements. It would, therefore, be economical to broaden the field of relief employment by extending it beyond the boundaries of public enterprise into various lines of production. Although production by the unemployed for their own use would probably raise the average standard of living in the community more than it could be raised by a work-relief program, such "self-help" activities have usually been opposed as "competition with business." Consequently, production by relief clients for their own use has been confined mostly to agriculture, where it has taken the form of subsistence gardening. For example, relief clients in New Jersey grew over ten per cent of the garden vegetables raised in that state in 1935.

Some farmers rightly complained that concentration of relief production on gardening tended to reduce the cash market for their crops. The savings from subsistence gardening left more money in the pockets of relief clients or taxpayers, but most of that saved money was spent for products not grown in gardens.

Producers in other lines gained what the farmers lost from this practice of relief gardening.

This experience indicates that it is necessary to pursue a well-balanced program of relief production, covering practically all lines of industry, if the relief authorities are to put the relief clients to work producing the things they so badly need. It is only by a general, over-all increase in production, that is in proportion to the demand of the newly employed for commodities, that the relief authorities can increase the total amount of employment in the country without assisting some groups at the expense of others not yet on relief. Such a general expansion in production and employment occurs in every normal recovery of business.

PUBLIC WORKS

Nature of Public Works. Public works are substantial construction projects rather than repair jobs or "manicuring" activities. They are usually built under contracts let to private firms. In contrast to work relief, public works are constructed in the most efficient manner, and workers are hired according to their fitness for the job. Since relief clients ordinarily are not given preference for jobs on normal public works, there is no tendency for better workers to be displaced by poorer ones — poorer in both wealth and workmanship. Instead of wages on the job amounting to about eighty per cent of all costs as under work relief, public-works pay rolls usually account for around thirty-five per cent of the total cost of the project. On the average, the cost of materials, such as iron, steel, and cement, accounts for more than fifty per cent of all expenses on public works. For this reason, the cost per man employed locally on the job ordinarily is more than twice as much under a public-works program as it is under a work-relief program.

As an Antidote to Depressions. Because such a high proportion of public-works expenditures goes for the products of heavy industry, public-works programs have been proposed as antidepression measures. Much of the unemployment during business depressions is concentrated in the heavy goods industries.

On the planned use of public works for the purpose of combating a depression, there are two schools of thought. One school would simply use public works as a balance wheel to private business, expanding them as business declines and reducing them as business revives. The balance-wheel group would not change the total amount of public works constructed during a complete business cycle from what otherwise would be constructed. They simply advocate distributing the same total expenditures for public works in a different manner — spending more of the total during depression periods.

The second school, which may be called the pump-priming group, would increase sharply the amount of public works constructed during a depression, without reducing them by a corresponding amount during the previous or succeeding periods of prosperity. Consequently, they would tend to increase the total amount of public works built from decade to decade. The pump-priming group would use public works as a lever to lift private business out of a depression. They would spend money on public works until industry recovers. The federal government's public-works program of 2.5 billion dollars,[7] begun in the latter half of 1933, was of the pump-priming variety, and probably represented the most ambitious attempt that has been made in any country to stimulate recovery by government spending on public construction.

In this discussion of planned public-works programs to combat depressions, it may help to have in mind the figures shown in the table on page 270, which indicate the relative significance of public works.

These figures indicate that public construction, in normal times, accounts for no more than one third of all construction and that it is but a small part of the total national income. An expanded public-works program during a depression cannot, therefore, fill the gap left by private business or even by private construction. Under the federal public-works program not as much was spent during any one year (the peak month was July 1934) as was spent for private construction in the low year of 1933 — about 1.3 billion dollars was spent under P.W.A. during the first year and a half of the program. The effectiveness of an

[7] A total of over 3.8 billion dollars was appropriated for public works in 1933 and 1934, but about 1.2 billion dollars was allotted for non-construction projects, such as relief and conservation.

IMPORTANCE OF PUBLIC AND PRIVATE CONSTRUCTION IN
THE UNITED STATES[8]

(Billions of Dollars)

	NATIONAL INCOME PRODUCED	PRIVATE CONSTRUCTION	PUBLIC CONSTRUCTION
1927		9.22	3.71
1928		9.39	3.63
1929	81.03	8.72	3.56
1930	67.92	6.58	3.63
1931	53.58	4.53	3.07
1932	39.55	2.06	2.00
1933	41.74	2.00	1.80
1934	48.40	2.00	2.60
1935	52.96	3.00	2.60
1936	63.80	4.30	3.20

expanded public-works program as a recovery measure, therefore, depends perhaps more upon the timing of its expansion than upon the absolute increase in the size of public-works expenditures.

Timing of the Program. There is no agreement among economists on the exact stage in the business cycle that public-works expenditures should be increased. Some would apply this stimulus at the beginning of a slump in business. Others advocate the increase of such expenditures after business has undergone "the strictly necessary degree of liquidation" but before the upturn in business has occurred. A third group would wait until business has definitely turned

[8] *National Income in the United States, 1929–1935,* United States Department of Commerce (Washington, 1936), and Gayer, Arthur D., *Public Works in Prosperity and Depression* (New York, 1935), p. 23. The more recent estimates for public and private construction and the national income have been supplied by the United States Department of Commerce.

the corner and is on the upgrade, before accelerating the rate of spending for public construction. This last group especially believes that depressions are necessary to purge the economic system of unhealthy conditions and that a public-works program should be used only to hasten convalescence.

It is evident that one's choice of the proper moment during the course of a depression to accelerate public-works expenditures depends upon one's theories about the business cycle and especially about depressions.[9] If one feels that depression and deflation serve a useful economic purpose, he will advocate waiting until late in the depression to initiate a public-works program. If, on the other hand, he believes that depressions are not self-corrective, or that deflation serves no useful purpose and leads to a vicious spiral of falling prices, he will advocate an expansionist program early in the depression.

The "depressions-are-necessary-and-inevitable" group believe that public-works programs cannot remove the causes of depressions nor restore the proper relationship among various prices. They believe that, until some costs are brought down and some inflated capital values are written off, there will be little prospect for profits, and business recovery will not occur. This "pessimistic" group believe that increased public-works expenditures, before such downward adjustments take place, is simply pouring money down a rat hole. In their opinion, such an acceleration of public

[9] *Cf.* McIsaac and Smith, *Introduction to Economic Analysis*, pp. 403–426.

spending early in a depression prolongs the period of liquidation or adjustment by supporting the market for construction materials and labor and thus preventing construction costs from falling as rapidly as they otherwise would.

On the other hand, the "optimistic" group deny that deflation is a necessary evil or that natural forces will soon mend matters if a hands-off policy is pursued. In their opinion a reflation of prices is the better way to restore the prospect for profits and to bring about business recovery. Instead of adjustment by bringing down those prices that seem too high, they would raise the prices that, in their opinion, have fallen too far. And they believe that an expanded public-works program started early in a depression will assist in arresting and reversing the cumulative downward movement of prices and production.

Effects of a Public-Works Program. An attempt to readjust prices upwards during a depression is likely to result in abandonment of the gold standard. The automatic international gold standard requires that all countries adhering to it have a common price level, so that prices cannot be raised appreciably in one country alone without endangering its monetary standard through loss of gold.[10] Adherence to gold serves as a drag on any national program to expand public spending and to raise prices during a depression.

The purchase of materials for public-works projects will stimulate many industries directly or indirectly

[10] See Luthringer, Chandler, and Cline, *op. cit.,* pp. 178–206 for a discussion of the gold standard.

and, by spending their wages, workers on the projects will stimulate many more branches of industry. Whether this increased spending will spread by a series of waves to cause increased spending throughout the economy will depend, of course, upon how business men and consumers view the future. If the future looks dark to them and they do not anticipate a rise of prices in the near future, they will hesitate to increase their expenditures, and the effects of the public-works program will not be felt throughout industry. Business men will not begin to buy and replenish their inventories if they believe that the public-works program will simply result in an artificially high demand, which will subside after the program has reached its peak.

Whether a public-works program results in increased business and general spending depends, in part, upon the way that the program is financed. If idle funds are put into circulation by enlarged public expenditures, a net increase in total spending may result. This might well be the case if the funds for the program were raised (either by taxation or bond issues) from funds that otherwise would lie idle or be hoarded. Sale of bonds to commercial banks, and especially to the federal reserve banks, is likely to increase the money supply and to ease the money market.[11] It is desirable for the government to follow an easy money policy, so that the financing of the public-works program will not adversely affect private industry either by causing

[11] See *ibid.*, pp. 108–109, 120–121, for the way purchases of government bonds by banks may increase the money supply and ease the money market.

a rise in market rates of interest or by reducing the supply of funds available for private investment.

An increase in public expenditures may even cause a reduction in total public and private spending. Business men may fear that an expansionist program will mean a continued unbalance of the budget and will have other results that seem disturbing to them. Their fears, whether justified or not, may inhibit them from making business commitments, which will cause a reduction in demand and further deflation. If the public-works program includes such projects as slum clearance and water-power developments, private investment in housing and in gas and electric utilities may be sharply reduced.

In order to spend large sums for worth-while projects under a public-works program, especially of the pump-priming variety, the government may be forced to undertake projects that seem to encroach upon vested rights and to compete with private enterprise, which then is not very active. That is more likely to be true if most of the government's projects are to be self-liquidating.[12]

Technical and Practical Difficulties. There are also a number of practical problems and difficulties in attempting to accelerate public-works expenditures at any particular time or to use public works as a balance wheel to private business.

It takes time to plan the projects, to let the contracts,

---

[12] "Self-liquidating" means that in time sufficient funds will be collected or earned from the use of that particular public work to pay the full cost of its construction.

and to begin operations. Such delays make accurate timing of the program very difficult. Once operations have commenced, it may be impossible to cease construction until the project is completed, even though business may be booming long before the project is finished. Furthermore, winter is the dull business season, yet in many sections of the country the weather is too cold for construction activity during that period.

The stimulating effects of public-works expenditures may be felt for the most part in localities that are suffering least from depression. The localities where public works can best be constructed may not be those with the most unemployment. And a construction program is bound to stimulate business in those areas in the few states (like Pennsylvania, Ohio, and Alabama) that produce most of the building materials, though such areas may not be the ones most urgently in need of the stimulus.

A public-works program of the balance-wheel type requires advance planning and budgeting of public works. Public-works expenditures must be reduced in good times; but some public-works construction cannot be shifted in time. It is not possible to cease building new highways for a while and then to construct them all at once. And the shifting of some public works forward or backward may mean that they will be completed at a time when they are not especially needed. If the program should involve the accumulation of a reserve in good times to meet the increased expenditures for public construction during depressions, there would be the problems of investing and handling such a reserve — problems that have already been discussed in connection with the old-age reserve account.

Finally, there are, according to the 1932 census figures, over 180,000 government units in this country, including 48 states; 3,062 counties, 16,442 cities, towns, villages, and boroughs; and 128,548 school districts. It would be difficult to induce all of these independent government bodies to expand and contract their public-works expenditures in unison. Presumably they would need to expand and contract all of their expenditures, otherwise the effects of increased spending for construction might be negated by a reduction in public expenditures for other purposes.

The federal government's expenditures for public works amounted to less than ten per cent of the aggregate public-works outlays of all government agencies during the 1920's. It is necessary, therefore, for the federal government to induce municipalities to spend. During the depression of the early 1930's the federal government offered a subsidy for the construction of municipal public works — first a subsidy of thirty per cent of total cost and later a subsidy of forty-five per cent of the cost of the project. Many municipalities accepted this subsidy for projects that they planned to do anyway. Consequently, the federal program did not increase municipal public works by the full amount that the official figures would seem to indicate.

Such are the practical difficulties that may beset a program to expand public works during a depression. In addition, there are the more theoretical problems, already discussed, such as the proper time to expand public works and the probable effect of the program on private spending. The successful operation of either a balance-wheel or a pump-priming program of public works would seem to be no mean task.

PART FOUR

SOCIAL REORGANIZATION

CHAPTER XII

The Attacks on Capitalism

CHARACTERISTICS OF CAPITALISM

THE economic system under which we live is commonly called "Capitalism." Because it is a term applied to a complex structure of economic and legal relationships, which varies from country to country and from time to time in the same country, it is difficult to define. Many of those who use the term give it a meaning that carries implications of either good or evil. The defenders of what they call "Capitalism" are prone to describe it as a system characterized by private property, economic freedom, individual initiative, progress in methods of production, and monetary rewards roughly corresponding to individual initiative, skill, energy, and thrift. As used by opponents of the system, the term "Capitalism" is ordinarily meant to imply the ownership of the essential means of production by a

very small minority under legal institutions that permit — and encourage — the exploitation of the toiling
masses by a small proportion of the population.

If we seek a statement of the characteristic features
of Capitalism that is free of implications as to its results
in the distribution of personal incomes or in terms
of social welfare, and free also of implications as to
its ethical justification or lack of it, we find rather
general agreement on four points. The first is the prevalence of methods of production and distribution that
require the possession of more capital than the general
run of manual workers can acquire. It may be capital
in the form of raw materials or stock in trade, or it
may be capital in the form of tools or machinery or
other equipment. Whatever the form of the necessary
capital, the lack of it on the part of the mass of the
manual workers means that they cannot be self-em-
ploying; their status is that of wage earners. To many
persons, this is the central fact of Capitalism.

The second characteristic is private property in the
means of production. This characteristic has to do with
a legal institution, not with technical methods. It can
exist, and has existed, under methods of production
and distribution that are not capitalistic — as under a
system of handicraft production for a local market.
But when capitalistic methods in the technological
sense have become common, the private ownership of
the capital stands out as an important characteristic of
the system. Indeed, it is to many persons the one distinguishing characteristic of Capitalism; private owner-

ship, as opposed to public ownership, is regarded by them as the essence of the capitalistic system.

The third generally accepted characteristic of Capitalism is legal freedom of economic action. The private owners of the means of production are legally free to produce what they wish and to insist on the best terms (for themselves) that they can get in the sale of their goods or services and in the purchase of equipment, materials, and labor. The wage earners are legally free, also, to work at any occupation they wish, for whom they wish, at the best terms they can get — and are free to reject the terms offered. Because capitalistic methods developed rapidly under a regime of freedom of contract or *laissez faire,*[1] this freedom of economic action came to be regarded as one of the characteristics of Capitalism.

Under private ownership and freedom of economic action, the motivating force in economic activity is private gain. This is true whether the units of production be large or small. Where the units are large enough to make the ownership or control of capital — rather than manual or technical skill — the essential qualification for conducting an enterprise, the direction of production is said to be motivated by the hope of private profit. This is the fourth characteristic of Capitalism — the predominance of the profit motive as the incentive to and the regulator of production. Many people consider that the direction of economic activity

[1] See Modlin and deVyver, *Development of Economic Society,* pp. 267–288.

by the private profit motive is the distinguishing feature of Capitalism. The discussions in recent years over the issue of a directed or planned economy versus an economy in which the decisions are left to private initiative, have led to an increase in the emphasis on this feature.

These four features together in an economic system make it Capitalism. However, to say that the system that exists in a particular country is Capitalism does not mean that all four of these characteristics are in exclusive occupation of their respective fields. It means merely that they predominate. Not all production units need be too large for ownership by the individual worker. Nor is public ownership of such services as communication and transportation excluded. Capitalism, as commonly understood, is also consistent with a considerable degree of government interference with freedom of contract in the sphere of price, as in public utilities, and especially in the sphere of working conditions, unemployment compensation, and so on. None of the large industrial countries has exhibited all of the characteristic features of Capitalism without any degree of exception to any of them. In other words, "pure" Capitalism has never existed. How far a country may go in the sphere of regulation and still be called capitalistic is an undetermined question in the field of terminology. But as yet no other generally accepted name has been applied to the complex of economic and legal institutions existing in such countries as the United States and Great Britain.

DESTRUCTIVE ANALYSES OF CAPITALISM

This section will be devoted to a brief survey of the analyses of Capitalism that lead to the conclusion that its inherent weaknesses make its replacement by another system either inevitable or socially imperative. The discussion of the systems that have been advocated, or actually attempted, as substitutes will be postponed to the next two chapters. The analysis at this point is concerned with the functioning of Capitalism itself, as viewed by its hostile critics. The order of treatment will be mainly historical.

Relatively few writers defend Capitalism in all its workings. Some of the objections presented by those who advocate the replacement of Capitalism by some other system have also been advanced by many who believe that Capitalism can be made to work acceptably, or at least that it contains more promise than any other system yet proposed. A survey of the literature of criticism of Capitalism will reveal attacks on some of its workings by men not advocating its replacement by another system, as stirring as any made by those advocating its overthrow. Doubtless the attacks by those who would reform Capitalism and those who would replace it have had their interactions.

It is usual to center the discussion of anticapitalistic theory around the doctrines of the socialists, using that term to cover those who believe that private owner-ship of the means of production must be replaced by some form of social ownership. This is because the socialist criticism is directed not only against the work-ings of Capitalism but against its essential founda-tions — private ownership and the private profit motive.

THE MARXIAN DOCTRINES

"Scientific" Socialism. The systematic analysis of Capitalism from a socialist standpoint is generally associated with the name of Karl Marx, whose writings began to attract attention in the middle of the nine-teenth century. Marx is called by his followers the father of "scientific" Socialism, because he presented a rounded body of doctrines that "exposed" the economic "laws" operating under Capitalism as inevitably causing the exploitation of the workers by the capitalists, and as inevitably leading to the downfall of Capitalism and its replacement by Socialism. There had been writers before Marx, of course, who attacked the validity of private property. There had been analyses, too, of the workings of the economic laws of the distribution of income under Capitalism that led to the conclusion that the capitalists were exploiting the wage earners by holding back from them part of the wealth pro-duced by the workers themselves. But the doctrines of Marx were based on "inevitable" social laws, and were related to each other as parts of a unified whole. For his followers at least, Marx put the attack on Capi-talism on a real scientific basis.

Economic Determinism. Many persons have regarded Marx's doctrine of surplus value (to be discussed below) as the foundation of his economics. Marx himself, however, insisted that the real basis of his economic thinking, and his greatest contribution to the science of human society, was his doctrine of "economic determinism." The essence of this doctrine is that economic forces are the fundamental cause of change in human institutions; social classes, political forms, the family, culture, and even religion are the results of — are determined by — methods of production and distribution. The state is but an instrument of coercion used by the class that controls the system of production, and therefore the economic life of the people, to keep the economically dependent classes in subjection. Religion, to Marx, is also but a means of keeping the people quiet — the "opiate of the masses."

Economic determinism is, of course, a materialistic interpretation of human institutions and human activities, one that excludes any spiritual or supernatural element. It is therefore often called the "materialistic interpretation of history." But economic determinism is more than an interpretation of the past. It is, to the Marxists, the key to the future; it is a law that explains the inevitable course that the development of Capitalism must follow.[2]

---

[2] Economic determinism, according to Marx, is but one aspect of a universal principle. This principle is that all things are subject to change through the clashing of opposing forces inherent in them. Out of this clash of opposing forces there emerges a new thing, which is different from what preceded it; then this new thing is changed in turn, through the clash of opposites, "contradictions", inherent in it, and so on. This system of reasoning is known as "dialectical materialism." It is called "dialectical" because it assumes that change is brought about by a clash of opposites; it is called "materialism" because it assumes that there is no ultimate force in the world that is not a purely material force.

leads to it?

The atheistic, materialistic basis of Marxism as a system of thought made Marx's doctrines anathema to religious people. He had declared war on religion. Consequently no religious people could accept Marxism, however much they deplored the injustices of Capitalism or however sharply they opposed the philosophical basis of economic individualism.[3] The identification of Marxism with materialism, and the assumption that Marxism and Socialism were identical, undoubtedly greatly hindered the spread of Socialism as a system of economic thought among those opposed to the existing Capitalism.

The Class Struggle. One of the manifestations of economic determinism, according to Marx, has been the conflict between economic classes. As far back in history as one finds a dominant economic class, one also finds below it a class that is waging a struggle to throw off the control of the dominant class and make itself the economically superior class. Before the coming of Capitalism the struggle had been between the bourgeoisie — the small capitalist trading and manufacturing class — and the feudal lords. The bourgeoisie eventually won economic independence and, establishing itself as the dominant class, developed Capitalism. In Marx's day the class struggle was between the proletariat — the capital-less wage earners — and their capitalist masters. This struggle, according to Marxian doctrine, would inevitably go on until the proletariat, just as inevitably, should overthrow the capitalists and take over the control themselves. Then

[3] See Modlin and deVyver, *op. cit.*, pp. 273–276.

the class struggle would be brought to an end, because the proletariat would establish a classless society. But until the capitalists were ousted, the class struggle must go on. Thus, the struggle between the proletariat and the capitalists is, according to the Marxists, an inevitable concomitant of Capitalism.

Surplus Value. Marx's doctrine of "surplus value" is one of the most important of the "exploitation" theories of distribution of income under private ownership and the system of wage labor. It was intended to be a scientific exposition of those laws of valuation inherent in Capitalism that give to the capitalists value created by the workers. But it was more than a piece of economic analysis. It was another manifestation of economic determinism. Marx's doctrine was not only an explanation of *how* the capitalist does it; it was an explanation of the reason for Capitalism.

Briefly, Marx held that economic laws inherent in the system of Capitalism keep wages always less than the value produced by the laborers. His explanation of what determines the amount of value produced by labor is based on what is known as "the labor theory of value." According to this theory, which was not peculiar to Marx, it is the amount of labor necessary for the production of a good that determines its value in comparison with other goods. In the case of goods produced for exchange, their relative value in exchange depends on the relative amounts of labor expended on them; a good that embodies twice as much labor as another will exchange for it at the rate of one for two.[4] Therefore, it is the laborers who create value in exchange. That is why the capitalists employ them. And the value created by the laborers for the capitalists is proportionate to the amount of labor expended.

With respect to the "exchange value of labor", or wages, Marx held that the exchange value of labor, like that of everything else, depends on the amount of labor necessary for its production. In the case of labor this means the amount of labor necessary to produce the bare essentials of living for the laborers. Marx thus arrives at a "subsistence" theory of wages by the application to labor of the general rule that value in exchange depends upon the amount of labor necessary for production. But — and this is important — Marx insisted that the laborers can produce the equivalent of subsistence in a smaller number of hours per day than the number of hours the capitalists compel them to work. In other words, the capitalists require the laborers to produce more value than the equivalent of subsistence. It is that additional amount above subsistence that is "surplus value." It is value produced by the laborers but expropriated by the capitalists.

Even if the validity of Marx's theory of value be granted, his explanation of surplus value under Capitalism requires two additional assumptions. The first is that the laborers can produce more than subsistence in a working day; this, as we have seen, Marx assumed.

---

[4] "Value in exchange" was distinguished from "value in use." It was recognized that there is no value in exchange unless the good has value in use; but, value in use being assumed, it was the amount of labor necessary for production that determined value in exchange, according to this theory.

The second assumption is that the capitalist has a superiority in bargaining position over the workers that enables him to compel them to keep on working after they have produced the equivalent of subsistence. Granted all that has gone before, if the workers quit when they have produced the equivalent of subsistence they would produce no surplus value for the capitalist. But, said Marx, the capitalist's ownership of the means of production — without access to which the capital-less workers can produce nothing — gives him the control over the workers that makes inevitable their production of surplus value for him. The bargaining superiority of the capitalists is strengthened by the presence of a "reserve army of unemployed" workers, an army that is continually augmented by the increasing use of machinery in production.

Marx's doctrine of surplus value undoubtedly did much to put Capitalism on the defensive, not only with many who welcomed this "scientific" explanation of what they had long accepted as a fact, but with some whose faith in the current explanation of the persistence of the low economic condition of the laboring masses in a period of amazing advance in production of wealth was shaken by the Marxian assertions. The "labor-theory-of-value" assumptions underlying Marx's explanation of the emergence of surplus value could easily be challenged. What could not easily be refuted were his assumptions that labor *does* produce more than subsistence but fails to get what it produces because of the superiority of bargaining power that the capitalist enjoys through his ownership of the means of production. Marx rejected the complacent assumption that what kept wages down was the tendency of man's fecundity to outrun his wealth-producing capacity. He put the blame squarely on the "law" governing the distribution of the product, not on productive capacity. And he insisted that this law of distribution is inherent in the system; it cannot be removed by good will or by any measure of reform within the system.

Crises and Depressions. According to Marx, the recurrence of crises and depressions is inevitable under Capitalism. They are due to a contradiction inherent in the system. On the one hand, there is the urge of the individual capitalists to continue accumulating capital. This they do by extracting surplus value from the workers and investing it. The addition to their capital equipment enables them to employ more labor and so to gain more surplus value, which is devoted in turn to enlarging production still further. But — and here is the contradiction — the capitalists are unable to go on increasing their production without bringing on the crises and depressions that waste much of the capital already accumulated in the form of productive equipment. Capitalist production is anarchic, in the sense that the capitalists, each acting independently of the others, enlarge their aggregate output beyond the limits of consumer demand. The blind following of the urge to increase production inevitably brings on a period of enforced idleness of capital equipment and widespread unemployment.

The inherent cause of the inability of consumer demand to keep pace with capitalist production is to be found, according to the Marxists, in the low buying power of the proletariat. Because wages are always below the exchange value of the goods produced — due to the expropriation of surplus value by the capitalists — the proletariat can buy only a restricted proportion of the goods they produce. The capitalists themselves do not use more than a fraction of the expropriated surplus value to buy each other's goods. They reinvest most of it in order to produce more goods. Thus, there is an inherent contradiction between the productive forces and the law of distribution of income, under Capitalism.[5] In an attempt to escape the limits imposed upon the home market by the low wages of the proletariat, the capitalists are constantly striving for markets in the noncapitalist regions of the earth and in countries less advanced in Capitalism. But this can afford no more than temporary relief. Crises must inevitably become more and more severe, and depressions more prolonged and more destructive, until Capitalism finds itself in a universal crisis from which it cannot emerge.

The Inevitable Collapse of Capitalism. So much for the workings of Capitalism, produced by its inherent laws. But there is more to the Marxian doctrines than an explanation of how Capitalism works in the present. There is also a statement of what is bound to happen.

[5] Marx apparently denied at one time that low wages are the fundamental cause of the recurrence of crises. The real cause, he said, is the "anarchic" character of production under Capitalism. But most followers of Marx have stressed the low buying power of the proletariat as the underlying inescapable cause of crises and depressions.

For Capitalism carries in it the seeds of its own destruction. Its inherent laws must inevitably lead to its downfall. Marx did not say that unless this or that is done, Capitalism will surely collapse. He said Capitalism *must* collapse; there is nothing that can stop it; it will itself generate the poisons that will kill it.

Briefly, the course of Capitalism will be as follows: There will be an increasing concentration of the ownership of capital; the capitalists will continually become "larger" and fewer. The process of concentration will be hastened by crises and failures; the larger capitalists will increasingly squeeze out the smaller. These ex-capitalists will be thrust down into the ranks of the proletariat. Eventually there will be only the few large capitalists on the one side and the proletariat on the other.

Crises and depressions will recur with increasing frequency and with increasing severity. With more and more capital in fewer and fewer hands, the system will become increasingly difficult to run. The capitalists will find themselves with a Frankenstein on their hands. Finally, there will come a crisis so serious that the capitalists cannot pull the system out of it. This will be the inevitable cataclysmic downfall of Capitalism. It will have worked out its own destruction.

Meanwhile the lot of the proletariat will have become worse and worse. The proletariat will have experienced continually "increasing misery and degradation." Thus will the proletariat have been prepared for its "historic mission" — to rise up in desperation and "expropriate the expropriators." With the capitalists gone — and Capitalism with them — the proletariat will proceed to establish Socialism. But first the "economic laws" inherent in Capitalism must themselves engender the economic collapse of Capitalism.

BROADENING OF THE SOCIALIST ATTACK ON CAPITALISM

Diversity in Economic Doctrine. Although the Marxian analysis of Capitalism was still accepted at the end of the nineteenth century by a majority of socialists, there was a considerable number of professed socialists who no longer held to the pure Marxian doctrine. There was, for example, a school of "Revisionists" who had "modernized" the Marxian teaching to bring it into conformity with the conditions and trends of the time, as they saw them. Marx was essentially right, they said, in holding Capitalism to be a system of exploitation and in predicting its ultimate supersession by Socialism, but he was too inflexible in his theories and was mistaken in some important respects in his statement of the inevitable lines of development of Capitalism. And in addition to the various groups generally included under the head of Marxists — ranging all the way from the strict constructionists to thoroughgoing Revisionists — there were many socialist thinkers whose approach to the analysis of the economics of Capitalism was independent of Marxism.

The best known group of non-Marxian socialists was the members of the Fabian Society, a small society of British intellectuals opposed to Capitalism. The

Fabians developed a theory of "unearned surpluses" that is much less rigid than the Marxian doctrine of surplus value. Instead of regarding surplus value as something created by labor alone and expropriated by capitalists, the Fabians insist that there are many types of surplus value under Capitalism and that this surplus is expropriated from the community as a whole rather than from the wage earners as such. The Fabians regard as surplus value any income exacted without an equivalent productive contribution; the surplus is the product of nature or of social forces, not the result of any productive effort on the part of those who receive it. Income that is "unearned" in this sense may be exacted not only by industrial capitalists but by owners of natural resources, by landlords, by middlemen, or even by well-organized craftsmen who are able to maintain stringent restrictions on entrance to their trade. To be sure, many employers gain unearned surpluses by paying too low wages to their employees, but unearned surpluses are also exacted at the expense of the great body of consumers.

The source of unearned surpluses, according to this analysis, is the ownership or control of something that society needs and that is relatively scarce — whether the scarcity be natural or due to monopolistic practices. The most flagrant examples are the surpluses received by owners of natural resources, or of land in industrial, commercial, and residential centers. These owners, according to the Fabians, receive incomes merely for owning; they contribute no service whatever to production. Absentee owners of industrial enterprises run

by hired managers are also put in the class of ex-
ploiters, if they receive profits. All profits from monopoly, whether industrial, trade or service monopo-
lies, are likewise classified as unearned surpluses. The
exaction of surplus value of these types by a small
minority is inevitable under private ownership and
production for profit.

It is not only with respect to surplus value that the
Fabians reject the Marxian formula. For example, they
hold that the cataclysmic downfall of Capitalism is not
inevitable. Economic and political forces have already
improved the condition of the masses; these forces can
be so directed as to transform Capitalism gradually
into a system of social ownership and "production for
use instead of profit."

Thus, by the beginning of the World War, there had
developed among socialists a considerable diversity in
economic analysis, marked by a decline in the relative
importance of the pure Marxian doctrine. The seizure
of power in Russia by a group of declared Marxists
and their subsequent increasing influence in the world
of Socialism has brought a distinct revival of Marxism. Nevertheless, there are still many socialists who
do not base their Socialism on such doctrines as economic determinism and surplus value as expounded
by Marx.

Shifts in Emphasis in the Economic Analysis. The
socialist attack on Capitalism reveals a changing emphasis from country to country and from time to time
as Capitalism itself has exhibited changes in its structure or in its operation. In some countries more is

made of the concentration of control through capitalistic combinations, or through control of finance and credit, than in others. In some countries, too, "land capitalism" is more under attack than in others.

In industrialized countries the emphasis has shifted, from time to time, as periods of relative prosperity have alternated with periods of depression. When employment is relatively good and workers' earnings as well as enterprisers' profits are increasing, there is likely to be more emphasis on the "inevitable" failure of the standard of living of the mass of men to rise as much as unearned incomes from ownership or control. And in time of depression, first place is given to "want in the midst of plenty." In recent years there has been, on the whole, a greater emphasis on the "inefficiency" of Capitalism, thus centering the attack on what has always been one of the leading arguments of its defenders — its efficiency in producing and distributing goods and services. The private profit motive is held more and more to be an antisocial force even in the sphere of production. The "inevitable" inequality in the distribution of the national income is now subordinated by some socialist writers to the "inherent" inability of the system to make the fullest use of the productive possibilities that the advances of science have made available to man.

Wider Effects of Capitalism. The narrower economic analysis of the workings of Capitalism as an economic system has been supplemented by criticisms of the effects of the economic system on human personality, on the political life of nations, and on the cultural life of peoples. To some extent these undesirable results are due to the methods of production adopted. But to the socialists they are the inevitable results of the concentration of ownership, or of economic control, and the private profit motive.

The system gives the absentee capitalists a dictatorship over men while at work — over what they shall make and how they shall make it — that is an offense against human dignity, beyond and above the "richness of the rich and the poverty of the poor." Exercised only with an eye to profit making, the control of the absentee capitalist forces men to produce luxuries, frivolities, and even shoddily made necessities, when millions are in need of well-made houses, furniture and clothing, and of sound, wholesome food. Therefore, according to these critics, production is misdirected, and consumption is distorted. Only by social control of production that would substitute "production for use" for "production for profit" can these evils be eliminated.

The control of the economic machine and the command of wealth that goes with it give the capitalists control also over the political life of the nation and of its cultural environment. This analysis does not necessarily go the full length of economic determinism. But real political democracy is impossible, it is contended, so long as a few have much wealth and keep the many in economic dependence upon them. This control extends to the press and to education in general. Obviously, this is an argument that does not have much point except in a country that boasts of political democracy, freedom of the press, popular education, and freedom of teaching. But in these countries, the socialists have emphasized that Capitalism is undemocratic in the political sense and undemocratic in the social sense as well, in addition to preventing the development of intellectually honest educational systems. The development of a sound, popular culture is also prevented, it is contended, by keeping the mass of people in economic subjection as workers, and at a low standard of living as consumers. It is hardly necessary to add that all groups of socialists hold that Capitalism is the fundamental cause of war; that the capitalists of the several nations, through their attempts to secure markets in other lands to supplement home markets restricted by the inherent contradiction between capitalist production and capitalist laws of distribution, and through their attempts to secure control of sources of raw materials, bring on conflicts that end in war.

It is clear, then, that the socialist indictment of Capitalism extends over a wide range. It has gathered in most of the criticisms leveled at the existing order by those who are not socialists. Exploitation of the worker, denial of the worker's instinct for sound production and craftsmanship, exploitation of the consumers, degradation of the public taste in consumption, waste of natural resources, exaltation of the pursuit of gain, enthronement of inequality, insecurity, thwarting of democracy, control of the press, suppression of freedom of teaching, class conflict, wars between nations — all these are charged by the socialists against private ownership and the profit motive. And all are found by the socialists to be inherent in the system.

NONSOCIALIST ATTACKS ON CAPITALISM

The nonsocialist attacks on Capitalism are sharply distinguished from the socialist analyses in that they do not attribute the evils of Capitalism to private property as such. In large part, they are centered on the free play given to the pursuit of private gain. Whether opposition to freedom of economic action, while still upholding private property as an institution, constitutes opposition to Capitalism is, of course, a matter of definition. Certainly many of those who occupy this position call themselves opponents of Capitalism. To them the whole spirit and practice of economic individualism is an integral part of what they mean by Capitalism.

Religious Reaction against Economic Individualism. The philosophy underlying economic individualism was never universally accepted. Many rejected economic individualism on the pragmatic ground that it did not work out well. The identification of the pursuit of individual interest with the promotion of the general good, that found expression in "the law of economic harmonies", was, they discovered, not supported by the results. But there were others who rejected economic individualism primarily because of the extreme individualistic philosophy on which it was based. The unregulated pursuit of self-interest was, they maintained, against the moral law. They still held to the older doctrine that self-interest must be restrained by moral obligation not to do injustice to others. And they denied that freedom of contract necessarily works justice.

Holding that complete freedom in economic affairs is wrong in principle, these critics of Capitalism found its workings to be frequently evil in practice. Like the socialists they found undue concentration of wealth, unfair distribution of income, bad working conditions and the degradation of human personality. But they found the "essential wrong" of nineteenth-century Capitalism not in private property but in economic individualism, or, as it was frequently called, economic liberalism. The best known indictment of the system from a religious standpoint is the Encyclical Letter of Pope Leo XIII on *The Condition of the Working Classes* (*Rerum Novarum*), issued in 1891. But this encyclical strongly defends the right to private property as a "natural right." It is a plea, not for social ownership of the means of production, but for reform within the institution of private property through the observance of moral standards and, where necessary, state intervention.[6]

The Distributist Attack on Capitalism. The "distributist" attack on Capitalism is centered on large-scale production.[7] Most of the distributists also reject the philosophy of economic individualism, holding it

[6] Pope Leo's analysis was reaffirmed and elaborated forty years later by Pope Pius IX in the encyclical *Quadragesimo Anno*. This encyclical is also referred to under the title *Reconstruction of the Social Order*.

[7] Not all distributists declare themselves opposed to Capitalism. Some prefer to say that they oppose "large-scale Capitalism" or "finance Capitalism" and favor "small Capitalism."

both the cause of the unwholesome structural development that characterizes Capitalism, and a force intensifying its evil results. However, they find the remedy not in any form of social ownership of the means of production but in a return to the ownership of the means of production by *individual* producers. The name "distributist" does not clearly indicate their program. It is not intended to suggest "dividing up" either income or existing property, but a gradual return to widely distributed ownership of production units by those actually using them.

The background of the distributist attack on Capitalism is to be found in a combination of reactions, religious, humanitarian, and cultural, against the existing system in the second half of the nineteenth century. They center around the dwarfing of human personality through making human beings cogs in a machine run by "soulless seekers after profit." They were reactions against both the motivating force of Capitalism and the capitalistic methods of production. The results of capitalistic methods, animated by ruthless disregard of all but profit, were not only exploitation and bad working conditions, but also bad products, degrading both those who made them and those who used them. This type of attack is well exemplified in the writings of John Ruskin.

The distributist movement was not the only "Anti-Capitalism" movement that developed against this background. As has already been pointed out, some of the socialists utilized much of this line of attack against Capitalism. The distinguishing mark of the distributist analysis is its conclusion that the prevalence of large-scale production, industrialism in the technical sense, is incompatible with human dignity. Its bad effects cannot be removed by transferring the ownership or the control of this economic structure to the public or to the workers acting collectively. The distributists are as much opposed to any form of collectivism as they are to Capitalism.

The distributists are also opposed to economic individualism, many of them on ethical grounds. They aim at individual ownership of the means of production, as the basis of economic organization, but not at individualism in the sense of reliance on unrestrained individualistic pursuit of gain. Restraint of acquisitiveness by moral obligation would still be necessary to maintain social justice between man and man, and for the preservation of the distributive economic system. But there would be less need of state intervention, they hold, under their system; the reorganization of the economic structure would largely obviate the necessity of governmental restraint. Indeed, to the distributist, the necessity of so much outside regulation under large-scale production is one evidence of the weaknesses of the system.

In their analysis of the weaknesses of Capitalism as an economic system, the distributists accept most of the socialist reasoning. They find conflict of interest between workers and absentee capitalists, and the same paradox of want in the midst of plenty. Capitalism has reached the stage in which its inefficiency as an economic system is glaring. Instability and insecurity, even for the capitalists, are its obvious marks. But unlike most of the socialists, the distributists find the prevalence of large-scale production uneconomic in and of itself. The boasted efficiency of large-scale operations is to the distributists an economic superstition, except in a few industries that cover but a small fraction of all production of goods and services.

In addition to its economic inefficiency and unwholesome social effects, Capitalism is also, according to the distributists, inimical to true political democracy. Much is made of that argument in the United States at the present moment. "Jeffersonian democracy" is impossible, the distributists hold, unless we return to the economic structure of Jefferson's time, omitting, of course, the plantation system of the South.

The Fascist Attack on Economic Individualism. If economic individualism is essential to Capitalism, then Fascism is opposed to Capitalism. Placing Fascism and Capitalism in opposition runs counter to the loose usage of "fascist" to mean "controlled by the capitalists." The term "Fascist" was introduced by a political party in Italy that called itself by that name, and control by or in the interest of the capitalists is not one of its tenets. But opposition to Socialism is one of its leading principles. Because the Fascists oppose Socialism so strongly, the socialists assert that the Fascist program is one of capitalistic control, and tend to identify Fascism with Capitalism; indeed many of them regard Fascism as Capitalism's last stand.

The doctrines of the Italian Fascists are primarily political; their economic principles are subordinated to their political philosophy. Their movement was at the start a movement of "action", not one growing out of a body of doctrines; the doctrinal side of Fascism was developed after the party had seized political control. Its foundation is the "totalitarian" concept of the state. The Fascist doctrine is that the state is everything, the individual nothing apart from the state. There are no human rights except those granted by the state. All human activity is subject to the control of the state, whether or not that control is carried to the point of active intervention.

No one who holds to this totalitarian doctrine can accept the philosophy of economic individualism; the two are in direct conflict. The Fascists scorn economic individualism, or, as they prefer to call it, economic liberalism, not on religious grounds — indeed, religion itself is subject to the control of the state in the full totalitarian philosophy, — but because economic individualism denies both the philosophical validity and the economic wisdom of state control. Fascist doctrine calls for a "disciplined economic life", with the discipline exercised, of course, by the state.

As to the practical results of economic liberalism, the Fascists agree with the other groups of unfavorable critics of Capitalism that reliance on individual self-seeking, under modern conditions of production and distribution, does not promote the economic welfare of the nation. They agree that it promotes class conflict; but they hold that class conflict can and must be suppressed by the state because it weakens the nation. The Fascists disagree with the distributists in that they believe that large-scale production must be re-tained, because, under state control, it makes for a stronger nation economically.

The Fascists do not oppose private property. This is one reason that the socialists call Fascism the last resort of a Capitalism with its back to the wall. But the Fascists do not regard private property as a natural right. They accept it, for the present at least, as the most expedient basis for the organization of production and distribution. With private property goes private initiative, stimulated by the desire for gain, as a force for economic efficiency. It must be directed and tempered by the state; but so controlled, it can be made to increase the wealth of the nation.

CHAPTER XIII

Socialism

To criticize the workings of an existing system is one thing; to outline a substitute system and prove that an untried system would work better than Capitalism is quite another. That is the position the socialists occupied until a few years ago. "Socialism" meant a body of doctrines, or a program, or a movement — and in none of these phases was it the same to all socialists — but it did not mean an existing economic order. Today the discussion of Socialism is dominated by the fact that there actually exists in one country, Russia, an economic system that is called Socialism by the party in control. The discussion of the forms Socialism should take in other countries, and how it would work, is conducted against the background of the Russian situation. And the program for attaining Socialism in other countries is profoundly affected by what has actually happened in Russia.

Socialism as a criticism of Capitalism was discussed in the preceding chapter. In this chapter we are concerned with socialist programs — programs for the attainment of Socialism and programs for the economic organization of society. Since there has been change and variety in the socialist program, just as there has been in socialist theory, the treatment of the program will also be approached historically.

EARLY MARXIAN PROGRAM

For the Attainment of Socialism. In the light of the Marxian doctrine of economic determinism and its application to the coming of Socialism, there was little to be done actively except to prepare the proletariat for the fulfillment of its "historic mission" when the workings of economic laws had brought about the inevitable collapse of Capitalism. The *ad interim* program was one of spreading the doctrines among the workers and effecting the "solidarity" of the proletariat.

This must be an international solidarity. "The proletariat has no Fatherland." The existing political organization of national states was looked upon as a form of capitalist control and, in addition, as a means of keeping the proletariat in the different countries disunited, even to the point of fighting each other in capitalistic wars. For the time being, the socialists must organize within each nation for the purpose of preaching the socialist doctrine to the workers. As a means of spreading their doctrines more effectively, they must organize a political party in each country, where that was permitted, and elect as many of their members as possible to the legislative assemblies. But there was no expectation that Socialism would be "voted in" peacefully in one country after another. The transition from Capitalism to Socialism would have to be brought about by a revolutionary movement of international scope and permeated by international solidarity of the proletariat.

Moreover, the transition to Socialism could not come until Capitalism had run its course. The economic collapse of Capitalism could be hastened but it could not be dispensed with. The concentration of the ownership of capital, the ever increasing severity of crises and depressions until the last great crisis, the increasing misery and degradation of the proletariat, must all be experienced before the world would be ready for Socialism.

Once the proletariat had seized control of the state it would set up the "dictatorship of the proletariat." This would be necessary in order to suppress all resistance to the establishment of a classless society. Marx thought of the dictatorship of the proletariat as a dictatorship exercised by an overwhelming majority of the people over a minority. By the time the economic collapse of Capitalism came, the great mass of men would be among the class-conscious, revolutionary proletariat. The state would thus be continued through the period of transition, as a necessary agency of coercion in the hands of the proletariat. This explains Marx's bitter feud with the anarchists, who held that the state must be abolished forthwith. Not until Socialism had been fully attained could the state be relinquished, according to Marx. Then it would "wither away."

Marx did not concern himself with the economic structure of the new society. Marx wrote about Capitalism, not about the details of the socialist order. The proletariat would take care of that when the time should come. The first stage of Socialism would be marked by the abolition of private property in the means of production and the substitution of state ownership; the state would become the employer of all the workers. Eventually there would emerge a classless society, in which all would work and each would share in the social product in accordance with his needs, and not in accordance with the quantity and quality of his effort. There would then be no state, as compulsion would no longer be necessary. This would be the second stage of Socialism; this would be the real "communism", the final goal of the social revolution.

EVOLUTIONARY PROGRAM

For the Attainment of Socialism. The non-Marxian approach to socialist doctrine, and the practical abandonment by the Revisionists of the Marxian formula for the economic collapse of Capitalism, cleared the way doctrinally for a consciously planned, gradual transition from Capitalism to Socialism without any sudden scrapping of the capitalistic system. In the last quarter of the nineteenth century, the argument for the feasibility of a gradual, peaceful transition was greatly strengthened by the spread of political democracy and the advance of public ownership, municipal and national. The growth of nonrevolutionary, organized working-class activity in the economic sphere, notably trade unionism and the consumers' co-operative movement, also contributed to the acceptance of the evolutionary, as contrasted with the revolutionary, program for the attainment of Socialism.

The Fabians were the leading exponents of the evolutionary program. The very name that these British socialists chose, "Fabian Society", indicates their confidence in a policy of strategic delay and attrition.[1] Their belief in the superiority of an evolutionary program was doubtless an outgrowth of British political democracy, of British working-class progress in economic organization, and of British aversion to sudden, revolutionary change. But their influence extended far beyond Great Britain.

The evolutionary program contemplates the transfer of the essential means of production from private to social ownership only as rapidly as the agencies of social ownership can be made ready to take care of them. There is to be no forcing of the pace, no dislocation of the workings of the economic system. Starting with the activities most essential to the economic life of the nation, such as transportation and banking, the transfer from private to social ownership is to be effected in one basic industry after another as the country becomes ready for it. And the extinction of the capitalists' title to their property is to be brought about by peaceful, constitutional means. The instru-

[1] The name "Fabian" comes from the name of the Roman general Quintus Maximus Fabius, who won ultimate victory over Hannibal by avoiding a decisive engagement.

ment of change is to be the ballot-box, not the bay-onet. Most of the evolutionary socialists, too, favor compensation for the capitalists, not ruthless "expropri-ation of the expropriators." However, they also favor the imposition of steeply progressive income taxes and inheritance taxes that would wipe out the ex-capital-ists' unearned incomes after a generation or two.

The public utilities of a local character are to be taken over by the local governments in the same way. For the supplying of most types of consumers' goods the already important consumers' co-operative movement is to be encouraged to extend its activities, even to the point of producing for itself in its own plants most of the wares that it would sell to its members. This would be one of the forms of social ownership, characterized by "production for use and not for profit."

The advantage of this program, the evolutionists contend, is that it avoids the chaos and suffering in-volved in a sudden break-up of the existing economic machine. Moreover, it has the practical advantage of a greater appeal to the middle class and the still con-servative portion of the wage-earning population. This has been especially important in Great Britain, for the Fabians have zealously sought the favor of the middle class for a socialist program. Not only would Social-ism be more efficient than Capitalism, they argue, but the transition would not be effected at the price of even a temporary loss of efficiency.

By the outbreak of the World War in 1914 the evo-lutionary program apparently commanded the support of the majority of the socialists. The forcible seizure, in November 1917, of political power in Russia by an extreme faction of socialists, who later adopted the name Communist and, in 1919, founded the Communist International, did not immediately check the more moderate movement. On the contrary, the outcome of the war seemed greatly to strengthen the hand of the evolutionary socialists. The program adopted in 1920 by the Labor and Socialist International, which then represented an overwhelming majority of the socialists, is substantially the program outlined above.

Structure of Socialism. The outline of the evolutionary program for the attainment of Socialism makes it clear that the evolutionary socialists look forward to a socialist order that would permit a diversity in forms of social ownership. The basic industries would be owned by the national government; there would also be municipally owned public utilities; and there would be nationally federated consumers' societies controlling not only the distribution of goods for household and personal consumption but also their production. But, whether the socialized units were owned by the government or by a nation-wide voluntary association of consumers, it would be *consumer* ownership, not *producer* ownership, whether by individual producers, private companies, or associations of workers.

The workers, "whether by hand or brain", would be organized into vocational associations with the right of collective bargaining. They would also have the right to participate in the administration of the socialized industries. But they would not control the administration. They would have the *right* to strike, but it is assumed that no workers would, in fact, strike against the community. All this is outlined in the program adopted by the Labor and Socialist International in 1920.

It is obvious that the kind of Socialism envisaged by the evolutionary socialists does not involve the abolition of the wages system. The managers and workers employed in the socially owned industries and services would still be working for salaries and wages. It is production for *private profit,* not working for wages, that the evolutionists want to abolish. Nor do they insist either on equality of monetary remuneration for all or on distribution according to needs. Most of them assume that there would be differences in salaries and different rates of wages for different classes of work, although the differences would be very much narrower than under Capitalism. The evolutionists do not depend on money incentives alone to get efficient management and good workmanship. The knowledge that they were working for the community instead of for profit-seeking capitalists would, it is assumed, lead both the workers by brain and the workers by hand to give their best efforts without holding out for "all the traffic will bear."

THE SYNDICALIST REACTION

Meanwhile there had been a reaction in some radical quarters against government ownership and control as the substitute for Capitalism. This reaction gave rise to a separate revolutionary movement known as Syndical-ism. It was a movement against Capitalism, but it was marked by a repudiation of "political" Socialism, both with respect to the economic structure of the society proposed as a substitute for Capitalism and with respect to the methods that were to be used to effect the change. So great was the antipathy of the syndical-ists to political action and to government ownership, that most of the socialists refused to recognize the syn-dicalists as socialists at all.

The syndicalist movement was developed within the French organized labor movement. It takes its name from the French term for labor organization — *syn-dicat*. The French labor movement, like most labor movements on the Continent, had been predominantly socialist. But in the last decade of the nineteenth cen-tury, the French labor federation expressed its dis-gust with the "political action" that was an essential part of the official socialist program, whether evolu-tionary or revolutionary. The syndicalists insisted upon "direct action" — that is, action against the capitalists directly in the economic sphere, as contrasted with political action.

The syndicalists held that political action would never accomplish the liberation of the proletariat. The capitalists would always be able to control the legis-lative assemblies. Socialists who were elected to them would lose their revolutionary zeal and become mere politicians, seeking their own political advancement. And such government ownership as might be at-tained by political methods would leave the workers under the control of politicians and bureaucrats, a control little, if any, better than that of the capitalists. Hence, political methods must be rejected in favor of direct action by the workers, the goal of direct action being the displacement of the capitalists in each industry by the workers themselves.

The method of ousting the capitalists and establishing worker control was to be the "general strike." This was to be the consummation of direct action. The general strike was to be the revolution. It was hoped that the revolution might be put through without bloodshed; but if not, the workers were to suppress all attacks. First, the workers must be organized into revolutionary industrial unions. And while perfecting their organization and preparing for the great general strike, the workers were to make the position of the capitalists more and more untenable economically by direct action on a minor scale. Strikes for better terms were to be spread as far as possible through sympathetic strikes by other workers. Even when not openly on strike, the workers were to "strike on the job" by resort to hidden means of crippling the operations — "sabotage."

As the years passed without revealing much progress toward the great general strike to overthrow Capitalism, some of the syndicalist leaders abandoned hope of spontaneous mass action by the proletariat for its own deliverance. The proletariat as a whole was too inert, too awed by the political and economic control exercised by the capitalists, to do anything for itself. There would be no revolution unless the proletariat were pushed into it by a "class-conscious militant minority of the proletariat." Thus, there developed the doctrine that the revolution must be accomplished by a revolutionary vanguard of the proletariat. The proletariat, willingly or unwillingly, would then have to follow the course laid out for it. Force would have to be used to suppress all attacks, from whatever quarter. This was a far cry from the peaceful transition from Capitalism through majority vote, and accompanied by compensation for the capitalists, that the evolutionary socialists favored.

The program of the syndicalists for the economic structure of society, like that of the evolutionary socialists, was closely related to their particular method of overthrowing Capitalism. Syndicalism was not concerned primarily with worker ownership in each industry, as "ownership" would then be meaningless, but with the *control* and *operation* of each industry by the workers actively engaged in it. The economic relations among workers in the respective industries would be settled by some sort of voluntary agreement. The syndicalists were a little vague about this; but in any event, there would be no super-control from outside the industry. Least of all would there be any government control. The syndicalists had no place in their scheme of things for state control. It is not surprising, considering the methods advocated and the kind of economic structure contemplated by the syndicalists, that many of the socialists regarded them not as socialists at all but as "anarchists."

The syndicalist ideas had considerable influence

upon labor movements outside of France, especially in the Latin countries. Whether or not the syndicalists may properly be called socialists, their doctrine also had an important effect upon Socialism. For one thing, it forced the socialists generally to give more attention to the degree of control that should be allowed the workers in the socialized plants. It also threw into the foreground the question of the use of the general strike as a means of overcoming hostile action or compelling favorable action by the government. But after the World War the syndicalist movement declined rapidly, even in France. The more revolutionary spirits seemed to be attracted to Communism, in spite of the fact that the communist program is very different from that favored by the syndicalists.[2]

Gild Socialism. In Great Britain, the advocacy of workers' control of socialized industry led to a somewhat distinct movement, called "Gild Socialism." As the name implies, Gild Socialism was one of the results of the "back-to-the-gilds" reaction against Capitalism that was noticeable in Great Britain in the first decade of this century. Many of those who shared in this reaction were really distributists. They wanted to return not only to the economic ideals of the gild era but also to small units of production. But the movement attracted many whose main interest was in workers' control of production and not in reducing the size of the units of production. Syndicalists joined the movement with a view to turning it toward the attainment of workers' control by direct action. Finally,

[2] See below, pp. 321–327.

Gild Socialism emerged as another form of Socialism, accepting technological industrialism with social ownership.

What differentiated the gild socialists from other socialists was their insistence that social ownership should be accompanied by workers' control in each industry. The gilds were to be national industrial gilds of workers, each gild controlling and operating its own industry, and not associations of craftsmen individually owning their instruments of production. In this respect the gild socialist structure resembled that advocated by the syndicalists. As socialists, the gild socialists differed sharply from the majority of the Fabians, who stood for consumer control as against worker control. After 1927 little was heard of Gild Socialism.

COMMUNISM

Communism is an extreme form of Socialism. The communist philosophy and the communist program are essentially Marxist. Indeed, Marx and his immediate followers called themselves communists. The famous Communist Manifesto, issued in 1848, was written by Marx and Engels for a small group of revolutionists that called itself the Communist League. The name afterwards became submerged until it was resurrected in 1918 by the Russian Bolshevists (the majority wing of the Russian Social Democratic Party). The Bolshevists were Marxists and they again took the name "Communist" to signify their rejection of the more moderate types of Socialism. In 1919 they organized the Communist International to spread their ideas and promote imitation of their own revolutionary program.

COMMUNIST PROGRAM

For the Attainment of Communism. The Communist program has passed from the original Marxian phase of preparation for the coming collapse of Capitalism to one of revolutionary action. For this Lenin, the leader of the Russian Bolshevist faction from 1903 to his death in 1924, is largely responsible. Lenin taught that the militant minority, the "vanguard of the proletariat", should seize power wherever and whenever the opportunity offered and use its control to introduce Socialism as rapidly as possible. When the World War broke out, he insisted that the time was ripe. The socialists should turn "this capitalistic war" into the "class war", that is, the socialist revolution.

Lenin even held that the socialists should seize control first in Russia, although Russia had not yet passed through the "capitalistic stage." Western Europe, he argued, was economically ripe for Socialism, and Socialism could therefore be established in Russia in conjunction with the rest of Europe. The seizure of power in Russia would lead to the class revolution throughout Europe. Russia could then be made socialist as a part of a socialist Europe. Most of the socialists, even Russian socialists, disagreed with Lenin, but this did not stop him from going ahead with his program. The fact that the Bolshevists succeeded in seizing control in Russia and maintaining control, even though the rest of Europe did not rise as he predicted, has made Lenin a communist idol second only to Marx — and a very close second.

We shall not detail here the circumstances under which the Bolshevists, in November 1917, succeeded in seizing the power in Russia. It must be emphasized, however, that the government overthrown by the Bolshevists was not the old Czarist government. That had been overthrown in the previous March. It had been succeeded by a "Provisional Government", which was apparently aiming at the establishment of a republican form of government on a democratic basis. The head of the Provisional Government, Kerensky, was a socialist, nominally at least, and it contained several other socialists; none of them was a Bolshevist. However, as the government had no deep roots, it was very weak and was overthrown by the Bolshevists without much resistance. There is no evidence that the majority of the Russian people, or even of the Russian socialists, wanted the Bolshevists to take control. On the contrary, such elections as there were resulted favorably for the government and against the Bolshevists. The Bolshevist *coup d'état* was a negation of democracy.

Once in power, the Communists, as they now called themselves, showed amazing vigor and equal ruthlessness. They defeated all attempts to unseat them by force of arms in a period of civil war running over three years. They suppressed all other opposition by terroristic methods. In a word, they established a dictatorship of the Communist Party. It cost millions of lives and a terrible suppression of human rights, but the Communists are still in control. The Russian Communist Party proved that it could be done, in Russia at least.

The Communist International, also called the "Third International", was founded by and is still controlled by the leaders of the Communist Party in Russia. Its program is the overthrow of all other governments and the seizure of power by the communists, whenever the opportunity is presented in any country. It is the business of the Communist International to promote the communist revolution everywhere. The orthodox Communist Party in each country is a section of the Communist International and is bound by iron discipline to follow the orders of the International. In recent years the Communist International has muted the note of revolutionary overthrow, but there is no convincing evidence that it has abandoned the program of bringing about a communist dictatorship in other countries by whatever means may seem most expedient at the moment. To do so would be to abandon one of the basic principles of Communism as an international movement.[3] And to accept the decision of the majority, when that majority is not communist, is not one of its principles.

Once having seized the power, the Communist Party will proceed to build up a communist society

[3] There are some communists, like Leon Trotsky, who denounce the Third International, under its present leadership, on the ground that it has betrayed the revolutionary cause.

as rapidly as this can be done. If Russian experience is any guide, the communist policy in this respect is one of opportunism. There the expropriation of the capitalists and the large landowners was undertaken at once, under the guise of the "economic disarming of the capitalists and the landlords" by the proletariat and the peasants, but the industrial plants were not brought under effective governmental control for some time thereafter, and the "collectivization" of agriculture was not attempted until ten years after the political revolution. Meanwhile, the Communist Party alternately accelerated and retarded the pace of socialization, because of the necessity of making "economic concessions" from time to time in order to retain the power politically. No doubt the fact that Russia was overwhelmingly a small-farm agricultural country, and that the technological basis of Socialism had to be built up from relatively small foundations, retarded the progress toward socialization. Large-scale production, with its technologically capitalistic methods, meant the raising of capital, and nearly all of that capital had to be raised through an "abstinence" imposed upon the Russian people by the Communist rulers; the rate of consumption had to be kept below the rate of production. And in agriculture the individual cultivation of small peasant holdings had to be superseded by some form of large holding in order to permit the use of capitalistic methods.

Another very important reason for the slow progress of socialization in Russia was the fact that only a tiny proportion of the population were Communists when that group seized the power. The political *coup d'état* left the real social revolution still to be undertaken. Over eighty per cent of the population were peasants. The industrial and urban wage workers proved fairly tractable, but the peasants' ideas were, for the most part, far removed from Communism. What they wanted was to divide up the large estates among themselves, and to be left then in undisturbed possession of their holdings, free to produce and trade their surplus products. Before the Communists could get very far with the establishment of a socialistic structure that they could operate, they had to remold the minds of the Russian people. They undertook that task with a total disregard of individual human rights. No opposition to communist teaching, in the fields of economics, politics, philosophy, or religion, was tolerated.

Whether or not the Communist Party has achieved in Russia an economic order that is superior to Capitalism may be debated. But that the present Russian system was established by the ruthless suppression of human rights and democratic processes cannot be questioned.

THE ECONOMIC STRUCTURE UNDER COMMUNISM

The question of what will be the ultimate economic structure under Communism is still unanswered. Communists do not seem to be generally committed to any rigid universal pattern of economic organization. Like Marx, they hold that economic life must first be socialized, but the forms to be followed are apparently a matter of opportunism. In Russia, after twenty years of dictatorship by the Communist Party, economic forms are still undergoing change. However, Russia is said to be in the "first stage of Socialism." [4] The Russian Communist Party does not contend that it has established Communism yet. The communists' ultimate goal is still, presumably, a classless society, in which there will be no coercion, and in which each will share in the common product in accordance with his needs.

COMMUNISM IS MORE THAN AN ECONOMIC PROGRAM

Communism cannot be judged as an economic program alone. Communism is far more than an economic program or an economic system; it is "a way of life." It is frankly materialistic and militantly atheistic. It is based on a totalitarian concept of society, and is therefore anti-individualist.

Because of the dictatorship in Russia many persons assume that the totalitarian state is part of the communist creed. This is incorrect. It would be more correct to say that the totalitarianism in Russia is that of the Communist Party, not of the state. The state is only a means to an end. According to the Marxian teaching, the state is eventually to "wither away" and disappear. If the state seems all powerful in Russia

[4] This is what is said by the Communist Party in Russia. There are communists elsewhere, like the followers of Leon Trotsky, who declare that the system in Russia is not Socialism at all, but merely "Stalinism."

now, it is because the Communist Party that controls it still finds use for it. The Russian Communist Party has undoubtedly become very nationalistic in its policies, and it may be that the older concept of the vanishing state will itself be shed by the communists. But Communism as a historical movement of international character had no place in its ideology for the nationalistic totalitarian state.

RUSSIAN ECONOMIC SYSTEM

The existing economic system in Russia must not be regarded as the summation of the communist economic program. Russian economic life is declared to be almost entirely socialized, but it is also acknowledged that Communism has not yet been attained. But whether or not the Russian system fulfills the hopes of communists for a new social order, it is a going system and as such must be briefly examined.

The Economic Organization. In "heavy" industry, mining, and transportation, state ownership is practically complete in Russia. In "light" industry — chiefly consumers' goods industries — state ownership is predominant. There is some production of goods and services by municipalities but this development is as yet relatively small; Russia lacks the background of municipal self-government found in most western countries. Nor has there been much development of production by consumer co-operatives for their own members. That has not been encouraged by the Communist Party. Another minor form of ownership is that by producer co-operatives of small handicraft or domestic producers. It is the policy of the Communist Party to encourage, if not to coerce, the formerly independent small producers into co-operative organizations and to transform these organizations as rapidly as possible into production units using advanced technological methods.

The leading form of socialization in agriculture is the collective farm. This is outwardly a co-operative organization of formerly independent peasant cultivators. In most collective farms the land and the equipment are held by the "collective", but each household is allowed a small plot to cultivate for its own consumption and each may keep its own poultry, goats, and other domestic animals. The main crop is cultivated in common and is the property of the group. The ownership of the land remains with the Russian people, but the present policy is to allow the collective to remain in undisturbed possession and to allow each household continued tenure of its own plot.

The collective farm is not the form of socialization preferred by the Communists originally. What they wanted was state farms, run on technologically capitalistic lines, with wage labor. However, they were confronted by the stubborn fact that the peasants had the land and would not give it up without resistance. When the Communists renewed their drive for socialization in 1928, they adopted the collective farm as the most feasible next step for the collectivization of agriculture in a peasant country. Whether it will remain as the final form, or be transformed eventually into a state farm, remains to be seen.

The drive for the collectivization of agriculture was motivated by a crying need to increase the productivity of agriculture, as well as by a desire to socialize a sector that had hitherto resisted socialization. It was necessary to increase agricultural exports in order to finance the rapid industrialization of the country and to feed the industrial population and the army. Undoubtedly the collective farm represented an advance, technologically, over the existing methods of individual peasant cultivation. It made possible the use of mechanical methods; collectivization and mechanization of agriculture were regarded as almost synonymous. If the peasants had developed the co-operative farm voluntarily, it would doubtless have been widely acclaimed as a great advance. But the coercion of the peasants to join and the measures taken to "liquidate" those opposed to collectivization, or even suspected of being opposed to it, is one of the blackest chapters in the history of social change. In spite of all resistance, however, collectivization has been attained over nearly all of the cultivated area of Russia. If this be socialization, then Russian agriculture is almost as much socialized as Russian industry.

The socialization of production has carried with it the socialization of trade. State-owned agencies now carry on nearly all the trade of the country. Individual middlemen have been almost entirely eliminated, although it is impossible to tell just how much illegal trading is secretly conducted. The voluntary consumers' co-operative movement, once very important, is being forced out. It was never entirely trusted by the Communist leaders. Lenin declared that it was infected with "bourgeois ideology."

The Question of Control. The outline of the economic structure in terms of ownership tells only part of the story. It has been realized for some years that the older concept of ownership has little significance in a socialized enterprise. The real question is, "Where is the control?" The answer in Russia is, "In the Communist Party." In Russia all production units, whether state, municipal, co-operative, or collective, have to conform to the policies of the Communist Party. In spite of the changes recently made in the constitution of the Union of Socialist Soviet Republics, there is no evidence that the real dictatorship of the Communist Party has been relaxed in either the economic or the political sphere.

The position of the so-called trade unions in Russia is a case in point. In capitalist countries the unions are not only collective bargaining organizations but agencies for working-class opposition to the policies of either employers or the government. Their protests may not be very effective, but the unions are at least legally free to make them. In Russia the unions are organizations for securing the co-operation of the workers in the production policy and in the execution of the Communist Party policy generally. They also carry on welfare work for their members and administer some types of social insurance. The unions go through the forms of collective bargaining, but all important policies with respect to wages, hours, and working conditions are determined by the Communist Party as part of the economic plan for the year. Strikes are not tolerated.

The kind of control that exists in Russia is obviously not producer control. Neither is it consumer control. Nor can it be called citizen control; Russia is far from a political democracy now, whatever the future developments may be. It is a form of control not considered in the debates among the socialists in the pre-war period over worker control versus consumer or citizen control. Behind all the outward forms of ownership runs the control by a highly disciplined party comprising but a small fraction of the population.

Shares in Distribution as Incentives to Production. One thing that may fairly be claimed for the Russian economic system is that it is a system that operates without the individual profit motive. There is almost no private enterprise in Russia in the ordinary sense. The direction of production is from above. There is no income-share in distribution for risk-taking.

What of interest, as a reward for "abstinence", to secure the accumulation and preservation of capital? The Russian Communists have given an amazing demonstration of the ability of a socialist administration to add to the capital of a nation by enforced abstinence. It was not by voluntary individual savings that the great increase in Russian capital has been brought about, but by "loading" the price of state-made goods and by taxation. There has been relatively little borrowing from individuals. The capital has been accumulated and preserved by keeping consumption below what it otherwise would have been — and that in a country for years close to the starvation line. That this accumulation would have been secured by voluntary individual action, under the stimulus of a higher rate of interest, seems hardly likely. In this matter of raising capital, the Communist dictatorshp has been more efficient than Capitalism itself. The amount of capital saved in Russia since the Revolution is apparently greater than the amount expropriated at the time of the Revolution.

The remuneration for work "by hand or by brain" is not left to freedom of contract. This does not mean, however, that monetary rewards are not held out as an incentive to effort. There is neither equality of remuneration nor the application of the old communistic principle of "from each according to his ability and to each according to his needs." "From each according to his ability" is stressed, but the appeal to "duty" is reinforced by variation of monetary rewards according to productive results, particularly in the case of the manual workers. There are graded scales of wages and piece-work payment within the grades. Even on the collective farms, the piece-work system of payment is widely used.

If an agricultural collective be looked upon as a group of individuals carrying on a joint enterprise, it may be said to be operated for private gain. If a collective produces a larger crop, its members, as a group, receive a larger reward in the form of a larger price for the joint product. And this reward may contain some of the elements of an unearned surplus, due to superior soil or more advantageous location. This apparent inconsistency is tolerated because of the desire to encourage maximum production. But the agricultural population as a whole must buy and sell at prices that are subject to control in accordance with a general plan.

Other Incentives to Production. The incentives to efficient production are by no means solely of a monetary character. Even the wage earners, and especially the manual workers in industry, are stimulated by motives ranging all the way from zeal for Communism to fear of punishment. It is difficult, of course, to separate the zeal for the success of a communist program from zeal for the success of the Russian nation. Citations for distinguished accomplishment are common. So are public denunciation and public ridicule for failure to meet the quotas set. Especially efficient brigades of workers are brought in to demonstrate to the less efficient what can be done. And there is always the fear of punishment for falling behind or spoiling a job, as "sabotage of the Revolution."

The weakest point in the Russian productive system seems to be what is ordinarily called management. The incentives for success are there. There is the usual incentive of the desire to hold one's place and to gain promotion. The salary range is not so great as in capitalist countries, but position means much more. "Position" in Russia means not only prestige, but preference in the allotment of scarce goods, from housing to seats in a railway carriage. On the other side is the fear of denunciation for sabotage, and severe punishment. The insecurity of position is more than mere economic insecurity. There is little of the easygoing, complacent, immune disregard of efficiency that many writers used to picture as the inevitable characteristic of management under Socialism. But in spite of the positive incentive to success, and the negative incentive through fear of punishment, management in Russian industry is still inefficient, whether judged by the standards of capitalistic countries or the standards set up by the Russian Communists themselves. Some Communists ascribe this to the alleged fact that the managers as a class are not wholeheartedly in sympathy with the communist ideas.

Economic Planning. The Russian economic system has all the institutional requisites of a planned economy. Inasmuch as production and the agencies of distribution are socially owned and subject to a unified control, the production and distribution of goods can be directed according to a central plan instead of being left to individual choice. And the Communist Party has subjected Russian economic life to direction, with definite objectives in view.

During recent years there has been much demand outside Russia for economic planning. The declared objective is such a co-ordination of production with consumption demands as will permit the full use of productive resources, insuring both stability and the fullest measure of abundance that productive possibilities will allow. This kind of planning assumes carefully prepared control estimates which will serve as a guide to production. It assumes a co-ordination in timing of the actual production in various branches of industry. If the estimates in any important branch of activity are not attained, or are exceeded, the other

related productive activities are thrown out of align-
ment with their control estimates, and the planning
is vitiated to that extent.

The Russian planning has not been of this kind.
Its main objective has not been the co-ordination of
production with predetermined estimates of consumption, but the attainment of the highest possible volume
of production. The quotas established are goals to
strive for, not figures that must be strictly adhered to.
When a quota is exceeded, it is a matter for great
rejoicing, not an evidence of a mistake in planning.
The quotas are ultimately fixed, not by statisticians or
technicians, but by the Party chieftains. The famous
first Five-Year Plan was a drive for greatly increased
production, not a planning of production to fit consumption needs. The original figures were later re-
vised upward in many respects. In some lines of production the quotas were exceeded; in others they were
not attained. The same is true, generally, of the second
Five-Year Plan, begun in 1933. The primary objectives of Russian planning have been the upbuilding of
capital equipment — the "material basis of Socialism"
— and the strengthening of the war machine. The
meeting of consumption needs has been a decidedly
secondary purpose. The plans for increased production
of consumers' goods have been sidetracked repeatedly
to allow greater concentration on the heavy industries
or production of war equipment. The production of
consumption goods has, in many particulars, lagged behind the figures of the plan.

One of the great obstacles to the execution of the

Russian plans has been the dependence on agriculture. It is the agricultural surplus — the surplus of production over domestic consumption — that has been mainly relied upon to pay for the great increase in capital equipment and the military preparations. And agricultural production is peculiarly unpredictable because of its dependence upon natural forces. But in Russia there has been the additional uncertainty as to what the peasants would do — whether they would sow all the available land and whether they would hold out their surplus instead of marketing it in ways that would permit the disposition of it according to the plan. In the past few years the results have been more satisfactory, largely because of the increased degree of effective control made possible by collectivization.

Although the objectives and character of economic planning in Russia have differed from those of the kind of planning advocated for the United States, one great advantage claimed for it is that it has kept the productive machine running at full speed while the capitalist countries have been floundering in a depression. This cannot be denied. One result has been the practical elimination of involuntary unemployment. Labor may not be free in Russia — and there may be countless instances of the coercion of individuals — but employment is there for those who want it, except those who have incurred the displeasure of the Party. No doubt this continuity of production and absence of unemployment are due in part to the fact that Russia has a great lack of even the commonest consumption necessities; the problem would be different if production were largely for a luxury or semi-luxury demand subject to rapid changes. But it is also due, in large part, to the fact that production is not for private profit. When estimates are shown to be mistaken, they can be corrected, and production redirected. There is no need to wait for the slow operation of natural economic forces. A socialized economy can put the loss of mistaken production on society as soon as the mistake is apparent, and readjust production immediately. It does not have to wait for the slow process of readjustment through liquidation. Socialism may not be worth the price, but the strongest challenge offered by the U.S.S.R. to Capitalism in other countries comes from the fact that production continued at an increasing pace right through a period of world-wide depression.

Economic Results. If the Russian system be regarded as merely an economic system, and the terrible cost of its establishment be overlooked, it must be admitted that it works. It produces far more goods and services than did pre-war Russia. And of the portion that is distributed among the people, as distinct from the portion that is added to capital or to national defense, a much larger share goes to the workers by hand or brain. The peasants in the collectives are better off materially than were the great majority of the peasants in pre-war days; and the industrial and urban workers now enjoy greater real wages, including everything from housing to insurance benefits. They have more opportunities for education. They have also the satisfaction of being members of a favored, instead of a despised, class.

If the Russian economic system had been brought about by voluntary action, without suppression of human rights, it would have to be recognized as an advance over the pre-war system. But pre-war Russia is not a fair basis of comparison. What the Communists have accomplished must be compared with a conjectural result; namely, what would have been attained if the Provisional Government had been allowed to pursue its avowed program of peaceful reform by democratic methods.

THE ECLIPSE OF EVOLUTIONARY SOCIALISM

In the last few years Communism has obtained a noticeable ascendancy in the world of Socialism. In the years immediately following the Bolshevist *coup d'état,* the majority of socialists were bitterly opposed to the actions and program of the Bolshevists and their Communist International. The Labour and Socialist International, the organization of the majority group, condemned dictatorship of whatever kind and repudiated "methods of violence and all terrorism." The break of the majority socialists with the communists on this point was more than a disagreement on principles; the Russian Bolshevists had executed a number of socialists and had suppressed all socialist parties but their own. The communists, for their part, were most scornful of the "yellow socialists" of the majority. The breach between the two wings of Socialism seemed too wide to be healed. The German Social Democrats and the British Labour Party (committed since 1918 to a program of evolutionary Socialism) seemed to have more in common with the democratic progressives in nonsocialist parties than with the communists.

But the march of events in the past decade, and more strikingly since 1930, has lowered the prestige of peaceful, democratic methods among the socialists. In Germany the Social Democratic Party, after having been in power for several months in the winter of 1918–1919 and close to power for a dozen years thereafter without appreciably promoting the advent of Socialism, was suppressed in 1933 by the so-called National Socialist government. In Austria the socialists revolted in February 1934, in order, they alleged, to anticipate an attempt to suppress them. They were defeated and outlawed as a party. In both Germany and Austria the socialists were denied the use of those democratic methods that the majority of socialists had so long espoused as the only proper means of attaining Socialism. In Italy, of course, this situation had prevailed since 1922. Even in England, where the Labour Party was still free to use democratic methods, several of its leaders had deserted it to join a national coalition government in 1931, and the party had suffered a severe defeat in the ensuing election.

In contrast to all this, the Communists have held on in Russia and have achieved socialization. In Russia "production for use instead of for profit" is in actual operation. There is more and more disposition among socialists to overlook the means and applaud the result.

Moreover, the Russian government is now less bent on promoting revolution in democratic countries than on seeking their support against governments that, bitterly hostile to Socialism, have suppressed all open socialist activity. Terming these governments "fascist", the communists now seek the support of all socialists in the expected struggle between Fascism and Communism. This is a marked change from the tactics the communists pursued in Germany prior to the coming of the Nazi dictatorship.

Thus, the present policy of the Communist International favors a united front of all socialist parties to combat Fascism. Undoubtedly the communists hope to take the lead in any such alliance. It may be that alliances with less extreme and less violent socialist groups outside Russia will soften the communist program. On the other hand, it is not unlikely that the more incisive character of the communist program, and the fact that communists are in control in a powerful nation, will attract those who put Socialism above democracy and will drive the more compromising reformers away from Socialism and into one or another of the social reform parties. Certain it is that we hear more of Communism today than of evolutionary Socialism.

Nonsocialist Systems

ITALIAN FASCISM AND THE
CORPORATIVE SYSTEM

FASCISM is primarily a political movement. Its program is first of all political and only secondarily economic. Just as its theories proceed from the central doctrine of the supremacy of the state in all human affairs, its economic system is one based on state control of economic life.

The Fascist method of establishing its system was that of force and dictatorship. The "March on Rome" in 1922 was a leaf out of the book of the Russian Bolshevists. The resort to force by the extreme wing of Socialism in Russia was followed a few years later by a resort to force in Italy by a party bitterly opposed to Communism. Each group set up a dictatorship of its own party in its respective country. In Russia it was a dictatorship of a class-conscious party bent on prosecuting the class war; in Italy it was a dictatorship of a nation-conscious party bent on suppressing class conflict. Both movements rejected the peaceful ways of democracy.

It is fair to say that with the Fascists the question of the particular form of the economic structure is less important than the principle that it shall be controlled, in the national interest, by the state. The particular economic structure now found in Fascist Italy has no more finality than has the collective farm in Communist Russia. For example, the transfer of the ownership of heavy industry to the state is not incompatible with fascistic doctrines; it is simply a question of whether it would promote the national interest to put this or that industry under government ownership rather than to leave it under private ownership and government control.

THE ITALIAN CORPORATIVE SYSTEM

The officially approved form of economic organization in Italy today is the so-called "corporative" system.[1] It is based on private ownership but it is a form of organization that places government control in the foreground. Whether the control be exercised in large or small degree, government control is a characteristic feature of the "corporative state." The dictatorship of the Fascist Party is also an outstanding feature of the system. One can conceive of a corporative system in a

---

[1] This term is less ambiguous than the term "corporate system." The term is not confined to the Italian system. There are so-called corporative systems in several other countries. There are also many advocates of what they call a corporative system in which government intervention would be but a last resort. The description here is restricted to the Italian system.

country in which the government itself is democratic and under which the internal organization and operation of the "corporation" are based on majority rule, but neither is the case in Italy. The Fascist Party controls both the internal operation of the corporations and the state that exercises the external control. And fascistic doctrine demands that this be so.

Structural Organization. The corporation in the Italian corporative system is not a joint-stock company. It is an expression of the solidarity of the owners, the salaried and wage-earning employees, and the state. The corporation controls the industry, but it does not own it. Ownership remains with those who supply the capital. They have the initiative in the operation of the system and they employ the workers. To this extent the system is based on private enterprise. But it differs from Capitalism in not permitting freedom of economic action to either owners or employees.

The employees and the employers are organized into parallel organizations. The organizations of the workers are called syndicates. The employers' organizations are also frequently called syndicates, but it will make for clearness to use the term "association" for them and confine the term "syndicate" to the organizations of workers. The local syndicates and associations are combined into parallel regional and national organizations. They deal with each other locally and, where necessary, regionally and nationally. The highest organization of employers or employees is the national confederation. The confederation is a co-ordinating and regulatory organization rather than a collective bar-

gaining unit. There are at present six national con-
federations of employers' associations and six of employees' syndicates.

The syndicates are recognized by the government
as having governmental functions and are under government control. They are, of course, under Fascist
control, for the Fascists virtually suppressed the former
unions — whether socialist or Catholic — and substituted Fascist syndicates for them. As few as ten per
cent of the workers in any group may, with government
approval, organize a syndicate that will be recognized
by the government as the only syndicate allowed to
function for that group of workers. The officers must
be approved by the government. The Fascist control
of the syndicates is thus complete. Similarly, those
enterprisers employing ten per cent of the workers in
any group may, with government approval, form an
association that will be given exclusive government
recognition as the agent of all the employers.

The terms of the labor contract are agreed upon
between the Fascist syndicates and the Fascist associations. They are binding on all employers and employees
in the area and industry covered and are enforceable
in a special set of courts. In case the syndicate and the
association are unable to agree, there is mediation by
the corporation. If that fails to bring about agreement,
there is what amounts to compulsory arbitration. Strikes
and lockouts are forbidden. There must be no class
war.

The respective syndicates and associations are linked
together, by industries or groups of industries, in the

corporations. Twenty-two such corporations were set up in 1934. Each corporation is intended to represent one division of production, commerce, or service. The production of the raw materials and the processing of them are under the same corporation. For example, the production of textile fibers and the manufacture of textiles are under a single corporation, although the first may be considered agriculture and the second manufacturing. Services such as water, gas and electricity are under a single corporation.

The governing body of the corporation is composed of representatives of the federated syndicates and associations, representatives of the government, and representatives of the Fascist Party. The function of the corporation is to unite the workers by hand and brain and the employers in co-operative effort in the national interest and to see that the government's policy — which is the policy of the Fascist Party — is carried out. The corporation is expected to reconcile the diverse economic interests within the industry, whether these involve disputes between employers and workers or between enterprisers at different stages of the productive process — such as growers of beets and refiners of sugar — or producers of competing products, such as silk and rayon. It has the authority to regulate prices.

The corporations are united under a Central Corporative Committee, with the Minister of Corporations at its head. Presumably the Central Corporative Committee will become the highest legislative authority in economic matters. It is called a "representative" legislative body on vocational instead of geographical lines.

It need hardly be said, however, that it is not a freely elected body, even on a vocational basis.

Operation of the System. Obviously this system is not based on freedom of economic action. It has been said by some opponents of the system that it means a servile status for labor and freedom of action for employers. There is not sufficient evidence to warrant the second conclusion. Labor is certainly not free to organize as it chooses for collective bargaining, nor free to strike. But the employers are not free to impose any terms they wish upon their workers or to sell their goods at whatever prices they wish. There is not even full freedom of investment. It is a system of disciplined economic activity under state control. Its purpose is not the highest economic gain for the individual but the strengthening of the nation. Under it the energy of the nation may be, and has been, diverted from maximum production for consumption to building up a greater productive equipment and greater military power — and this in a nation poor in natural resources.

The profit motive is not abolished, but every effort is made to subordinate it to the attainment of the national purpose. This is true of the wage motive also. The incentive of individual gain is held in check by, and supplemented by, a sense of national duty on the part of each person to give his best efforts. The Fascist Party attempts to keep all employers and workers at a "high ideal tension" for the aggrandizement of the nation.

The results of the operation of the system in raising

the standard of living have not been noteworthy. Real wages, including insurance benefits, which are not as extensive in Italy as in Russia or Germany or England, have not been appreciably raised, if, indeed, they did not fall during the world-wide depression. For Fascist Italy did not succeed in avoiding the depression. Whether the workers in a poor country like Italy are better off materially than they would be under Capitalism, is a question difficult to answer.

FASCISM AS "A WAY OF LIFE"

It has been repeatedly emphasized that Fascism is more than an economic system. Like Communism it is "a way of life." It has its own distinctive social philosophy. It has a concept of the state that is essentially pagan. And it holds that war is necessary for national realization, regarding war as the highest test of manhood and of national virtue. Fascism is not atheistic like Communism. It suits the policy of the Fascist leaders to encourage rather than to oppose religion. But the Church, like the individual, has no rights except those the state chooses to give it. Like Communism, Fascism asserts its right to control the education of youth, the press, all agencies that mold opinion, and all instruments of culture. It thus seeks to assimilate the minds of the people to its will. The fascist ideology is in these respects remarkably similar to that of the communists. Like Communism, and German National Socialism, it bows to no superior right, whether of the individual or of the majority.

NATIONAL SOCIALISM IN GERMANY

German National Socialism closely resembles Italian Fascism in its subordination of the economic to the political, in its glorification of the nation, in its contempt for nineteenth-century political democracy, in its dictatorship by a party, and in its bitter opposition to class conflict. It differs noticeably from Italian Fascism, however, in its emphasis on racial superiority.

German National Socialism is not Socialism in the generally accepted meaning of the term. It denounces all Marxism. Its philosophy is decidedly antisocialistic, whether Marxian or evolutionary. Its economic program is not socialistic, but is based on private ownership of property. The party took the name "National Socialist" in order to emphasize its nationalistic character as opposed to Marxism. Its central doctrine is not social ownership, but national solidarity based on race.

Before its rise to power the National Socialist Party attacked "big business" and "finance capitalism." It especially denounced "interest slavery." It was making its economic appeal primarily to the agricultural population and the professional and salaried middle classes. And the appeal was later widened to attract as many of the workers as possible from the Social Democrats and the Communists. It held out the hope of economic liberation to a people that had suffered from extreme inflation and was then suffering from a severe economic depression. The liberation was to come not only from throwing off the economic chains imposed upon Germany by the Allies but also from economic reorganization and a fairer distribution of the national income. However, the economic program was far from definite.

Outwardly there has been little change in the economic structure in Germany since the Nazi dictatorship was established in 1933. Big business has not been broken up. The most marked change is in the status of labor. The old labor organizations have been suppressed, and a "German labor front" under National Socialist control has been set up in their place. The employers also belong to the "labor front"; this reflects the rejection of any conflict of interests between employees and employers. The enterpriser is given full control over his workers; he is the "leader", they are merely followers. There is no real collective bargaining, although there is provision for appeal to special labor courts against injustice; strikes are not tolerated.

It must be remembered that there was a large measure of government control in economic matters in Germany before the Nazi dictatorship. Now, all business is potentially subject to the control of a party committed to a totalitarian nationalism, even though that control is not expressed through a corporative structure as in Italy. It may be that in time all economic life in Germany will be directed from above and bent toward national self-sufficiency and ever increasing military strength.

DISTRIBUTISM

The distributist program differs radically from Communism, Italian Fascism, and German National Socialism in that it rejects totalitarianism of any kind. It also rejects large-scale production except where its technological superiority is so great as to make its replacement by small units practically impossible. It is a program for diffused ownership as opposed to concentrated ownership, whether social or private. The distributist ideal is the small unit, whether in manufacture, agriculture, or trade, operated by the individual who owns it. Factory production methods may have to be tolerated for essential machinery, automobiles, and the like, but the ownership should not be concentrated; it should be diffused, preferably among those actively carrying on the production. Large units will also be necessary for the production of power, and for railroads, but these should be owned by the active workers or by the government. Consumer co-operative ownership is also favored for the present as an alternative to ownership by large distributing corporations. However, the small unit should be the *prevailing* type, both in production and in trade.

To make the small shop and the small farm, each individually owned, an efficient economic unit, it should be supplemented for purchasing and marketing, and for agricultural-product processing, by co-operative societies of the producers. But the ideal is the processing and preparation of as many things as possible in the home. The economic life of the nation should be centered in the household.

The distributists' program is not a revolutionary one. It calls for no dictatorship to put it into effect. It demands first of all that the nation use all legal means to check concentration. Much of the concentration that has been brought about in ownership or in financial control has been effected, they insist, in contravention of the law. The law should be enforced to stop the process.[2]

Beyond that, the government should take positive measures to encourage the growth of small units under individual ownership. It should aid tenant cultivators to become owners. It should encourage co-operative societies, especially producers' co-operatives. Differential taxation should favor the small shop and the small store. Electric power should be supplied cheaply to small production units. These are but examples of what might be done. The resultant economic organization will not be rigid or all of one pattern. But it will be one in which ownership of productive property will be widely diffused, and "private property in the means of production" will once again mean *individual* ownership of the means of production used by the producer.

It should hardly be necessary to add that Distributism, too, is "a way of life." The only wholesome society, the distributists maintain, is one based on a wide diffusion of productive property; that is the only enduring support of family life and of democracy. It is the

[2] *Cf.* McIsaac and Modlin, *Social Control of Industry* (1938).

only way of preserving individual freedom, and is the only economic system that will permit the full development of human personality.

IN CONCLUSION

It was pointed out above that pure Capitalism exists in no important country. Even in countries still called capitalistic, like Great Britain and the United States, there is no longer, if there ever was, full freedom of economic action. Nor is large-scale production all pervasive. In some other countries that are not communistic, nor patterned after Fascist Italy, small-scale production is still predominant, as in Denmark. Sweden is often referred to as a country with a "mixed" economic system. Side by side in Sweden are found large units under corporate ownership, small business units, consumers' co-operatives that do a considerable proportion of the retail business of the country and also produce for themselves some of the goods they sell, and a large degree of government ownership in transportation, communication, power production and natural resources. But these forms of ownership are found, to some degree, even in predominantly capitalistic countries. It is a question of proportions.

Capitalism in the United States and England is still undergoing change. Certainly it is not characterized by the freedom of economic action that featured nineteenth-century Capitalism. The tendency seems to be toward more, rather than less, government regulation. The glorification of profit making for its own sake is less conspicuous. The necessity of recognizing "obligations", whether moral or merely social obligations, is increasingly recognized.

The present economic structure is also likely to be modified to some extent. Social ownership, national or municipal, may increase. There may also be a greater development of small units along the lines advocated by the distributists and a greater development of both producers' and consumers' co-operative societies.

In large-scale industry under private ownership, progress may be made toward participation by workers' organizations in the formulation and execution of industrial policies. Several starts have been made in this direction, both in England and in the United States, but none of them has yet gone far. Joint action by associations of owners and organizations of workers would seem to require the check of potential governmental intervention, in the interest of the public at large. And the problem of reconciling regulation of industry by those in industry with the power of veto by government over the policies initiated within industry is as yet far from a solution. Nor has the problem of safeguarding individual economic freedom to the degree that is desirable, under regulation by either industry or government, been solved.

Moreover, any proposal for government control of the conduct of industry and of the workers' organizations is suspect today in democratic countries because of its close association in Europe with state absolutism and the dictatorship of a single party. The same is true of the conduct of industry, generally, by the government itself. And yet the democratic countries must face the fact that extreme *laissez faire* will not answer. Nor is it wholesome to have powerful workers' organizations restricted in function to bargaining with employers over the terms of employment. Some way must be found of reconciling, in proper proportions, private ownership, private initiative, participation by voluntary associations of workers in the determination of industrial policies, and government regulation in the public interest. This is the challenge, in the economic field, to democracy in industrial countries.

Whatever changes are made, it is to be hoped that they will be made peacefully, without confiscation and without the suppression of individual rights. There is no gainsaying that, beginning with the Bolshevist seizure of power in Russia in 1917, there has been a tendency over a large part of the earth's surface to become impatient with democratic methods and to force a change in the economic, political, and social system through a dictatorship. And where force and dictatorship are necessary to effect a change, the necessity of maintaining the dictatorship seems to remain for a long time thereafter. We cannot expect that a party that will resort to force to put through a change will, if it succeeds, tolerate any other party that is committed to a different program. Moreover, a country cannot afford to change its economic system every few years.

The great social and economic cost involved in the reorganization of the economic system, if it needs to be reorganized, would seem to be a sufficient reason for proceeding slowly and with the consent of a substantial majority of the people. Economic injustice should not be tolerated any longer than it takes to remedy it. But to change a whole economic order without working other injustices takes time. No economic system is worth the suppression of fundamental human rights. An economic system is a means to an end, not an end in itself.

INDEX

Absentee capitalists, and criticisms of Capitalism, 299; and distributists, 304

Accident compensation, *see* industrial accident compensation

Accidents, and economic insecurity, 179–180; and industrial accident insurance, 201–209; casualties from industrial, 201; common law on, 201–202; the movement for compensation for industrial, 202–204; and advantages of industrial accident compensation, 204–205

American Federation of Labor, 46–54; based on autonomy for national trade unions, 46–47; local unions directly affiliated with the, 47–48; limitations of powers and functions of the, 48–50; nonpartisan policy of political action of, 50; jurisdictional disputes between unions in the, 50–52; and the conflict over industrial unionism, 53–54

Anti-Injunction Act of 1932, the, 118–119; and the use of nonunion materials, 134–135; and picketing, 136; and the use of the injunction, 138–139; and damage suits, 139

Arbitration, 110–112; defined, 110; primary, 111–112; secondary, 111–112; voluntary, 141; compulsory, 142–143

Associations, of employers in the Italian corporative system, 343–346

Bargaining unit, and the Railway Labor Act, 129–130; and the National Labor Relations Act, 130

Black-Connery Bill, and child-labor legislation, 158 *n.*; and a maximum of forty hours a week, 162 *n.*

Bolshevists, and Communism, 320–322; and the Provisional Government, 322

Boycott, the, defined, 108; primary, 108; secondary, 108–109; legislation concerning the, 109; legality of the, 137

Brookings Institute, estimates of, on earnings of employed people, 185

NOTES ABOUT THE MAKING OF THIS BOOK

The text of the book was set on the linotype in Granjon type, named purely out of compliment to Robert Granjon, a sixteenth century typefounder and printer. George W. Jones designed this type, neither copying a previous face nor creating a new one. The characteristics of the letters follow more closely a type used by Claude Garamond, a French craftsman, than do the numerous adaptations of types named after him. Granjon type was introduced in England by Linotype and Machinery, Limited, in 1926 and its obvious merit was quickly recognized there as well as in America.

Choice of Granjon type for this book, using the twelve point size, aims toward a page easy to read and pleasant to look at, with headings and subheadings in simple unison with the text.

This book was set, electrotyped and printed by The Norwood Press; paper was made by S. D. Warren Company; bound by The Riverside Bindery and designed by Arthur Williams.